D0864059

ITUMELENG J. MOSALA

Biblical Hermeneutics
and
Black Theology
in
South Africa

WILLIAM B. EERDMANS PUBLISHING COMPANY
GRAND RAPIDS, MICHIGAN

Library of Congress Cataloging-in-Publication Data

Mosala, Itumeleng J. (Itumeleng Jerry)
Biblical hermeneutics and black theology in South Africa.

Bibliography: p. 194
1. Black theology.   2. Bible—Hermeneutics.
3. Theology, Doctrinal—South Africa.   I. Title.
BT82.7.M67   1989   220.6'089968   88-33521
ISBN 0-8028-0372-5

*Organized religion is not about to give us access to the full story of the Bible. We have to recover the Bible through our own efforts to penetrate and unlock its full resources. The clue to the Bible as a social class resource is the recognition of an inner affinity between life struggle in the biblical world and life struggle today. The biblical world only looks placid when viewed from the composure of an established class perspective. If we are comfortable with having "arrived" at a reasonable end of our lives, biblical communities will appear to us as similarly secure and "realized" communities. If we are engaged in identifying and overcoming the splits and barriers to imperfect community, biblical communities may "open up" to us as **kindred struggle contexts**. . . . To a large extent, what the Bible is depends on who you are.*

—Norman K. Gottwald and Anne Wire (emphasis added)

To my parents:
Montlaletsi and Mosai Mosala

Contents

Contents

Acknowledgments

I WOULD LIKE TO ACKNOWLEDGE THE DIRECT AND INDIRECT DEBT I owe to a number of individuals and groups for their contributions and support in the development of this study.

I am deeply grateful to my mentors and comrades across the Atlantic, on the American continent, for the theoretical guidance and support they gave me both from a distance and at closer quarters from time to time in the past four years. These mentors and comrades include Norman K. Gottwald, Herman Waetjen, Anne Wire, Marvin Chaney, and Robert Coote. To them I say: "Aluta Continua! I hope this study will re-emphasize our mutual conviction that the Bible and the black church remain the terrain as well as the weapon of struggle for the liberation of the poor and exploited."

Not least among those I owe a special word of gratitude are my students and my colleague Takatso Mofokeng at the University of Botswana in Gaborone. The thesis of this study was in fact originally conceived in the debates and discussions I participated in during my stay in that country. Even more importantly, in the Botswana context, I must thank the members of the Bible-study group with which I was associated for two and a half years. Their inspiration, support, and, above all, their theoretical contributions will be reflected in the pages that follow. They are: Frank Youngman, Sefapano Gaborone, Isa, Olebile Gaborone, Takatso Mofokeng, Onalenna, and Otto.

Contrary to appearances, a gynecological metaphor is not entirely out of place in the context of a department of religious studies. After this baby was conceived and the natural processes of development were set in motion, I needed a clinic —and eventually midwives—to do a periodic checkup and to see the whole thing through. My colleagues in the department of religious studies at the University of Cape Town served this purpose in different ways. Charles Villa-Vicencio and Chuck Wanamaker deserve a word of gratitude for reading the drafts of this study and providing critical comments. Bill Domeris and the postgraduate students provided the forum for debating and refining my ideas. A very special word of gratitude must go to three other people. First, my colleague and mother—indeed a mother to many others who have gone through the Religious Studies Department at the University of Cape Town — Mrs. Shaan Ellinghouse. She typed and retyped the various drafts of the work. I am also deeply grateful to my colleagues and comrades Dr. Brenda Cooper and Glenda Kruss. Both Brenda and Glenda read drafts of this study and contributed significant theoretical and ideological comments, criticisms, and stylistic suggestions.

This list of acknowledgments would be incomplete without a mention of four sites of struggle from which I benefited during the writing of this book. I refer here to the National Youth Leadership Training Programme (NYLTP) in Durban, where many of the ideas contained here were tested; the Black Theology Project of the Institute for Contextual Theology (ICT) in Johannesburg; the black church, that refuge to which black people escape from the brutalities of racism and capitalist exploitation, and which also serves as a resistance base; and, not least, the Black Methodist Consultation.

I would also like to thank the following for their financial support during my research: the British Methodist Church Overseas Division Scholarship Fund, the United Church of Canada, and the University of Cape Town.

Above all, when all is said and done, I must salute

Bakubung and Bakgwatleng, Mmakgotha, Montlaletsi and Ole-
bogeng. Without their commitment to the production and reproduction of the labor power necessary for the creation of this
work, needless to say, it would never have seen the light of day.

Itumeleng J. Mosala
University of Cape Town

Abbreviations

JThSt	*Journal of Theological Studies*
NTS	*New Testament Studies*
OTWSA	*Ou testamentiese Werkgemeenskap van Suid Afrika*
PEQ	*Palestine Exploration Quarterly*
SBLSP	*Society of Biblical Literature Seminar Papers*
SBT	*Studies in Biblical Theology*
SNTS	*Society for New Testament Studies*
USQR	*Union Seminary Quarterly Review*
VT	*Vetus Testamentum*
VTSup	Vetus Testamentum, Supplements
ZAW	*Zeitschrift für die alttestamentliche Wissenschaft*
ZNW	*Zeitschrift für die neutestamentliche Wissenschaft*

Prologue

BACKGROUND

BLACK THEOLOGY IN SOUTH AFRICA FIRST EMERGED IN THE CONTEXT of the black consciousness movement during the late 1960s and early 1970s. It came into being as a cultural tool of struggle propounded by young black South Africans who were influenced by the philosophy of the new black consciousness. The immediate target of black theology was the Christian church, and especially Christian theology. The point of contention was the perceived acquiescence of the Christian church and its theology in the oppression and exploitation of black people. Black theologians argued, justifiably, that not only was the church relatively silent on the question of oppression but that the thoroughly Western and white outlook of its theology helped to reproduce the basic inequalities of an apartheid society. Consequently, black Christian activists emphasized the need for a black theology of liberation.

The tasks of this theology were to be measured against the broad goal of the national liberation of black people. Included among those tasks, then, was the critical function of exposing the imposition of the cultural forms of the dominant classes on the oppressed. Black theologians considered the question of cultural dependency, among others, to be at the base of the oppression and exploitation. It stood to reason for them, therefore, that one of the critical tasks of black theology would be to work toward the cultural autonomy of black people. The creation and development of black theology itself would also be part of the wider task of creating autonomous weapons of social and cultural struggle. The Christian churches, and especially the theological seminaries, were to be the starting point for this activity and the reflection on the new black theology. The wider black community, however — and especially the most oppressed sections of it — was to be the real ground in which black theology would take root and develop. There was never any doubt, therefore, that black theology was to be developed as an instrument of struggle for the liberation of the oppressed and exploited black people in South Africa.

It is now just over fifteen years since black theology first emerged in South Africa. Many articles, theses, and books have been written on the subject. Various projects, albeit few in number, have been undertaken in the name of black theology. In short, black theologians have not stopped working since the task of creating and developing a black theology of liberation was first enunciated. In fact, the task continues and is gaining momentum. But, notwithstanding this flurry of black theological activity, black theology has not yet properly emerged as an autonomous weapon of struggle. Evidence of this is its inability to become a useful weapon in the hands of the oppressed and exploited black people themselves. It has remained the monopoly of educated black Christians and has often been unable to interest the white theologians against whose theology it was supposedly first developed. Further, it has been unable to develop organic links with the popular struggles of especially the black working-class people, the most exploited segment of the black community.

In the meantime, the oppressed black masses relentlessly continue their struggle against apartheid and capitalism — with or without the leadership and cultural equipment of black theology. As one might expect, however, many forms of resistance that the oppressed create for themselves remain open

2

to co-optation and undermining by the dominant classes. The latter are able to co-opt and undermine the discourses of the oppressed on the grounds of intellectual and theoretical superiority. Needless to say, the oppressed are very often unable to contest this claimed intellectual and theoretical superiority. In the realm of religious practice, this state of affairs underscores the absolute necessity of a theoretically well-grounded and culturally autonomous black theology of liberation.

This study, therefore, seeks to address the need to develop a black theology of liberation that is capable of becoming an effective weapon of struggle for black liberation. I argue here that the reason for black theology's failure among the oppressed has to do with its class and ideological commitments, especially with respect to its biblical hermeneutics. I contend that, unless black theologians break ideologically and theoretically with bourgeois biblical-hermeneutical assumptions, black theology cannot become an effective weapon of struggle for its oppressed people. And hence I undertake to develop a distinctive biblical hermeneutics of liberation for black theology.

MAIN ISSUES

Two main issues form a structure for the development of my thought in this work. First, there is the question of the historical-cultural foundations and links of black theology and how these affect black theology's biblical-hermeneutical assumptions, which I regard as very important in developing a biblical hermeneutics of liberation. It comes from an understanding that people's reading of the Bible is framed by their history and culture. This is as true of white people as it is of black people. Consequently, it is ultimately wrongheaded to fail to take history and culture into account when identifying biblical-hermeneutical factors. Latin American liberation theology, for instance, has failed precisely on this point: it presupposes European history and culture and not the indigenous Latin American history and culture; thus blacks and Indians are missing from the Latin American theology of liberation. Similarly, Western social and political theologies have failed to become instruments of liberating praxis because they have been premised on the dominant and patriarchal class histories and cultures at the expense of the oppressed and women's histories and cultures. The rise of a feminist theology of liberation is an appropriate counter-response to this state of affairs. And in order to become a weapon of struggle for oppressed black people, black theology needs to relocate itself within the historical and cultural struggles of these people.

Second, black theology must openly declare where it stands ideologically and theoretically. It is not enough to be on the opposition side in societal struggles. The very fact that a specifically black theology of liberation is needed, in spite of the existence of opposition theologies in traditional Christian circles, underscores this point. Existential commitments to the liberation struggles of the oppressed are inadequate because those who are committed in this way are often still ideologically and theoretically enslaved to the dominant discourses in the society. In the case of black theology—and specifically with respect to the biblical-hermeneutical aspect I deal with here—this means that the liberating power of this theological discourse becomes limited. Even more serious, the ideological and theoretical enslavement of black theology to the biblical hermeneutics of dominant theologies often leads to a promotion of those theologies rather than black theologies. Hence I argue that a clear ideological and theoretical break with the dominant practices and discourses is necessary if a biblical hermeneutics of black liberation is to emerge.

METHOD

I have chosen the historical-materialist method of analysis usually associated with the name of Karl Marx rather than the idealist framework that makes the history of ideas—abstracted from concrete historical and social relationships—the focus of its analysis. If black theology is to become an effective weapon in the struggle to critique and transform present realities, it needs to employ analytical concepts that can get to the bottom of real events, relationships, structures, and so forth. I give priority to this method of exposing fundamental social relationships because, in the case of both the Bible and black theology, there are communities and networks of relationships that must be brought to the fore. Only such an exposure of the underlying material relationships can throw light on the problems of which the biblical texts are a solution and can enable black theology to become the kind of critical discourse that is capable of contributing meaningfully to black liberation struggle.

I should remind the reader, however, that the proponents and the forms of historical-materialist methods vary, and that there are important historical, cultural, racial, and gender variations in the way the historical-materialist method is used. I find it particularly important in this study, therefore, to include the cultural, racial, and gender relationships as part of the material relationships that the historical-materialist method undertakes to analyze. I invoke various perspectives on the sociology of literature, discourse analysis, empirical sociology, and political literary criticism that are associated with such scholars as Terry Eagleton, Willis and Corrigan, Stuart Hall, Cornel West, Stanley Aronowitz, and Edward P. Thompson, among others. On the specifically biblical side of this methodological approach, I invoke materialist and sociological methods associated with the names of Norman K. Gottwald, Robert B. Coote, Marvin Chaney, Herman Waetjen, and others. This study insists, however, that all of these perspectives must be tested on the grid of black history and culture in order for them to enable the development of a specifically black biblical hermeneutics of liberation.

STRUCTURE

The work is divided into three parts, which include seven chapters plus an epilogue. In Chapter One I attempt to show that the fundamental problem underlying the present impotence of black theology lies in its hermeneutical captivity to the ideological assumptions of white theology and Western civilization. These assumptions are reflected in the idealist epistemology characteristic of white theology and Western culture. The notion that the Bible is simply the revealed "Word of God" is an example of an exegetical framework that is rooted in such an idealist epistemology. I criticize that position in this study because it leads to a false notion of the <u>Bible as nonideological,</u> which can cause political paralysis in the oppressed people who read it. In addition, it leaves the privilege of a political reading of the Bible to the hegemonic sectors of society; and they often do not have to strain after an explicitly political reading since the texts of the Bible are themselves already cast in hegemonic codes. Thus black theology, by colluding with a dominant epistemological view of the Bible, has helped to reproduce the status quo—in contradiction of its own goals. It does so not because of where its own commitments lie but as a result of the contradictory insertion of its proponents within the bourgeois social order. This leads to the failure to recognize a similar contradictory nature of the Bible as an ideological product.

In order to avoid a mechanistic reductionism and determinism in the view that the contradictory insertion of black theologians in bourgeois society explains the weaknesses in their theology, I have chosen as examples the most celebrated and undoubted activists in the struggle for liberation, Allan Boesak and Desmond Tutu. I scrutinize the biblical hermeneutics of these two activists' theology to highlight the fundamental problem of a theological discourse whose class basis is *ambiguously* rooted in the black working-class struggles. Their discourse is committed to the goals of these struggles but draws its weapons of combat from the social class assumption with which these struggles are in conflict. This point must be made emphatically, even though it is not automatically true that black working-class discourses provide liberating weapons of struggle. It is rather to say that bourgeois or ruling-class discourses place limits, *ab initio*, on the range of possible liberating weapons of struggle that can be derived from them.

I thus conclude that biblical appropriations and interpretations are always framed by the social and cultural locations and commitments of those who do them. For black theology the relevant base is in the historical, cultural, and ideological struggles of black people. The category of "struggle" at all levels and through various phases of black history should be taken as the key hermeneutical factor. Thus this study seeks to probe the nature of the struggles behind and beneath the text; the struggles in the pages, the lines, and the vocabulary of the text; the struggles that take place when readers engage the text by way of reading it; and the struggles that the completed text represents.

Chapter Two critiques the dominant direction of the new sociological approaches to the Bible. While welcoming the sociological concern shown by the proponents of the new methods, this study laments their methodological reproduction of the same ideological and cultural assumptions that undergird the traditional biblical methods. This chapter argues that sociological idealism is no real improvement on philosophical idealism. We need an approach to the biblical texts that recognizes that they are the products of definite historical and social *material conditions*. This approach should also recognize that these texts are *productions,* or "signifying practices," that reconstitute in very specific ways the realities of the material conditions of which they are products. Such an awareness would negate the possibility that the use of sociological methods would become no more than a new scholarly fashion, with nothing substantive to contribute. This is true because, while the concern with social systems and realities that the new methods bring is welcome, their failure to effect a theoretical break with the underlying idealist framework prevents the creation of new knowledge through the use of these methods.

Just as in the case of the failure of black theologians to break theoretically with the dominant approaches, we need an explanation of the failure of biblical scholars to break with traditional assumptions. Social scientific approaches to the Bible seem to have failed to recognize the ideological character of even the social science methods themselves. The result has been that issues of ideology, race, gender, class, and politics have not been sufficiently integrated, if raised at all, in the application of these methods to the Bible. This failure, however, is itself a function of the position and commitments of the proponents of the sociological methods in actual human struggles today.

Thus the biblical hermeneutics of a black theology of liberation cannot be adequately served by a mere shift from the "humanities" method to a "sociological" method in the study of

7

texts. Rather, it is necessary that fundamental questions of ideology, culture, gender, race, and politics be integral to a liberating methodological approach. Again, I insist that a base and an engagement in actual contemporary struggles is a necessary, though not a sufficient, condition for the development of such a black biblical hermeneutics of liberation.

Chapter Three represents the beginning of a long but indispensable process that needs to be followed in developing a biblical hermeneutics of liberation. A fundamental aspect of my argument is that "the black struggle for liberation" is a basic biblical hermeneutical factor. Thus no formulation of this hermeneutics can afford to ignore the nature and forms of the black struggle over time and in the contemporary context. I undertake a historical retreat, therefore, in this chapter to trace the "trajectory of struggle" in black history and culture from the precolonial period to the present. I argue that the category of struggle provides the lens for reading the text in a liberating fashion as well as the codes for unlocking the possibilities and limitations of the biblical texts. This chapter offers the weapons of struggle for engaging the text as a cultural discourse in the process of one's participation in the wider social and historical struggles. The point here is that biblical texts do not suddenly become politically supportive of the black struggle just because they are being appropriated from its perspective. The relevance of the Bible in the black liberation struggle may be as much a negative factor as it is often a positive one. To engage a biblical text in the light of the black struggle for liberation may be to take sides in and to connect with kindred struggles that were being waged in very ancient communities. Doing this, however, may be one way of taking sides in and connecting with contemporary struggles. For this reason it is liberating to recognize that not every God of every biblical text is on the side of the poor; nor is it desirable that this should be so.

Thus the search for biblical-hermeneutical weapons of struggle must take the form, first of all, of a critical interrogation of the history, culture, and ideologies of the readers/appropriators of the biblical texts. The key category in this process is that of *struggle,* because struggle is the motive force of human societies. Furthermore, one can avert the danger of a romantic and uncritical embracing of one's history and culture by invoking this notion of struggle to determine the configuration of forces in black history and culture.

The value of applying the category of struggle as a tool for reading black history and culture is that such application allows for a *critical* appropriation of the Bible. In such an appropriation one can hope for a genuine liberation project. This approach leads to the important understanding that not all black historical and cultural readings of the Bible are liberating. Armed with this insight, we can clearly see a biblical hermeneutics of liberation for black theology as liberating neither because it is black nor on the grounds simply that it is biblical. Rather, it is a *tool of struggle* in the ongoing human project of liberation.

The category of struggle becomes an important hermeneutical factor not only in one's reading of his or her history and culture but also in one's understanding of the history, nature, ideology, and agenda of the biblical texts. Consequently, a biblical hermeneutics of liberation, using the same tool of struggle as was used to interrogate the readers' history, culture, and ideology, must now address the question of the material conditions that constitute the sites of the struggles that produced the biblical texts. Operating with the hypothesis that the Bible is the product and the record of historical, cultural, gender, racial, and social-class struggles, Chapters Four and Six set out to interrogate the material and ideological conditions of production of the texts of Micah and Luke 1 and 2. In the case of Micah, we identify the conjunctural historical contours that the hegemonic cast of the text suggests as falling within the eighth century B.C.E. Luke 1 and 2 presents itself as a story of the events of the early years of the first century C.E. in Palestine. In both cases the identifiable dominant mode of material production is the tributary mode characterized by monarchical political superstructures.

The biblical texts of Micah and Luke 1 and 2 come out of the sociohistorical situations in which there was a struggle between those who exacted tribute, through control of a state machinery as well as through control of *latifundia* (large estates) acquired by the dispossession of others, and those who tilled their own land but were reduced to bare subsistence by heavy taxes and rents, as well as dispossessed employed laborers, the unemployed, petty criminals, bandits, and other *lumpen-*proletariat. These material conditions, together with the struggles that they produced—and were in turn produced by —are inscribed in particular ways in the texts of the Bible. A reading of the Bible that utilizes the category of struggle as a hermeneutical key is able to plumb the depths and thus feel the impulse of the struggle behind and in the text.

The struggles that produced the text and those that are part of the nature of the text express themselves in terms of certain internal contradictions. Traditional biblical scholarship saw these in purely logical and empiricist ways. The quests for the historicity and authorial integrity of texts define a hermeneutical method rooted in contemporary Western ruling-class anxiety about authenticity; this authenticity resolves itself racially as "purity of the breed" and ideologically as hegemonic "universality." Thus contradictions and logical inconsistencies in the texts were treated by the historical-critical method of the Bible as evidence of different literary sources or different historical provenances only. The issue of different social class, cultural and gender sources, and provenances that would raise the important factor of struggle in and beneath the texts was never seen as a possibility. The reason, of course, is that these questions of class, culture, race, and gender were not raised in relation to the readers of the Bible themselves in the first place.

I argue in Chapter Four and Six that the biblical texts are products of contradictory and struggle-ridden conditions of production. Nevertheless, I also contend that the finished textual products are, in spite of their conditions of production, still cast in hegemonic codes. This, therefore, raises the fundamental problem of how hermeneutical appropriation of hegemonic texts can be undertaken by nonhegemonic sectors of contemporary societies.

Chapters Five and Seven address this problem. I suggest that a materialist-biblical hermeneutics such as this study has been concerned to develop can only be liberating if it again employs the category of struggle. This category must be chosen over other hermeneutical possibilities that either uncritically co-opt the texts to one's side of the struggle or simply collude with texts in their dominant ideological agendas. The concept of struggle as a tool of hermeneutical appropriation of texts also avoids the escapist option of textual selectivity, an option that simply rejects as irrelevant those parts of the text that seem unsupportive of one's cause and accepts as the "Word of God" those parts that appear supportive. The notion of struggle as an instrument of biblical-hermeneutical appropriation means that one *is* appropriating a text, however negatively, when one engages it critically on the basis of the questions and agenda emanating out of the history and culture of struggles today. It means being galvanized by the configuration of historical and social forces today to identify the nature of and to take sides in the struggles that are signified by the text. This is true whether or not the victorious forces in the struggles of the biblical texts are antithetical to one's concerns and aspirations. Equally, it means being dialectically galvanized by the struggles beneath and in the text to identify the nature of and take sides in the struggles occurring today.

Chapter Five and Seven, in light of the contradictions and questions of the black struggle and of the struggles of the biblical communities in Micah and Luke 1 and 2, suggest ways of appropriating these texts as part of the liberation project of black theology. The form of biblical-hermeneutical appropriation suggested in these chapters is deliberately oblivious to the notion of "scriptural authority," which is at the heart of traditional biblical scholarship. The reason for this is that the fundamental presupposition of a biblical hermeneutics being developed here is not only that the Bible is the product and record of class, race, gender, and cultural struggles, but also that it is the site and weapon of such struggles. The Bible is the place where—and the means whereby — many contemporary struggles are waged. Therefore, this study recognizes that the historical, cultural, racial, gender, and social-class character of the Bible is so central that the need for a theological relocation of the Bible within other sociohistorical and cultural aspects of human life is crucial.

*   *   *

I hope that the approach to the biblical texts proposed in this study will open up greater liberating possibilities in the use of the Bible. In particular, I hope that black theologians will take black history and culture seriously enough that they will use it more to interrogate the texts of the Bible. I propose that, in this appropriation of black history and culture for purposes of appropriating biblical texts, the category of struggle will serve as a critical grid. It is necessary to take sides in the struggles inscribed in black history and culture as a prior step to taking sides in the struggles that produced the Bible and are signified in it.

PART I

1
The Use of the Bible
in Black Theology

IN THIS CHAPTER I PRESUPPOSE THE IMPORTANT CONTRIBUTION OF black theology to the black struggle for liberation and therefore will make no attempt to catalog the virtues of this theology. But it is appropriate to mention that among its key contributions is its insistence on the necessary *ideological* roots of all theology. Black theologians have not always identified this in an explicit way. They have, however, exposed the cultural assumptions of white theology and shown its link with white society and white values. In this way black theology has exploded the myth of rational objectivity in theology, which presumes to preclude cultural and ideological conditioning.

But black theology does not take its own criticism of white theology seriously enough. This is particularly true with regard to the use of the Bible. The first part of this chapter, therefore, extrapolates features of black theology that represent an ideological captivity to the hermeneutical principles of a theology of oppression. I will argue that it is precisely this slavery to the hermeneutics of white theology that is responsible for the inability of black theology to become a viable theoretical weapon of struggle in the hands of the exploited masses themselves. In this respect it is appropriate to consider the words of Marx:

The weapon of criticism cannot, of course, replace criticism of the weapon, material force must be overthrown by material force; but theory also becomes a material force as soon as it has gripped the masses. Theory is capable of gripping the masses as soon as it demonstrates *ad hominem,* and it demonstrates *ad hominem* as soon as it becomes radical. To be radical is to grasp the root of the matter. But for man the root is man himself.[1]

It is incontestable that, although black theology has made a vital contribution to the black struggle,[2] it has not yet, as a weapon of theory, become the property of the struggling black masses. To this extent it is a theory that has not yet become a *material force,* because it has not gripped the masses. It has served its purpose well as a weapon of criticism against white theology and white society. That activity, however, does not replace criticism of the weapon itself. Part of the reason black theology has not become the property of the toiling masses may lie in the class positions and class commitments of its proponents.[3]

BLACK THEOLOGY'S EXEGETICAL STARTING POINT

All major black theological studies in South Africa draw in some way on the work of James Cone. Cone cannot be faulted for omissions in South African black theology; it is nonetheless necessary to trace the trajectory of the biblical hermeneutics of black

1. Karl Marx and Friedrich Engels, *On Religion* (New York: Schocken Books, 1964), 50.
2. See Ishmael Noko, "The Concept of God in Black Theology" (Ph.D. diss., McGill University, 1977); Lulamile Ephraim Ntshebe, "A Voice of Protest" (M.A. thesis, Rhodes University); Stanley Mogoba, "The Faith of Urban Blacks" (M.A. thesis, Bristol, 1978); Takatso A. Mofokeng, "The Crucified among the Crossbearers" (Ph.D. diss., Kampen, 1983); and numerous articles in the various issues of the *Journal of Theology for Southern Africa.*
3. I have argued this in "Black and African Theologies" (paper read at the University of Cape Town, 1982). See also the "Final Statement of the Black Theology Seminar," *Institute for Contextual Theology News* 1 (No. 2, Sept. 1983):9ff. Sam Noplutshungu, writing on the political interpretation of the so-called black middle class, corroborates this contention. He writes: "As things stand, it is not surprising that attempts to define a modern cultural sensibility for Blacks in the

theology back to its first and most outstanding exponent in order to see how it has been uncritically reproduced in South Africa. Black theology's exegetical starting point expresses itself in the notion that the Bible is the revealed Word of God. The black theologian's task is to reveal God's Word to those who are oppressed and humiliated in this world.[4] For Cone, the Word of God, therefore, represents one structuring pole of the biblical hermeneutics of black theology, while the black experience constitutes the other. He summarizes black theology's hermeneutical position in this way:

> The Bible is the witness to God's self-disclosure in Jesus Christ. Thus the black experience requires that Scripture be a source of Black Theology. For it was Scripture that enabled slaves to affirm a view of God that differed radically from that of the slave masters. The slave masters' intention was to present a "Jesus" who would make the slave obedient and docile. Jesus was supposed to make black people better slaves, that is, faithful servants of white masters. But many blacks rejected that view of Jesus, not only because it contradicted their African heritage, but because it contradicted the witness of Scripture.[5]

Thus the black experience of oppression and exploitation provides the epistemological lens through which to perceive the God of the Bible as the God of liberation. This process, however, does not alter Cone's perception of the nature and function of the Bible as the Word of God. Rather, Scripture in its status as the Word of God "establishes limits to white people's use of Jesus Christ as a confirmation of black oppression."[6]

Paradoxically, black theology's notion of the Bible as the

---

late 1960s and early 1970s were so derivative in idiom and style — deep and authentic through the anguish which they expressed. 'Middle class' Blacks remained, even so, firmly attached to the common culture and even in the area of religion where much was written about the need for a black theology, radical dissent was still expressed by separatist churches that were predominantly non-middle-class in following." *Changing South Africa* (Cape Town: David Philip, 1983), 125.

4. Cf. James Cone, *God of the Oppressed* (New York: Seabury Press, 1975), 8.

5. Ibid., 31.

6. Ibid.

Word of God carries the implication that there is such a thing as a nonideological appropriation of Scripture. Black theologians condemn white people's view of God and Jesus Christ as *apolitical*, that is, above ideologies, on the one hand; but they maintain a view of Scripture as the absolute, nonideological Word of God that can be made ideological only by being applied to the situation of oppression, on the other hand. Even the most theoretically astute of current black theologians, Cornel West, takes this position. He argues:

> An interpretation of the black historical experience and the readings of the biblical texts that emerge out of this experience constitute the raw ingredients for the second step of black theological reflection. By trying to understand the plight of black people in the light of the Bible, black theologians claim to preserve the biblical truth that God sides with the oppressed and acts on their behalf.[7]

To be fair to West, one must add that he goes a step further than do Cone and other black theologians by not resting the case at interpreting the black experience in the light of the Bible; he also interprets the Bible in the light of the black experience. Nevertheless, West, like Cone, insists that it is a biblical truth that God sides with the oppressed in their struggle for liberation. This is true as far as it goes; but, as any hermeneutics deriving from the crucible of class struggle will attest, the biblical truth that God sides with the oppressed is only one of the biblical truths. The other truth is that the struggle between Yahweh and Baal is not simply an ideological warfare taking place in the minds and hearts of believers but a struggle between the God of Israelite landless peasants and subdued slaves and the God of Israelite royal, noble, landlord, and priestly classes. In other words, the Bible is rent apart by the antagonistic struggles of the warring classes of Israelite society in much the same way that our world is torn asunder by society's class, cultural, racial, and gender divisions.

What, then, do we mean by the Bible as the "Word of God"? The ideological import of such a theological question is

7. Cornel West, *Prophesy Deliverance* (Philadelphia: Westminster Press, 1982), 109.

immense, because presumably the Word of God cannot (by definition) be the object of criticism. Furthermore, the Word of God cannot be critiqued in the light of black experience or any other experience. The only appropriate response is obedience. At best, the black experience can be seen in the light of the Word of God but not vice versa. Does the definition of the Bible as the Word of God, therefore, mean that even the "law and order" God of David and Solomon cannot be the object of criticism in the light of the black experience? Does it mean that the black struggle cannot be hermeneutically connected with the struggles of the oppressed and exploited Israelites against the economic and political domination of the Israelite monarchical state, which was undergirded by the ideology of the Davidic-Zionist covenant (II Sam. 7)? Does it mean that no hermeneutical affinity can be established between working-class blacks and landless peasants, exploited workers, and destitute underclasses that made up the followers of Jesus? One cannot select one part of the "Word of God" and neglect others.

It is clear that South African black theologians are not free from enslavement to the wider neoorthodox theological problematic that regards the notion of the Word of God as a hermeneutical starting point. Sigqibo Dwane displays this exegetical bondage when he writes:

> Liberation theology as an aspect of Christian theology cannot play to the gallery of secular expectations. It seeks to understand and to articulate what in the light of this revelation in the past, God is doing now for the redemption of his people. Liberation theology is theocentric and soundly biblical insofar as it points out that God does not luxuriate in his eternal bliss, but reaches out to man and to the world. To say that liberation theology is not a Gospel of liberation is to state the obvious. The Gospel, it is true, is good news for all men. And no theology, Western or African, has the right to equate itself with the Gospel. The entire theological enterprise is concerned with the interpretation of the one Gospel for all sorts and conditions.[8]

The attempt to claim the *whole* of the Bible in support of

8. "Christology and Liberation," *Journal of Theology for Southern Africa* 35 (1981):30.

black theology is misdirected because it ignores the results of biblical scholarship over the last century and has its roots in ruling-class ideology. By ruling-class ideology I mean the desire and attempts by the dominant classes of society to establish hegemonic control over other classes through a rationalizing universalization of what are in effect sectional class interests. James Joll makes this point succinctly:

> The hegemony of a political class meant for Gramsci that that class had succeeded in persuading the other classes of society to accept its own moral, political and cultural values. If the ruling class is successful then this will involve the minimum use of force, as was the case with the successful liberal regimes of the nineteenth century.[9]

The insistence on the Bible as the Word of God must be seen for what it is: an ideological maneuver whereby ruling-class interests evident in the Bible are converted into a faith that transcends social, political, racial, sexual, and economic divisions. In this way the Bible becomes an ahistorical, interclassist document. Sergio Rostagno exposes the ideological roots of this line of thinking when he argues:

> Historically speaking, the church has always been a church of the bourgeoisie, even when it claimed to transcend class barriers or labored under the illusion that it pervaded all classes in the same way. Indeed it has been a truly bourgeois church, if the notion of interclassism is taken as part of bourgeois ideology. . . . The church has been the church of the class which has identified itself with the history of the West, in which Christianity may have been considered to have been a major force. Only those members of the working class who accepted this view of history attended church. But most of the working people never accepted this view and only gave the church the kind of formal allegiance subjects give to the claims of their rulers. They could not really belong to the church of another class.[10]

Just as the church has always been the church of the bourgeoisie, theology and biblical exegesis have always represented bour-

9. James Joll, *Gramsci* (Fontana Paperbacks, 1977), 99.
10. Sergio Rostagno, "The Bible: Is an Interclass Reading Legitimate?" in *The Bible and Liberation*, ed. N. K. Gottwald (New York: Orbis Books, 1983), 62.

geois theological and exegetical interests. And it is a tragedy that rebel theologies like black theology and liberation theology should uncritically adopt the biblical hermeneutics of bourgeois theological interests. According to Rostagno, bourgeois exegesis shows the sterility of its ahistoricism in that

> It claims to consider humanity in certain typical existential situations which provide analogies for all historical situations resulting from the human condition. It deals, therefore, with *humanity*, rather than with *workers* as they try to wrest from the dominant class its hold on the means of production and its hold over the vital spheres of human life. In this sense, it could be said that exegesis was an interclass affair. . . . This was an indication that biblical exegesis had been effectively estranged from the labor movement.[11]

The belief in the Bible as the Word of God has had similar effects. It is pro-humanity but anti-black-working-class and anti-black-women. It has, to all intents and purposes, been bourgeois exegesis applied to the working-class situation. The theoretical tragedy of such a state of affairs is that claims in that direction have been made with confidence and pride. Allan Boesak, for instance, states unashamedly:

> In its focus on the poor and the oppressed, the theology of liberation is not a new theology; it is simply the proclamation of the age-old gospel, but now liberated from the deadly hold of the mighty and the powerful and made relevant to the situation of the oppressed and the poor.[12]

An approach to the study or appropriation of the Bible that begins with the theological notion of the Bible as the Word of God, therefore, presupposes a hermeneutical epistemology for which truth is not historical, cultural, or economic. For such an epistemology the Word of God is pre-established. The political, cultural, economic, or historical relevance of this Word of God comes out of its capacity to be applied to the various facets of human life, and in this case of black human life. Its relevance does not issue out of its very character as a historical, cultural,

---

11. Ibid.
12. Allan Boesak, *Farewell to Innocence* (New York: Orbis Books, 1976), 10.

political, or economic product. Because Boesak sees the Word of God as above history, culture, economics, or politics, he resorts to a mere contextualization approach in biblical hermeneutics, which he rightly perceives as nothing new but simply the proclamation of the age-old gospel.

The problem with the contextualization approach is that it conceals the hermeneutically important fact that the texts of the Bible, despite being overladen by harmonizing perspectives, are problematical—if only because they are products of complex and problematical histories and societies. By this I mean that as products, records, and sites of social, historical, cultural, gender, racial, and ideological struggles, they radically and indelibly bear the marks of their origins and history. The ideological aura of the Bible as the Word of God conceals this reality. A black biblical hermeneutics of liberation must battle to recover precisely that history and those origins of struggle in the text and engage them anew in the service of ongoing human struggles.

The point, therefore, is not that Boesak and other black theologians are mistaken in finding a liberating message in the Bible. Rather, I contend that the category of the Word of God does not help to bring out the real nature of the biblical liberation because it presumes that liberation exists everywhere and unproblematically in the Bible. I argue here that this category is oblivious, even within biblical communities themselves, to the history of ruling-class control and co-optation of the discourses and stories of liberation of the ancient Israelite people. The appropriation by the exile community in Babylon of the exodus story to express their yearning for freedom to return to Zion and rebuild the Davidic dynasty, for example, conceals—with devastating ideological effects—the class and political differences between the first exodus and this second exodus. This kind of reuse of the exodus story goes against the invectives of the prophets and their view of Jerusalem and Zion: "Listen to me, you rulers of Israel, you that hate justice and turn right into wrong. You are building God's city, Jerusalem, on a foundation of murder and injustice" (Mic. 3:9-10, Good News Bible). The ethos of the original exodus theology is incompatible with the ideology and culture implied in the struggle for the reconstruction of Zion and Jerusalem.

Black theology needs a *new* exegetical starting point if it is to become a material force capable of gripping the black working-class and peasant masses. Such an exegetical point of departure must itself be grounded in a materialist epistemology that is characterized, among other things, by its location of truth not in a world beyond history but indeed within the crucible of historical struggles.[13] The social, cultural, political, and economic world of the black working class and peasantry constitutes the only valid hermeneutical starting point for a black theology of liberation.

THE PROBLEM OF UNIVERSALITY AND PARTICULARITY IN BLACK THEOLOGY

The abstract exegetical point of departure of black theology leads inevitably to problems concerning the validity of the particularistic character of this theology. If the Word of God transcends boundaries of culture, class, race, sex, and so forth, how can there be a theology that is concerned primarily with the issues of a particular race? Conversely, if black people are correct when they claim that in their struggle for liberation Jesus is on their side, how can the same Jesus remain the supreme *universal* disclosure of the Word of God?

This simultaneous concern for a cultureless and culture-bound, classless and class-based, raceless and race-oriented Jesus manifested itself fairly early in the development of black theology. Simon Gqubule says:

> Black Theology is not an attempt to localize Christ in the black situation, but to make him so universal that the Red Indian, the Pigmy, the Maori, the Russian, the Hungarian, the Venda and the American, may each say: "This man Jesus is bone of my bone; he speaks in my own accent of things that are true to me!" Viewed in this way Christianity can never be a white man's religion although it was brought to us by a white missionary. It is natural that any white artist would portray Jesus as a white man.[14]

13. Marx and Engels, *On Religion,* 42.
14. Simon Gqubule, "What is Black Theology?" *Journal of Theology for Southern Africa* 8 (1974):18.

Elliot Khoza Mgojo endorses this line of thinking when he sees black theology as contextual. By this he seems to understand that it is the application of universal theological principles to a particular situation. Consequently, he traces the development of universal theology from the Age of Apology through to the period starting in 1720, which he characterizes as the era of evolving theological responses to a technological society. He concludes:

> In looking at the history of doctrine we can see in every period, theology developed in response to challenges from the larger society. This being the case there is nothing strange in a particular segment of the Christian community reflecting on the nature of God in relation to its experience of suffering and oppression. Hence today there is Black Theology.[15]

Thus Mgojo's understanding of the origins and function of black theology is rooted in a belief in the fundamental universality of the gospel. This understanding stems from a hermeneutical commitment to the Bible as the "Word of God." As a result, he sees the emergence of black theology as a logical historical development of Christian theology, not a rebellion against Christian theology. There is thus no theoretical break with traditional Western theology. Indeed, black theology is simply *contextual* theology, that is, white theology in black clothes. It is little wonder that he applies the following strictures against James Cone:

> Cone's understanding of the theological task in his early work is in conflict with our definition of theology, in fact it is in direct opposition. His focus is on the analysis of the black man's condition, ours is on God as revealed in Jesus Christ and his relationship to the world and man. Cone's approach here could be classified as christian sociology rather than christian theology.[16]

This apologetic attitude on the part of black theologians is related to their enslavement to traditional biblical hermeneutics, which we discussed above.[17] There are also forms of coloni-

---

15. Elliot K. M. Mgojo, "Prolegomenon to the Study of Black Theology," *JTSA* 21 (1977): 26f.

16. Ibid.

17. See also Ephraim K. Mosothoane, "The Use of Scripture in Black Theology," in *Scripture and the Use of Scripture* (Pretoria: Unisa, 1979), 32.

zation that are connected to this hermeneutical bondage. In South African black theology the debate between African theologians, whose emphasis is more heavily cultural, and black theologians, whose focus—like that of the Afro-American theologians—is predominantly sociopolitical, exemplifies this crisis of cultural identity. Gqubule, for instance, in addressing one of the points of conflict between Christianity and African religion, locates himself unproblematically in a framework that reflects at once a cultural desertion and a biblical hermeneutical position based in the dominant Western culture. He argues:

> There is a widespread belief about the role of the ancestors. One view is that they are an object of worship. Another view is that they are intermediaries who, because they know our lot on earth, are better able to mediate to God on our behalf. However, for the Christian only the Triune God can be the object of worship; moreover, the Christian Scriptures say: "There is *one God,* and also *one mediator* between God and men, Christ Jesus" (I Tim. 2:5). [italics mine][18]

The most explicit and often-quoted criticism of African theology and religion, which feeds on this cultural self-deprecation, is the one made by Manas Buthelezi. Buthelezi correctly directs his strictures against tendencies to reify the African past, especially African culture. However, the terms of his strictures display an uneasiness about culture that characterizes the conflict between the universal and the particular in black theology. He writes:

> There is a danger that the "African past" may be romanticised and conceived in isolation from the realities of the present. Yet this "past" seen as a world view is nothing more than a historical abstraction of "what once was." Rightly or wrongly, one cannot help but sense something panicky about the mood which has set the tenor and tempo of the current concerns about "indigenous theology."[19]

Notwithstanding this rigorously antiabstractionist stance,

---

18. Gqubule, "What is Black Theology?", 17.
19. Manas Buthelezi, "Toward Indigenous Theology in South Africa," in *The Emergent Gospel* (New York: Orbis Books, 1978), 62.

Buthelezi proceeds to suggest equally abstractionist solutions to the problem of indigenous theology in South Africa:

> The shift from the "ideological" to the "human" expressions of ecclesiastical kinship solidarity will serve as a freeing factor for indigenous theology. Considerations of *esprit de corps* will no longer be a haunting spector for theological freedom in Africa, since there will be another way of expressing this kinship solidarity.[20]

The abstract universalizing category of the "human" as opposed to the concrete particularizing concept of the "African" helps Buthelezi maintain ties with what is "universal"—and for him nonideological—while simultaneously intending his theology to address the indigenous—and therefore ideological—situation. One might even argue that for Buthelezi the "human" or "anthropological" is finally given in the Word of God, which, he asserts, addresses him within the reality of his blackness.[21] That is why, in his view, black theology is no more than a methodological technique of theologizing.[22]

Bereft of a theoretical perspective that can locate both the Bible and the black experience within appropriate historical contexts, Buthelezi and other black theologians are unable to explode the myth of the inherent universality of the Word of God. In so doing they are surpassed by the largely illiterate black working class and poor peasantry who have defied the canon of Scripture, with its ruling-class ideological basis, and have appropriated the Bible in their own way by using the black working-class cultural tools emerging out of their struggle for survival.[23] To be able to reopen the canon of Scripture in the interests of black liberation, black theologians will need to take the materialist-hermeneutical significance of the black experience much more seriously.

*   *   *

Black theology's inability to connect adequately with the culture

20. Ibid., 73.
21. Ibid., 74.
22. Ibid.
23. For a helpful study of this process, see Matthew Schoeffeleer's "African Christology" (unpublished paper, Free University, Amsterdam, 1981), *passim.*

of resistance of the oppressed and exploited black people needs to be considered in the light of the class bases and commitments of the black theologians. Thus, while they oppose the racial exclusiveness of social privileges and how these are legitimated by the existing white theology, they are uncritical of their own structural lines to the societal institutions that produce these privileges. The contradictory insertion of black theologians into the social structure of the South African capitalist society and its cultural institutions, including the churches, accounts for the contradictory character of their theological practice. On the one hand, black theology represents a revolutionary rhetoric against social discrimination and oppression. On the other hand, it is the mechanism through which black theologians try to deal with an identity crisis occasioned by their exclusion from the privileges of white culture despite their secret admiration of and class qualification for it. This conflict between a critique of oppression and a hunger to occupy and control the institutions of power that produce this oppression has affected black theologians' choice of biblical hermeneutical tools.

Thus the problem of an absence of a black biblical hermeneutics of liberation has its roots in the inherent crisis of the petite bourgeoisie of all shades, but especially those of the colonized countries. Amilcar Cabral diagnoses the inherent malaise of this class when he says:

> As I said, regarding culture there are usually no important modifications at the summit of the indigenous social pyramid or pyramids (groups with a hierarchical structure). Each stratum or class retains its identity, integrated within the larger group, but distinct from the identities of other social categories. By contrast in urban centers and in urban zones of the interior where the colonial power's cultural influence is felt, the problem of identity is more complex. Whereas those at the base of the social pyramid — that is, the majority of working people from different ethnic groups—and those at the top (the foreign ruling class) keep their identities, *those in the middle range of this pyramid (the native lower middle class)—culturally rootless, alienated or more or less assimilated—flounder* in a social and cultural conflict in quest of their identity. [italics mine][24]

24. Amilcar Cabral, "The Role of Culture in the Liberation Struggle," *Latin American Research Unit Studies* 1 (Toronto, No. 3, 1977), 93.

Cornel West has raised the same question of the cultural crisis of the petit-bourgeois class in relation to Latin American liberation theology. The problem there expresses itself in terms of the conspicuous absence of blacks and Indians—or the issues related to them—in liberation theology. He suggests that when Marxists are preoccupied with an analysis that denigrates the liberating aspects of the culture of oppressed people, they share the ethos not of the degraded and oppressed minorities but of the dominant European culture.[25]

Thus universal abstract starting points derived presumably from the biblical message will simply not work for a biblical hermeneutics of liberation. Black theology will have to rediscover the black working-class and poor peasant culture in order to find for itself a materialist-hermeneutical starting point. The particularity of the black struggle in its different forms and faces must provide the epistemological lens with which the Bible can be read. Only this position seems to represent a theoretical break with dominant biblical hermeneutics; anything else is a tinkering with what in fact must be destroyed.

OPPRESSION AND OPPRESSORS, EXPLOITATION AND EXPLOITERS IN THE TEXT OF THE BIBLE

The need for a biblical hermeneutics of liberation rooted in the cultural and political struggles of the black oppressed and exploited people is underscored when we realize that black theology's propensity to appeal to the same ideology as do its oppressors in fact represents the extent of its slavery. For while the deceptions of the theology of oppression concerning its basis especially in the Yahwistic and Jesus movements must be exposed with all the might that can be mustered, it is equally crucial—if not more so—to recognize the presence of the oppressor and oppression in the text itself. It is fatal to mistake oppression for liberation and an oppressor for a liberator. Boesak exemplifies how some black theologians are hermeneutically ill equipped to make this identification:

25. "The North American Blacks," in *The Challenge of Basic Christian Communities* (New York: Orbis, 1981), 256.

26

Can the whites succeed? How can they succeed if the gospel itself rejects everything that white society attempts to maintain and
defend? How can the whites succeed if the gospel of liberation
that Jesus Christ effects condemns white "Christianity"? Against
what paganism does white society struggle if its "Christian civilization" can be maintained only by trampling justice underfoot?
This "Christian civilization" is established on self-centredness,
selfishness, murder, and the theft of the land.... To defend what
I have been describing, you must be alienated from the gospel.[26]

Indeed, one wishes it were really true that, to defend
what Boesak describes, one must be alienated from the gospel.
That is in fact what most innocent Christians assume is the case.
The real reason the dominant groups in society are able to claim
to be grounded in the best traditions of Christianity and at the
same time to be part of structures and societal processes that al-
ienate and impoverish others is that that accommodation happened in the formation of the biblical texts themselves. Thus to
overlook that internal biblical contradiction is to be in danger of
uncritically — albeit often inadvertently — transmitting such
struggle-ridden texts as part of the unproblematical Word of
God. There is a trajectory of struggle that runs through all biblical texts, and a recognition of this fact means that it is no longer
accurate to speak of the gospel or the Word of God unproblematically and in absolute terms. Both the Word of God and the
gospel are such hotly contested terrains of struggle that one cannot speak in an absolutizing way of being alienated from the
gospel. What one can do is take sides in a struggle that is not con-
firmed by the whole of the Bible, or even of the Gospels, but is
rather encoded in the text as a struggle representing different
positions and groups in the society behind the text. That pro-
vokes different appropriations of those texts, depending on one's
class, gender, culture, race, or ideological position and attitude.

Underlying Boesak's assertion is the assumption that
there exists a "gospel" that all social classes, genders, and races
can recognize equally as representing the essential message of
Jesus of Nazareth. This perspective derives from the assumption

26. Allan Boesak, *Black and Reformed* (Johannesburg: Skotaville Publishers, 1984), 5.

that the entire biblical text is, in an unproblematical way, God's message to and intention for the world. Once black theology colludes with the text in obscuring its oppressors and oppression and in presenting the text as divine discourse emanating from among the poor and oppressed, then the way is open for it to defend and claim, as part of the underclass, the program of the dominant classes.

The impotence of black theology as a weapon of struggle comes from this useless sparring with the ghost of the oppressor, whom black theology has already embraced in the oppressor's most dangerous form, the ideological form of the text. There is a real sense in which it does not bother the oppressors that black theologians attack their "Christian civilization" for being established "on self-centredness, selfishness, murder, and the theft of land." It does not matter, as long as before or after this attack, blacks or oppressed peoples can embrace and own the same processes and their agents in the text as part of the "Word of God" or as integral to that "gospel."

The issue of social class, race, and gender *struggles* is the single most undetected feature of the biblical literature. It is overlooked even by those theologies that originate from contexts of fierce struggles and come into being specifically as weapons of struggle. Among these theologies is black theology. The problem is illustrated by the manner in which black theologians speak and write of the "biblical message" rather than the "biblical messages" (plural); the "biblical God" rather than "biblical Gods"; the "biblical right" rather than "biblical rights." As a consequence, for example, Boesak, attacking the brutalities perpetrated by white people on black people, argues that despite their manipulation of God (by which he means their false claims to the favor of God) and their economic and military power, white people cannot escape God's judgment. A biblical hermeneutician of liberation cannot but ask, Which God— Baal, or El, or Yahweh? the white God or the black God? the male God or the female God? No theology of struggle can any longer afford not to recognize the biblical texts' witness to the fact that there are many Gods.

Motivated by what is undoubtedly a politically righteous conviction, Boesak asserts further:

The right to live in God's world as a human being is not the sole right of whites that eventually, through the kindness of whites, can be extended to "deserving" (obsequious?) Blacks as a "special privilege." *Human dignity for all is a fundamental biblical right.* Nevertheless, many whites seem to think that Blacks live by the grace of whites. [italics mine][27]

As a matter of historical, political, and ideological fact, blacks in South Africa *do* live by "the grace of whites." Boesak is correct in arguing that there is no *ontological* reason why this should be so; nevertheless, the Bible is not an ontological product in which the human dignity of all is ontologically inscribed.

The reason the Bible cannot be read as a bill of rights pertains to the very nature of the Bible itself. A century of historical-critical scholarship has demonstrated beyond any doubt that the Bible is made up of a multiplicity of varying and often contradictory traditions that are a function of both a long history over which they were produced and a variety of situations that produced them. Recent sociological and materialist exegeses of biblical texts have added to this understanding the role of contradictory and conflicting social and political interests, even within the same time frame or society, in the production of the Bible. Thus, while many texts of the Bible clearly represent human rights values, there are surely many others that emanate from the biblical counterparts of our contemporary oppressors and violators of such human rights. The biblical story of the settlement of Israelite tribes in Canaan, for example, is totally oblivious of any understanding of human rights until it is rescued by the kind of sociological reassessment of the rise of ancient Israel such as Norman K. Gottwald undertakes in his *The Tribes of Yahweh.*

In South Africa the use of the story of settlement to justify the colonial dispossession of blacks by whites and the maintenance of an ideology of white people's superiority over black people is well known. Protestations to the effect that white people are misusing the Bible have neither empowered black people to deliver themselves from this white slavery nor successfully explained to anybody, except the beneficiaries of

27. Ibid., 6.

apartheid, why such a tradition of conquest exists in the Bible in the first place. My contention is that the only adequate and honest explanation is that not all of the Bible is on the side of human rights or of oppressed and exploited people. Recognition of this is of vital importance for those who would use the Bible in the service of the struggle for the liberation of oppressed and exploited people.

Existentialist uses of the Bible in the struggle for liberation cannot be allowed to substitute for a theoretically well-grounded biblical hermeneutics of liberation. The reason for this is that, while texts that are against oppressed people may be co-opted by the interlocutors of the liberation struggle, the fact that these texts have their ideological roots in oppressive practices means that the texts are capable of undergirding the interests of the oppressors even when used by the oppressed. In other words, oppressive texts cannot be totally tamed or subverted into liberating texts.

For this reason a biblical hermeneutician of liberation must respond, "Yes, but . . ." to Boesak when he writes:

> God acts openly, not secretly. God does this as a challenge to the powers that be and to the powerful ones who think that they can manipulate God's justice, or that they can escape God's judgement. God acts openly so that the world may know that Israel's God lives—lives for the people of Israel; that Yahweh is the liberator of the oppressed and the warrior who fights for justice on behalf of the downtrodden. God is not ashamed to be called "the God of the oppressed." "You have seen what I did to the Egyptians, and that I have brought you to me" (Exod. 19:4, 5). Of course! You have *seen!*[28]

Boesak's argument must be embraced to the extent that it expresses, albeit inadvertently, something of what Gottwald describes when he argues that Yahweh is unlike other gods because Israel is unlike other social systems; Yahweh forbids other gods because Israel forbids other social systems; Yahweh is so different from other gods because Yahweh is the God of such a different social organization. In Israel Yahweh acted for and through the people instead of for and through kings and dynas-

28. Ibid., 8.

ties and centralized political entities. "Moreover, Yahweh acts for and through a whole people acting on their own behalf." Yahweh brings a people into being because Yahweh is a God of a people who bring themselves into being. Yahweh is at once the cause and the effect of a particular historical choice. Israel in the premonarchic period created a just and egalitarian society because it trusted in Yahweh, and Israel trusted in Yahweh because it had created a just and egalitarian society.[29]

To the extent, however, that Boesak's existential appropriation of the Bible is founded on questionable historical and theoretical grounds, one must agree with Hugo Assmann, contrary to Boesak, that there is a

> need to reject a "fundamentalism of the Left" composed of short-circuits: attempts to transplant biblical paradigms and situations into our world without understanding their historical circumstances. It is equally false to state that the whole biblical framework, with its infinite variety of paradigms and situations, is an adequate basis for establishing a satisfactory complex dialectics of hermeneutical principles.[30]

In a recent study, Gottwald has driven home Assmann's point with an even more poignant clarity. He says of liberation theologians, including black theologians:

> While invoking biblical symbols of liberation, liberation theologians seldom push those biblical symbols all the way back to their socio-historic foundations, so that we can grasp concretely the inner-biblical strands of oppression and liberation in all their stark multiplicity and contradictory interactions. . . . A thinness of social structural analysis and a thinness of biblical analysis combine to give many expressions of liberation theology the look of devotional or polemical tracts. . . . The picking and choosing of biblical resources may not carry sufficient structural analysis of biblical societies to make a proper comparison with the present possible. Likewise, those most oriented to biblical grounding for liberation theology may lack knowledge or interest in the his-

29. Norman K. Gottwald, *Tribes of Yahweh: A Sociology of the Religion of Liberated Israel, 1250-1050* B.C.E. (London: SCM Press, 1980), 692f.

30. Hugo Assmann, *Theology for a Nomad Church* (New York: Orbis Books, 1976), 104.

tory of social forms and ideas from biblical times to the present, so that unstructural understanding of the Bible may simply reinforce and confirm unstructural understanding of the present.[31]

My fundamental objection to the biblical hermeneutics of black theology is that not only does it suffer from an "unstructural understanding of the Bible," but—both as a consequence and as a reason—it also suffers from an unstructural understanding of the black experience and struggle. In point of fact, black theologians fail in what Terry Eagleton has called the threefold task of a revolutionary cultural worker. According to Eagleton, a revolutionary cultural worker must 1) participate in the production of works and events, thereby intending those effects commensurate with the victory of socialism; 2) function as a critic, exposing the rhetorical structures of works and combating whatever deceptions are intended through them; 3) interpret works and events "against the grain." Presumably, in making this last point Eagleton seeks to remind us that the appropriation of works and events is always a contradictory process that embodies in some form a "struggle."[32]

I will argue that this struggle is a key category in developing a biblical hermeneutics of liberation. The struggle is, depending on the class forces involved, either to harmonize the contradictions inherent in the works and events or to highlight them with a view toward allowing social class choices in their appropriation. In brief, then, Eagleton summarizes the tasks of a cultural worker as "projective, polemical, and appropriative."

The interrelatedness of the tasks of a revolutionary cultural worker can scarcely be overemphasized. There is no doubt that black theology is "projective" and "appropriative," albeit vaguely and loosely, in its use of the Bible. It is certainly *not* polemical—in the sense of being critical—in its biblical hermeneutics. Rather, it lifts and appropriates themes from the Exodus, the prophetic, and the Jesus traditions into the service of

31. Gottwald, "Socio-Historical Precision in the Biblical Grounding of Liberation Theologies" (an address to the Catholic Biblical Association of America at its annual meeting, San Francisco, August 1985), 5f.
32. Terry Eagleton, *Walter Benjamin, or Towards a Revolutionary Criticism* (London: Verso, 1981), 113.

a liberation project. It uncritically enlists the rhetorical structures that inhere in and circumscribe those themes—and which have an inbuilt proclivity to produce politically undesirable effects—on the side of the struggle for the liberation of the oppressed. And it fails to detect oppression and oppressors, exploitation and exploiters in the text of the Bible. Nothing, of course, could be more subversive to the struggle for liberation than enlisting the oppressors and exploiters as comrades in arms. Eagleton identifies this danger with enviable precision in his analysis of Samuel Richardson's *Clarissa*. Eagleton comments on Clarissa's forgiveness of her aristocratic rapist, a forgiveness symbolizing a victory that takes the form of a spiritual submission of which the rapist himself is incapable:

> If the bourgeoisie are to attain spiritual hegemony over the squirearchy, this is an essential inversion: *you must not fight the class enemy with his own weapons,* and the fact that the bourgeoisie are in practice indistinguishable from their superiors on this score counts heavily against them. Clarissa's forgiveness of Lovelace thus reflects something of the bourgeoisie's impulse to make peace with the traditional ruling class; *it also of course frustrates it, since, given her death, no actual alliance will ensue.* [italics mine][33]

The most glaring example of this fighting of the class enemy with his own weapons is Boesak's appropriation of the text of Genesis 4:1-16, the story of Cain's killing of Abel. Boesak's reading of this story is in complete ideological collusion with the text and its rhetorical intentions: to legitimate the process of land expropriation by the ruling classes of David's monarchy from the village peasants in the hill country of Palestine during the tenth century B.C.E. Boesak maintains that Cain shirked his responsibility for his brother: "Cain rejects this human responsibility in the most abominable manner: he murders his brother."[34] According to Boesak, God's punishment was justified: Cain had to be ruptured from the land. But what is more, he had to be made a wanderer, a vagabond, in the world. Boesak then draws this hermeneutical conclusion:

33. Eagleton, *The Rape of Clarissa* (Minneapolis: University of Minnesota Press, 1982), 90.
34. Boesak, 149.

What does that mean for us? I think the story meant to tell us that oppressors shall have no place on God's earth. Oppressors have no home. Oppressors do not belong to, are not at home in God's objectives for this world. They have gone out of bounds. They have removed themselves from the world. Cain did not only break his relationship to the land, but also his relationship to God.[35]

"Kgakgamatso! Mohlolo! Isimanga! What a miracle!" Africans would say. The story of the oppressed has been stolen by the oppressors and is being used as an ideological weapon against the oppressed in subsequent histories. The point is that there is no historical basis in this period of Israel's history to support the argument that the oppressors were made homeless, wanderers, and vagabonds. Neither is there any historical evidence in previous or subsequent epochs to support the assertion that oppressors can be made homeless, even by their murder of the oppressed. On the contrary, there is ample evidence to suggest that the Davidic monarchy, which forms the historical backdrop of the J-story we encounter in Genesis 4, inaugurated a relentless process of land dispossession of the village peasants in Israel.[36] The story as it stands is a ruling-class author's attempt to validate this landlessness of the village peasants on the grounds—hardly convincing—that their harvest was not an acceptable offering to the Lord.

A correct theological appropriation of Genesis 4 should begin with a historical-critical exegesis of the text. The importance of doing this is underscored by Anthony Mansueto when he states that "existential or religious commitment to social revolution will not substitute for scientific analysis of the valence of a tradition in the class struggle."[37] The category of social struggle

35. Ibid., 151.
36. See Mosala, "Social Justice in the Early Israelite Monarchy" (unpublished M.A. thesis, University of Manchester, 1980), ch. 4; Marvin L. Chaney, "Latifundialization and Prophetic Diction in Eighth Century Israel and Judah" (Sociology of the Monarchy Seminar, Anaheim, CA, 1985), *passim;* "Systemic Study of the Sociology of the Israelite Monarchy" (Sociology of the Monarchy Seminar, Dec. 1981), *passim;* N. K. Gottwald, "Social History of the United Monarchy . . ." (Seminar on the Sociology of the Monarchy, Dec. 20, 1983), *passim.*
37. Anthony Mansueto, "From Historical Criticism to Historical Materialism: Towards a Materialist Reading of Scripture" (seminar paper, Graduate Theological Union, Berkeley, 1983), 2.

M.B. — The Western insistence on hist'l verfability is shared by the author

34

as a biblical hermeneutical tool necessitates a historical-critical starting point for an exegesis of Genesis 4. The questions that emanate from this approach are, among others: What historical point is reflected by the discursive practice this text represents? what are the social, cultural, class, gender, and racial issues at work in this text? what is the ideological-spiritual agenda of the text, that is, how does the text itself seek to be understood?

It is generally accepted within biblical scholarship that Genesis 4 is part of the *J*-document of the Pentateuch. Most scholars also concur that the *J*-document is to be located historically in the Davidic-Solomonic era of the Israelite monarchy. The royal scribes of Solomon, in particular, are credited with having undertaken to write the history of the united monarchy using the traditions of the various groups. This production of the history of Israel by the royal scribes is acknowledged to be dominated in its discursive practice by the concerns of the Davidic-Solomonic state. These concerns involve such matters as the change of socioeconomic structures, for example, from the premonarchical egalitarian tribal system to the semifeudal tributary-exploitive monarchical system. They also involve the need for an ideological explanation of the creation in Israel of large estates *(latifundia),* which were privately owned, and the simultaneous large-scale dispossession of the majority of the peasant producers of Israel from their *nahalahs* (II Kgs. 21), or inherited plots of land. Included in these concerns are matters such as the development of the social division of labor on which was predicated deep class distinctions. New social struggles developed around this division of labor in the monarchy, into which the prophetic movement was to insert itself in very specific ways, most of them not necessarily revolutionary.

Genesis 4 represents one such production of the royal scribes of Solomon and David's monarchy. The question of the division of labor is excellently inscribed in this text through the struggle between the pastoral sector and the agricultural sector of the economy. The agenda of this story seems to be the legitimation of the process of dispossession of freeholding peasants by the new class of estate holders under the protection of the monarchical state. Clearly, Cain the tiller of the soil must be seen to represent the freeholding peasantry who became locked in a

life-and-death struggle with the emergent royal and latifundiary classes, represented in this story by Abel. Obviously, the text
favors Abel and enlists divine pleasure on his side. The reason
Abel is depicted as a pastoralist must have something to do with
the division of labor mentioned above and the way in which it
fed the regional specialization so important to the ruling classes.
Marvin Chaney, commenting on these dynamics from the point
of view of the text of II Chronicles 26:10, says:

> Here we learn that under royal tutelage, herding was increased
> in the steppe by means of guard towers and cisterns, plowing—
> the cultivation of cereal crops, the predominant of which was
> wheat—was intensified in the plain and piedmont region, and
> viticulture and orcharding were pressed in the uplands. In each
> case, the economic exploitation of a given region was specialized
> to the one or two products by whose production that region could
> contribute maximally to the export trade and/or to the conspicu-
> ous consumption of the local elite.[38]

Expropriating the lands of the peasant producers for purposes
of increasing and intensifying ruling-class herding, plowing, vi-
ticulture, and orcharding was a practice that is very well attested
in Israelite traditions, not least in Genesis 4. The problem, of
course, is that these traditions must be understood as ideological productions—spiritual ideological productions certainly, but
ideological productions nonetheless. Thus their signification of
the historical and social processes of Israel is necessarily in some
way reflective of, even though not exhausted by, the class and
political interests of the conditions of their production.

In the case of Genesis 4 roles are changed around. The
story chooses to depict the victorious and successful groups of
the tenth and ninth century B.C.E., the Israelite monarchy, as the
victims and vice versa, thus lending ideological legitimacy to
the process of latifundialization and peasant land dispossession
that took place.

On the issue of whether an offering was acceptable or
unacceptable to the Lord, a critical biblical hermeneutics of liberation would have immediately thought of the question of the

---

38. Chaney, "Latifundialization and Prophetic Diction," 5.

Israelite monarchy's ruling classes' practice of exacting a tribute from the village peasants. This perspective would have raised the question of the class struggle in monarchical Israel and how its reality is signified in a discursive ideological textual practice such as Genesis 4 represents.

There is also evidence that village peasants often resisted encroachments on their *nahalahs*. While no indications of their victories exist in the texts of the Bible, except in the New Testament (Matt. 21:33ff.), it is reasonable to believe that the murder of Abel may stand for one such victory. But, of course, the text comes to us from the hands of the ruling class, and thus one can hardly expect a celebration of Abel's representative demise. The class and ideological commitments of Genesis 4 are unequivocal. This factor, however, is not immediately obvious to the reader. It requires a reading that issues out of a firm grounding in the struggle for liberation, as well as a basis in critical theoretical perspectives that can expose the deep structures of a text.

*   *   *

Desmond Tutu is even more deeply steeped in traditional biblical hermeneutics than is Allan Boesak. Like Boesak, he also fails to identify the oppressor in the text. At a memorial service for Steve Biko, the leader and founding member of the Black Consciousness Movement in South Africa, Tutu likened the sacrifice that Biko had made of his life to that of Jesus of Nazareth. While Jesus the liberator of the oppressed in certain parts of the New Testament is indeed comparable to Biko in hermeneutical ways that can spell liberation for present-day black South Africans, not all Jesuses of the New Testament have such effects. The point is that the ideological appropriations of Jesus by the various New Testament authors are different and do not all always adequately represent the ideological concerns of Jesus' own earthly program. There are, therefore, different approximations of Jesus' ministry by the different discourses of the New Testament. The argument here is that Luke's signification of Jesus' program, in particular, is problematical in terms of the liberation struggle of black people in South Africa.

The tradition that Tutu appropriates in the service of this struggle is especially problematical. Having made the Jesus connection, he proceeds to collude with the oppressors in the Bible by describing Jesus—as do other black and liberation theologians—in terms of Isaiah 61:1-7. He ignores the class basis of the text, as it now stands, in the royal ruling-class ideology (the Hebrew term *masiah* is thoroughly royal). This is true notwithstanding the liberating aspects of the text. For although the text appeals to a tradition of liberation that probably goes back many centuries, it is now framed by the interests of a formerly Zion-based elite, a ruling-class people now displaced from Jerusalem. This group is in Babylonian exile, where an ideology of return—not liberation—is being hammered out on the basis of the old liberation traditions of Israel and the political and ideological interests of a formerly Zion-based ruling class: "To appoint unto them that mourn in Zion—to give unto them beauty instead of ashes, the oil of joy for mourning, the garment of praise for the spirit of heaviness; that they may be glorified. And they shall build the old wastes, they shall raise up the former desolations, and they shall repair the waste cities, the desolation of many generations."[39]

Surely it is the liberation—if one may speak of it as that —of the exiled elites that this text has in mind. It is their restoration to the luxuries and privileges of Zion that the text predicts. If this text had had in mind the oppressed and exploited peasants and underclasses of monarchical Israel, their vision of the future would have been different. It would certainly not have been symbolized by the possession of luxury items such as oil, a garment of praise, buildings, and cities. Rather, it would have been the repossession of land, the tools, the control of their labor for productive use, and their security (Mic. 4:3b-4; I Sam. 8:11-22).

Of course, the real difficulty in criticizing Tutu's biblical hermeneutics here is one's assumption that he shares an ideological uneasiness about ruling-class values. This assumption is based on his speaking of liberation as the goal of his theology.

39. See Desmond Tutu, *Hope and Suffering* (Grand Rapids: Eerdmans, 1984), 7.

It is, however, sometimes difficult to maintain that assumption in the face of assertions such as the following:

> My dear Brothers, you are being prepared for one of the most wonderful moments in your life—when you will be ordained priests. This means that you will have a special share in *the one royal priesthood* of our Lord and Saviour Jesus Christ, the true High Priest of our faith who ever lives to make intercession for us. . . . [italics mine][40]

The basic question here is: which side of the class struggle in the social history of the biblical communities do we hermeneutically connect with when, like Tutu, we describe our vision in terms of a share in the *royal* priesthood of our *Lord* (i.e., our ideological landed nobility)?

In all fairness to Tutu, Boesak, and black theologians in general, I am not questioning their personal intentions here. The problem is basically one of contradiction. It has to do with the difficult area of the interface between personal existential commitments and structural-ideological locations as well as frameworks of political activity. It is not enough to be existentially committed to the struggles of the oppressed and exploited people. One must also effect a theoretical break with the assumptions and perspectives of the dominant discourse of a stratified society. Thus, unless the nature of this contradiction at the heart of the theologies of Boesak and Tutu is identified and dealt with adequately, the effect of black theology will be no more than what Cornel West describes regarding the black American scene in the 1960s:

> The working poor and underclass watched as the "new" black middle class visibly grappled with its identity, social position and radical political rhetoric. For the most part, the black underclass continued to hustle, rebel when appropriate, get high and listen to romantic proletarian love songs produced by Detroit's Motown; they remained perplexed at their idolization by the "new" black middle class which they sometimes envied. The black working poor persisted in its weekly church attendance, struggled to make ends meet and waited to see what the beneficial results would be after all the bourgeois "hoopla" was over.

40. Ibid., 17.

In short, the black nationalist moment, despite its powerful and progressive critique of American cultural imperialism, was principally the activity of black petit bourgeois self-justification upon reaching an anxiety-ridden middle-class status in racist American society.[41]

Gottwald offers a way out of the dilemma of black and other liberation theologians: that is, gleaning liberation themes and perspectives from biblical texts. Specifically regarding feminist biblical hermeneutics, he says:

Instead of straining after possible "feminine" elements in the overwhelming masculine deity of Israel, women and men who care about the future of feminism in our religious communities should be examining the techno-environmental and socio-political conditions of ancient Israel to see what parameters actually existed for a feminist movement and to assess the extent to which Israelite women benefited or lost from the transition between elitist hierarchical Canaan and a generally much more egalitarian intertribal Israel. A careful calculus of these gains and losses will ultimately be of far more significance to the contemporary religious feminist movement than attempts to make ancient Israelite religion look more feminist than it actually was. . . . For feminists who wish to keep in continuity with their religious heritage, I believe it is sufficient to assert that contemporary feminism in church and synagogue is a logical and necessary extension of the social egalitarian principle of early Israel, which itself did not exhibit any appreciable independent feminist consciousness of praxis.[42]

Clearly, however, black theologians are correct in detecting glimpses of liberation and of a determinate social movement galvanized by a powerful religious ideology in the biblical text. The existence of this phenomenon is not in question; rather, the problem here is one of developing an adequate hermeneutical framework that can rescue those liberating themes from the biblical text. One cannot successfully perform this task by denying the oppressive structures that frame what liberating themes the texts encode. The need for such a framework can be

41. West, "The Paradox of the Afro-American Rebellion," in *The 60s Without Apology,* ed. S. Sayres et al. (Minneapolis: University of Minnesota Press, 1984), 53.

42. Gottwald, *Tribes of Jahweh,* 797, n. 628.

seen from the use of even a semiological approach to texts. Describing how this approach underscores the urgency of *materialist* readings, Michel Clevenot says:

> But the reading that is interested only in the meaning is idealist, believing in the innocence and transparency of the text. The exchange is governed here by the general equivalent—just as on the economic level, fascinated by the signifier "gold," workers are unable to see the real process of production; and just as on the political level, fascinated and intimidated by power and its signifiers such as king and Caesar, the subjects find the established order natural. So on the ideological level, fascinated by a "god" or the "truth" and by the false evidence of the signified (the meaning of the text), people read with the eyes of faith and "good sense."[43]

It is this manner of reading the biblical text as an innocent and transparent container of a message or messages that has caused black and liberation theologians not to be aware of—or, more correctly, to appropriate as otherwise—the presence and significance of oppression and oppressors, exploitation and exploiters in the *signified practices* that the biblical texts really are. In reading a biblical text, one can decode its message using any number of reference codes. One can read the text accepting the code in which its message has been inscribed, thus colluding with it. Stuart Hall calls this the "dominant" or "hegemonic" code of a text. According to him, there are at least three other codes within which the messages of a text or discourse can be decoded: 1) The professional code attempts to communicate messages that are already signified in a hegemonic manner. While this code has a relative autonomy, it nonetheless operates within the hegemony of the dominant code. As Hall aptly puts the matter,

> Indeed, it serves to reproduce the dominant definitions precisely by bracketing the hegemonic quality, and operating with professional codings. . . . It may even be said that the professional codes serve to reproduce hegemonic definitions specifically by not overtly biasing their operations in their direction: ideological

43. Michel Clevenot, *Materialist Approaches to the Bible* (New York: Orbis Books, 1985), 67f.

reproduction therefore takes place here inadvertently, uncon-
sciously, "behind men's backs." Of course, conflicts, contradictions, and even "misunderstandings" regularly take place between the dominant and the professional significations and their
signifying agencies.[44]

2) The negotiated code combines within itself adaptive and oppositional elements. It takes dominant codes as a starting point,
while it allows itself "a more negotiated application to 'local
conditions.'"[45] Hall succinctly captures its essence when he says
that negotiated codes

> ... operate through what we might call particular or situated log-
> ics: and these logics arise from their differential and unequal re-
> lation to power.[46]

3) The oppositional code is another means by which a message
may be decoded. This particular framework, while understanding perfectly the preferred code inherent in a text or discourse, may choose to read such a text or discourse in a contrary
and often alternative framework. "This is the case of the viewer
who listens to a debate on the need to limit wages, but who 'reads'
every mention of the 'national interest' as 'class interest.'"[47]

*   *   *

My effort in the later chapters of this study to develop a materialist black biblical hermeneutics of liberation takes its cue from
an understanding of the existence of these various ways of reading a text. The next chapter, however, is a critique of the recent
sociological approaches to the Bible that have not taken seriously the materialist framework of analysis.

---

44. Stuart Hall, *Encoding and Decoding in the Television Discourse*
(Birmingham: Centre for Contemporary Cultural Studies, 1973), 22.
    45. Ibid., 23.
    46. Ibid.
    47. Ibid.

2

Social Scientific Approaches to the Bible: One Step Forward, Two Steps Back?

Modern criticism was born of a struggle against the absolutist state; unless its future is now defined as a struggle against the bourgeois state, it might have no future at all.

—Terry Eagleton[1]

THE RISE OF MODERN BIBLICAL CRITICISM IN THE EIGHTEENTH AND nineteenth centuries was an inextricable part of a new, emerging capitalist world in the West. This world was socially and politically pitted against an older, historically disappearing, feudal world. Thus the emergence of modern biblical criticism was never simply an isolated mental act. It was a manifestation of and a self-conscious response to a historical and social movement—the rise of the bourgeois society. Viewed in this way, biblical criticism can justifiably occupy its place within modern criticism in general and thus be included in Eagleton's statement above. Few biblical scholars who are aware of the links between forms of consciousness and forms of social and cultural institu-

---

1. *The Function of Criticism* (London: Verso, 1984), 124.

43

tions will deny Eagleton's identification of the circumstances of the origin of biblical criticism. Anthony Mansueto corroborates Eagleton's contention when he says:

> The roots of both historical criticism and the sociological tradition can be traced to the crisis of 19th century liberalism. The tremendous development of the productive forces unleashed by modern industry, and in particular steam power, and the great revolutions of the later eighteenth and the nineteenth century undermined the older, ideological theories of social life—e.g., natural law doctrines—and sparked a wave of historical studies and theoretical investigations struggling to come to terms with the diversity of human social existence, the dynamics of social change, conflict and integration: i.e. with the new world of bourgeois society, and its manifest difference from the old world of the-ancient regime.[2]

The present era of the modern world, which may well be the last phase of this modern world and the womb in which is developing the "new world," is witnessing the emergence of new biblical critical methods. A new criticism has begun to operate that expresses itself in various ways. In this chapter I propose to examine the form of new criticism generally referred to as the "sociological" or "social scientific" approach to the Bible. We will view Eagleton's warning that "unless modern criticism is now defined as a struggle against the bourgeois state, it might have no future at all" as an appropriate grid for an assessment of the social scientific approaches to the Bible. In fact, the title of this chapter already betrays the judgment we propose to offer.

SOCIAL SCIENTIFIC METHODS: THEIR USEFULNESS

Robert R. Wilson has warned that the use of social scientific approaches in biblical studies is still in its infancy. It is, therefore,

---

2. Anthony Mansueto, "From Historical Criticism to Historical Materialism," 3; see also Robert Wilson, *Sociological Approaches to the Old Testament* (Philadelphia: Fortress, 1984), 10.

too soon to predict the influence that these methods will have.[3] But it is not unreasonable, in light of what has been produced in a somewhat systematic manner for about a decade now, to try to judge whether there is a future for biblical criticism that is not simply a newly phrased reiteration of a past. Biblical criticism cannot afford to continue to engage its energies—uselessly— against the kind of absolutist state whose material conditions have been virtually eroded. If it chooses to do so, it does so in defense of the bourgeois status quo in conjunction with which it came into being in the first place. In that case, however, the boundary between it as *criticism* and as *ideology* (the latter being the glue that holds existing social relationships together) will be precariously thin.

There can be no doubt that the present deliberate and sometimes systematic application of sociological insights to the Bible has brought about a new atmosphere in biblical criticism. There is a new climate of freedom from what Gottwald has termed the "distinctly individualizing tendency of the humanities, a perspective reinforced and complicated by the attachment of biblical scholars first to monarchic and aristocratic class interests and then to bourgeois class interests."[4] As we shall observe later on, the presence of this atmosphere does not mean that the proponents of the social scientific methods have necessarily taken advantage of it. The recognized legitimacy of these methods, however, does create conditions under which such freedom is possible.

In addition, a greater social-historical relativism, in opposition to the dominant positivist empiricism of the historical-critical method, has been introduced to the understandings of ancient Israelite and early Christian communities. This means the possible emergence of a healthier attitude toward the biblical texts that sees them as ideological products of social systems and of the configurations of social relations internal to these systems. Such an attitude is in opposition to the atomizing and ideologically reductionist approach of the historical-critical methods.[5]

3. Wilson, *Sociological Approaches*, 81.
4. Gottwald, *Tribes of Yahweh*, 11.
5. Itumeleng J. Mosala, "Social Justice in the Early Israelite Monarchy," ch. 2.

Some may argue that the most crucial contribution of the social science methods is that they may finally free biblical criticism from the neoorthodox theological problematic that, in Mansueto's words, "set the terms for biblical research during the period after the First World War."[6] As Mansueto makes clear, this theological starting point of biblical criticism stifled even the implicit sociological concerns of form criticism and tradition history. By questioning the premise of biblical criticism that the Bible is the "Word of God," the new methods have also called into question the idealist epistemological framework that undergirds such criticism. Real living human communities whose histories and struggles are represented in the biblical texts may soon be seen to constitute the goal, if not the starting point, of modern social science criticism of the Bible. It is important that we are referring to whole communities rather than just prominent individuals.

The social science methods may enable us to see that the historical-critical methods, however much they may seem antithetical to the biblical criticism of the prebourgeois era, were born, ironically, of political consensus and served as a catalyst in the creation and unifying of the new bourgeois ruling bloc. While it called for the emancipation of biblical study from its feudal prisons, historical criticism was "uplifting the profligate aristocracy by retaining the latter's fundamental doctrinal assumptions as a starting point and goal of its activity."[7] The use of the social science methods may enable us to discern the central irony of all Enlightenment criticism, including the historical-critical methods as applied to the Bible. The essence of this irony is that while the Enlightenment criticism is characterized by its resistance to absolutism on the one hand, it has nevertheless itself grown intolerant of forms of criticism that appear dissident in its sphere of dominance on the other hand.[8]

Having briefly assessed the contribution of the social science methods of biblical understanding, most of which are methodological, we still need to address the question of whether

6. Mansueto, "From Historical Criticism to Historical Materialism,"1.
7. See Eagleton, *Function of Criticism*, 11.
8. Ibid., 12.

these methods as they are used in biblical criticism represent a *theoretical* break with the past. In other words, viewed theoretically, how new are these methods?

THE HISTORICAL AND SOCIAL CONTEXT

Late monopoly capitalism constitutes the wider social-historical matrix of the social science methods in biblical study. On the nondiscursive level this social-historical context is characterized by the movement of the "subsumption of many capitals into one capital based on a vastly expanded reproduction process; the progressive abolition of capital as *private* property and the socialization of the accumulation process; and the transformation of the whole of society into a sort of 'social factory' for capital."[9] Historically, this is the period characterized by the universal market. The dominant tendency of the capitalist mode of production is to transform and subordinate the individual, family, and social needs to the market and to the needs of capital. It is the mode of the total commodification of life. By extending the commodity form to all aspects of life, capital gives fresh energy and scope to its operations. Late monopoly capitalism is the era of the obsolescence of the family and the subjection of its members to productive activity under the direct supervision and control of capital. Everything is for selling and for buying. As Harry Braverman so succinctly articulates it,

> . . . the population no longer relies upon social organization in the form of family, friends, neighbours, community, elders, children, but with few exceptions must go to market and only to market, not only for food, clothing, and shelter, but also for recreation, amusement, security, for the care of the young, the old, the sick, the handicapped. In time not only the material and service needs but even the emotional patterns of life are channeled through the market.[10]

9. Stuart Hall, et al., eds., *Policing the Crisis* (London: Macmillan, 1978), 371.

10. Braverman, *Labor and Monopoly Capital: The Degradation of Work in the Twentieth Century* (New York: Monthly Review Press, 1974), 276.

This era is the era of large-scale capital accumulation; its dominant rule is the ever-expanding valorization of capital. If human life must be devalued in order for increased surplus value to accrue, so be it. As Marx pointed out when this process was still in its very early stages,

> It is not the diminished rate either of the absolute, or of the proportional increase in labour-power or labouring population, which causes capital to be in excess, but conversely the excess of capital that makes exploitable labour-power insufficient. . . . It is not the increased rate either of the absolute or of the proportional, increase in labour-power, or labouring population, that makes capital insufficient; but, conversely, the relative diminution of capital that causes the exploitable labour-power, or rather its price, to be in excess. . . . The rate of accumulation is the independent not dependent variable; the rate of wages, the dependent, not the independent variable.[11]

The sine qua non, the *differentia specifica,* of the capitalist mode of production is increasing accumulation. The specific form of accumulation characteristic of late monopoly capitalism is that all of social and individual life is subjected to the dictates of accumulation and structured through market relations. Braverman summarizes the point exquisitely:

> In the period of monopoly capitalism, the first step in the creation of the universal market is the conquest of all goods production by the commodity form, the second step is the conquest of an increasing range of services and their conversion into commodities, and the third step is a "product cycle" which invents new products and services, some of which become indispensable as the conditions of modern life change to destroy alternatives.[12]

Given the unprecedented levels of accumulation and the total involvement of exchange relationships at all levels of social and individual life, the traditional role of the state has become expanded and more complex under monopoly capitalism. The accumulation process churns out more economic surplus than can be absorbed. This leads to crises of disorder in the economy, which express themselves in terms of the lack of "ef-

11. Marx, *Capital* (London: Penguin/New Left Books, 1976) 1:679.
12. Braverman, 281.

fective demand." The gap created by this lack of demand has since World War II been filled by government spending—accompanied, of course, by increased taxation.

The increased accumulation of capital has in the last hundred years also led to the internationalization of capital. The latter process has created economic competition among capitalist nations that has in turn led to military clashes over spheres of economic influence. Also, the rise of people's revolutions, especially in Third World countries, has led to an interest in what Braverman calls "policing the world structure of imperialism." Government is thus able to absorb the economic surplus and guarantee "effective demand" by playing this international role. The capitalist state under monopoly conditions has also had to intervene domestically within capitalist countries in a situation of permanent poverty and insecurity in order to diffuse local political bombs and simply to sustain life.

Government-sponsored services like education have become imperative under modern conditions. As Braverman puts it, "The minimum requirements for 'functioning' in a modern urban environment—both as workers and as consumers—are imparted to children in an institutional setting rather than in the family or community."[13] Eagleton summarizes the cultural effects of late monopoly capitalism in the following quotation:

> Late capitalism overcomes the sheer separation of the symbolic from the economic, but does so by bringing the symbolic under the dominance of the economic. The processes of this subsumption are precisely designed to block the overcoming of the subjective divisions inaugurated by capital. It is here that the cultural processes of late capitalism are most crucial: Through its dominant *cultural* norms and practices, late capitalism strives to sever social experience from the formation of counter-ideologies, to break collective experience into monadic isolation of the private experiences of individuals, and to pre-empt the effects of association by subsuming the discourses and images that regulate social life. [italics mine][14]

The effects of late capitalism were felt at two different levels in

13. Ibid., 287.
14. Eagleton, *Function of Criticism,* 120ff.

different parts of the world. In the Third World capitalism caused dislocations at the structural levels of society; the First World experienced alienation at the level of discursive practices. The peasants and workers of the Third World, on the one hand, arose in revolution against capitalism. During colonization, sub-structural and discursive uprootings of the indigenous life had been combined as a condition of the success of colonization. Students and professors in the institutions of higher learning in the West, on the other hand, encountered the alienating and totalizing force of monopoly oligarchy primarily at the discursive level. This was true because even that last bastion of Western privilege, the college and university, had been invaded by the dominant cultural forms and practices of the armed, repressive state of late monopoly capitalism.

*   *   *

It is thus not unfair to characterize modern criticism in terms of Roland Barthes' view of it as the criticism that expresses itself as "text." And according to him, text "is . . . that uninhibited person who shows his behind to the Political Father."[15] But, as Eagleton indicates,

> That reference to the Political Father is not fortuitous. *The Pleasure of the Text* was published five years after a social eruption which rocked France's political fathers to their roots. In 1968 the student movement had swept across Europe, striking against the authoritarianism of the educational institutions and in France briefly threatening the capitalist state itself. For a dramatic moment, that state teetered on the brink of ruin; its police and army fought in the streets with students who were struggling to forge solidarity with the working class. Unable to provide a coherent political leadership, plunged into a confused melee of socialism, anarchism and infantile behind-baring, the student movement was rolled back and dissipated; betrayed by their supine Stalinist leaders, the working class movement was unable to assume power. Charles de Gaulle returned from a hasty exile, and the French state regrouped its forces in the name of patriotism, law

15. Quoted in Eagleton, *Literary Theory: An Introduction* (Minneapolis: University of Minnesota Press, 1983), 141.

and order. Poststructuralism was a product of that blend of eu-
phoria and disillusionment, liberation and dissipation, carnival
and catastrophe, which was 1968. Unable to break the structure
of state power, poststructuralism found it possible to subvert the
structure of language.[16]

It would appear that this sense of the inability or
powerlessness to break the structure of monopoly capitalism
on the one hand, and the feeling of strength and enthusiasm
about ransacking and subverting the social systems and social
worlds of literary texts on the other, remains the defining
characteristic of modern criticism. It has not been able to live
down the experience of the 1960s; it is sometimes even uncer-
tain about its moment of *Entstehung* and thus is generally unable to theorize this moment. Robin Scroggs, for instance, expresses this uncertainty when he says, about the new
sociological criticism in biblical study:

> Today the pendulum has swung again. Whether this is the result
> of a neo-liberalism, or social tensions such as the Vietnam war,
> student revolutions, and severe economic and political oppres-
> sion in various parts of the world, or all of these, is not clear as
> yet. Nevertheless, Gerd Theissen speaks for many of us when he
> notes a rising *Unbehagen* about a discipline which limits the ac-
> ceptable methods to the historical and theological.[17]

Systematic theology responded to the cultural and political convulsions of the 1960s by evolving a twentieth-century secularism that was clearly distinguishable from the secularism of eighteenth-century Enlightenment rationalism. The new secularism
was a search and plea for an accommodation within the discursive structures of late monopoly capitalism. It was a cry for freedom from the captivity of pre-Enlightenment religious ideology
to which it had returned in the nineteenth century, but also especially in the period after World War II. It was an embracing of
the metaphors, symbols, and controlling notions of the so-called
technopolitan civilization, a euphemism for late monopoly capitalism. The subtitle of Harvey Cox's most celebrated book, *The*

16. Ibid.
17. Robin Scroggs, "Sociological Interpretation of the New Testament:
The Present State of Research," *New Testament Studies* 26 (1979/80): 165.

Secular City, is very revealing in this regard: "A celebration of its liberties and an invitation to its discipline."

Cox argues, as would most secularists of the 1960s, that a theology developed around the symbols of "secular city" would be better able to deal with the social change of the modern world. He summarizes his position in the following:

> The idea of the secular city exemplifies maturation and responsibility. Secularization denotes the removal of juvenile dependence from every level of a society; urbanization designates the fashioning of new patterns of human reciprocity. Combined in the symbol of the secular city, they portray man's continuing effort to find a basis for common life as archaic order and sacral ties disappear. The secular city emerges as tribes and towns vanish— and the process is never over.[18]

The process that Cox has invited us to celebrate is the moment of "statification" of society and socialization of the state that is characteristic of late capitalism. The disappearance of archaic order and sacral ties is the transgression of traditional boundaries between private and public that happens under conditions of monopoly capitalism. Eagleton aptly describes the real nature of this process:

> As bourgeois society develops into the modern epoch, the relations between public sphere, "intimate" sphere and state undergo significant changes. With the increasing "statification" of the public sphere, the "intimate" sphere becomes progressively marginalized; state education and social policy take over many of the functions previously reserved to the family, blurring the boundaries between "public" and "private" and stripping the family of its social, productive roles. The "intimate" sphere is in this sense deprivatized, pulled into public society—but only, in a notable historical irony, to be reprivatized as a unit of consumption. Private consumption and leisure, based upon the now shrunken space of the family, replace the forms of social discussion previously associated with the public sphere.[19]

Be that as it may, systematic theology saw the changes

---

18. Cox, *The Secular City: A Celebration of its Liberties and an Invitation to its Discipline* (New York: Macmillan, 1965), 109-110.
19. Eagleton, *Function of Criticism,* 117.

wrought by monopoly capital as the creation of new liberties that were to be embraced and celebrated. Biblical criticism, in the meantime, stuck to the idealist theological terms set for it by the neoorthodoxy of post-1945 systematic theology on the one hand, and continued to abide by the norms of positivistic empiricism endowed upon it by the rationalism of the eighteenth-century Enlightenment on the other. No real, new developments were widely felt in response to the social and political movements of the 1960s. Change in biblical criticism had to wait for the unprecedented rise—and in some instances success—of the liberation movements in the Third World and the concomitant questioning of the assumptions of Western theology as a whole, including biblical studies.

The response of biblical criticism to the revolutions and economic crises of the 1970s was in line with the convulsions of the 1960s: it was of the same type as the stock responses that were generated in order to deal with the world reality of the 1960s. These were represented by studies in phenomenology, hermeneutics, reception theory, structuralism, semiotics, and, most recently, poststructuralism. Politically the so-called sociological approaches to the Bible belong within the same framework as these new literary-critical approaches to the Bible. Like them, sociological approaches have not really honestly addressed the question of the politics of cultural and ideological discourses. Cornel West's strictures against the Marxist hermeneutics of Fredric Jameson apply without qualification to our sociological approaches, if not more so:

> In my view, Jameson goes wrong in trying to relate epistemological moves to ethical ones in ideological terms without giving an account of the collective dynamics which accompany these moves. From the Marxist perspective, all metaphysical, epistemological, and ethical discourses are complex, ideological affairs of specific groups, communities, and classes in or across particular societies.[20]

Eagleton levels a similar criticism against the deconstructionists, which is also relevant to our sociological criticism:

20. West, "Fredric Jameson's Marxist Hermeneutics," *Boundary 2: A Journal of Post-Modern Literature* (Winter 1983): 189.

If deconstruction is telling academic liberal humanism that it does not know quite what it is doing, or whether it is doing anything or not, or whether it can know whether it is doing anything or not, then this is not only because of the topical, fictive nature of all discourse; *it is also because of an historical uncertainty in the wider social functions of academic humanism, which neither it, nor much deconstruction, will fully acknowledge.* [italics mine][21]

Thus the social science approach to the Bible literature often gives one the impression that it is wading through no more than sociological—as opposed to literary or textual—deconstructionism. The feeling that the terms of debate are still set by the problematics of the eighteenth and nineteenth century is difficult to avoid. In a simple but brilliantly written article, Richard Rorty affirms this:

I have been saying, first that idealism and textualism have in common an opposition to the claim of science to be a paradigm of human activity, and second, that they differ in that one is a philosophical doctrine and the other an expression of suspicion about philosophy. I can put these two points together by saying that whereas nineteenth century idealism wanted to substitute one sort of science (philosophy) for another (natural science) as the centre of culture, twentieth century textualism wants to place literature in the centre, and to treat both science and philosophy as, at best, literary genres.[22]

This turning of criticism, literary or sociological, into "critically ingenious but politically deluded" ideology or, to put it another way, "imaginative response to once pertinent but now defunct problematics,"[23] does no more than play the role of the "anthropological . . . tiger which regularly disrupted a tribal ceremony by leaping into its midst; after a while, the tiger was incorporated into the ritual."[24]

Sociological approaches to the Bible often raise and address political issues in the Bible. They do not, however, address the issue of the politics of the sociological approaches

21. Eagleton, *Function of Criticism*, 106.
22. Richard Rorty, "Nineteenth Century Idealism and Twentieth Century Textualism," *The Monist* 64 (No. 2, 1981): 157.
23. West, "Jameson's Marxist Hermeneutics," 193.
24. Eagleton, *Function of Criticism*, 102.

themselves. The question is: On whose side, politically and so-cially, are these critical methods? As West puts it,

> To resurrect the dead, as bourgeois humanists try to do, is im-possible. To attack the dead, as deconstructionists do, is redun-dant and, ironically, to valorize death. To "go beyond" the dead is either to surreptitiously recuperate previous "contents" of life in new forms (Nietzsche), or to deceptively shrug off the weight of the dead whether by promoting cults of passive, nostalgic "dwelling" (Heidegger), or by creative self-rebegetting and self-redescribing (Emerson, Bloom, Rorty).[25]

Our contention, therefore, is that the new methods of biblical study under the rubric of sociological approaches do not really take us a step forward. They fail to constitute a criticism that "aims at transforming present practices—the remaining life — against the backdrop of previous discursive and political practices, against the dead past."[26] Biblical study under repres-sive, totalizing, commodifying conditions of late monopoly capitalism cannot afford to be reduced to an attack on the dead past of ancient Israelite history or early Christian discursive and political practices.

SOCIAL SCIENTIFIC METHODS: A CRITIQUE

Now it remains to show how the politics of our sociological ap-proaches are constantly symbiotic with the object of their criti-cism: the dead past of ancient biblical societies on the one hand, and the dead past of the nineteenth-century historical-critical methods on the other. The point of my argument is that in their present form the sociological approaches cannot serve as ade-quate tools of a black biblical hermeneutics of liberation.

Anthony Mansueto has convincingly shown that these methods do not represent a theoretical break with the past; rather, they "amount to no more than the sociological potentiali-ties of liberal biblical criticism along interpretive sociological or

25. West, "Jameson's Marxist Hermeneutics."
26. Ibid.

structural functionalist lines."[27] Max Weber, the chief theoretician of interpretive sociology, has defined it as

> . . . a science concerning itself with the interpretive understanding of social action and thereby with a causal explanation of its course and consequences. We shall speak of "action" insofar as the acting individual attaches a subjective meaning to his behaviour—be it overt or covert, omission or acquiescence. Action is "social" insofar as its subjective meaning takes account of the behaviour of others and is thereby oriented in its course.[28]

While Weber shared with his contemporaries a belief in "positive science," he nevertheless objected to the use of the methods of the natural sciences in the cultural sciences. In this he shared similar concerns with nineteenth-century metaphysical idealism, which "wanted to substitute one sort of science (philosophy) for another (natural science) as the centre of culture."[29]

But interpretive sociology, as a product of and response to the social disruptions of emerging late capitalism, exhibits the modified features of idealism that we have discerned in the textual idealism of twentieth-century literary criticism. It seeks not an Archimedian point from which to pontificate over culture, but it locates itself midway between the metaphysical idealism of philosophy and the positivist empiricism of natural science.

> "Meaning" may be of two kinds. The term may refer first to the actual existing meaning in the given concrete case of a particular actor, or to the average or approximate meaning attributable to a given plurality of actors; or secondly to the theoretically conceived *pure type* of subjective meaning attributed to the hypothetical actor or actors in a given type of action. In no case does it refer to an objectively "correct" meaning or one which is "true" in some metaphysical sense. It is this which distinguishes the empirical sciences of action, such as sociology and history, from the dogmatic disciplines in that area, such as jurisprudence, logic, ethics, and esthetics, which seek to ascertain the "true" and "valid" meanings associated with the objects of their investigation.[30]

27. Mansueto, "From Historical Criticism to Historical Materialism," 7.

28. Max Weber, *Economy and Society* (New York: Bedminster Press, 1968), I, 4.

29. Rorty, 157.

30. Weber, *Economy and Society*, I, 4.

Weber sought to have sociology accorded the status of positivist science in general, while he preferred to have it refrain from using the methods of this science. He struggled to distance sociology from metaphysical idealism while not really disagreeing with the importance of the latter's role. Archie Mafeje summarizes Weber's sociological attempt succinctly:

> In his attempt to cut off sociology from German metaphysics, Weber succeeded in relativizing and abstracting ideology in such a way that it ceased to be a question of class conflict and became merely a problem of interpreting individual intellectual reflexes under determinate social conditions. Now that history was no longer seen as an intelligible totality held together by social struggles, what remained was the subjective freedom of each individual to act according to his reason.[31]

The Weberian sociological approach manifests itself in a number of the works of biblical sociologists. Wayne Meeks is Weberian to the core in his study *The First Urban Christians:* he seeks to meet ordinary early Christians as individuals, but since they did not write the texts that we have about them, we must rather seek to find them "through the collectivities to which they belonged and glimpse their lives through the typical occasions mirrored in their texts."[32] Meeks's approach is inimical to social structures: its point of departure is individuals and their subjective choices. It is self-confessedly eclectic. According to Meeks, "Society is viewed as a process in which personal identity and social forms are mutually and continuously created by interactions that occur by means of symbols."[33] Meeks argues that this view of the social structure makes him a moderate functionalist.[34]

This theoretical and methodological eclecticism seems to me a new way of concealing old theoretical and ideological perspectives. It moves us one step forward to the extent that it focuses our attention on the social nature of our texts; but it pulls

31. Archie Mafeje, "The Problem of Anthropology in Historical Perspective: An Inquiry into the Growth of the Social Sciences," *Canadian Journal of African Studies* 10 (No. 2, 1976) 313.

32. Wayne A. Meeks, *The First Urban Christians* (New Haven: Yale University Press, 1983), 2.

33. Ibid., 6.

34. Ibid., 7.

us two steps backward in that it not only reintroduces the old ideological hunches inherent in the historical-critical methods, but it hides them under the cloak of a more systemic approach. Thus it blunts the edge of a possible new social and political biblical hermeneutics that could liberate the Bible itself to become a more liberating tool.

A more positivist aspect of the Weberian approach is discernible in the work of Edwin Judge, who complains about Bengt Holmberg's failure to "bestride ideas and facts in an equally secure manner." According to Judge, the fundamental question that remains unasked in many of the biblical sociology approaches, especially the New Testament, is this:

> What are the social facts of life characteristic of the world to which the New Testament belongs? Until painstaking field work is better done, the importation of social models that have been defined in terms of other cultures is methodologically no improvement on the "idealistic fallacy."[35]

The idealist-positivist problematic of the historical-critical methods and of most of eighteenth- and nineteenth-century science remains the structuring pole of the new sociological approaches. Scroggs is at pains to prove that the use of new sociological methods is not a turning of the idealistic tables; it does not reduce Christianity to social dynamic. "Rather it should be seen as an effort to guard against a reductionism from the other extreme, a limitation of the reality of Christianity to an inner-spiritual, or objective-cognitive system. In short, sociology of early Christianity wants to put body and soul together again."[36]

As we have argued above, this twentieth-century idealism, like nineteenth-century idealism, is a response to the social-historical crisis caused by the expansion of capitalism and its conquest of every aspect of life, especially as it made itself felt in the 1960s in the West. In biblical studies, it is a belated response to the 1960s. The most staggering example of this idealist sociological eclecticism seems to be John G. Gager's study

---

35. Edwin A. Judge, "The Social Identity of the First Christians: A Question of Method in Religious History," *Journal of Religious History* 20 (1980): 210.
36. Scroggs, "Sociological Interpretation of the New Testament," 165.

Kingdom and Community,[37] where he describes early Christianity as a millennial movement. It is, however, a movement that lost its eschatological vision as a result of the cognitive dissonance experienced by Jesus' followers as a result of his death. The result was a disconfirming of the belief that Jesus was the Messiah. As a means of rationalizing that experience of dissonance, the movement turned to a proselytizing mission. In the process it also engaged in activities to deeschatologize the message of Christ. According to Gager,

> The success of these efforts may be seen in the fact that by the year 150 C.E. not only was Christianity no longer an eschatological community, but, as the reaction to the apocalyptic fervour of Montanism clearly reveals, that it had come to regard eschatological movements as a serious threat. Toward the end of the first century Christians could still pray, "Thy Kingdom come" (Matt. 6:10). But at the end of the second century, Tertullian tells us that Christians prayed "for emperors, for their deputies and all in authority, for the welfare of the world, and for the delay of the final consummation" (Apol. 39.2; cf. 32.1).[38]

Gager combines models such as the sociology of millenarianism,[39] cognitive dissonance,[40] interpretive sociology,[41] and revitalization[42] without regard to the need for a systematic theory of social structure and development. As Mansueto correctly points out,

> Many of his models—e.g. millennialism—are based on comparative data drawn from societies which have little in common with the Roman Empire, while his account of the social structure of the Empire itself fails to take into account the tremendous diversity of landholding patterns and means of surplus extraction, as

37. John G. Gager, *Kingdom and Community: The Social World of Early Christianity* (Englewood Cliffs, NJ: Prentice-Hall, 1975), 45.

38. Ibid.

39. Kennelm Burridge, *New Heaven, New Earth.*

40. Leon Festinger, *A Theory of Cognitive Dissonance* (Stanford University Press, 1957).

41. Weber, *Economy and Society.*

42. Anthony Wallace, "A Revitalization Movement," *American Anthropologist* 58 (1958).

well as the very substantial evolution the Empire underwent, especially in its last stages.[43]

It is, moreover, the sociological idealism of Gager's Weberian approach, in political collusion with the status quo under present monopoly capital conditions, that requires critical attention. Gager's approach, like that of Weber, relativizes and abstracts ideology in the Roman Empire and in our societies. The result is that it ceases to refer to questions of class conflict and of the material conditions of production of the Christian literature and theologies. Instead, it confines itself to the subjective reflexes of Christians. This is a necessary logical position on the part of Gager and other Weberian biblical sociologists. For they themselves purport not to be engaged in their scholarly labors in the interests of any specific social class today. In other words, they conceal their real class commitments.

In the area of Old Testament studies, Robert Wilson's study of prophecy stands as an example of this sociological idealism. Wilson abstracts activities and institutions from societies of one kind (horticultural) and compares them with similarly abstracted phenomena in a society of a vastly different kind (tributary agrarian social formation of Israel). He neglects the question of social structure and of the complexity of social relations and contradictions. For this reason, Marvin Chaney's strictures against Wilson are justified:

> A recent and distinguished work, for example, purports to be a study of *Prophecy and Society in Ancient Israel* (Wilson, 1980). In fact, it is no such thing, but rather a learned study of the role of the prophets. Wilson's failure to take macrosociology seriously leaves two serious and related deficiencies in his work. a) The prophetic roles delineated with such care are not adequately articulated within the larger web of society, its conflicts and its changes. b) Just these latter considerations are demonstrably a major concern of the prophetic texts themselves. The same cannot be said of the prophetic roles in and of themselves, a fact which leads to no little speculation in any attempt to describe such roles.[44]

43. Mansueto, "From Historical Criticism to Historical Materialism," 8.
44. Marvin Chaney, "Systematic Study of the Israelite Monarchy" (unpublished SBL seminary paper, 1981), 3.

Wilson's attempt to locate prophecy within society is extremely generalized and disappointingly sketchy and brief. He asserts that ancient Near Eastern intermediaries articulated with their societies in complex ways and functioned in a number of different ways. For example, he makes the following vague statement:

> Some intermediaries, such as the Mesopotamian diviners and the Palestinian seers, were part of the central social structure, which they helped to regulate and maintain. Such figures were carefully selected, trained and supported by the whole society or at least by the ruling elite. On the other hand, some intermediaries, . . . were peripheral figures who delivered messages aimed at reforming the political and religious establishments.[45]

The theoretical poverty inherent in this descriptive account of phenomena in ancient societies is staggering. What is more, it is not clear what advantage a sociological method that works in this way has over the traditional humanities approaches.

Another group of biblical sociologists pays greater attention to questions of social structure. They deploy the Durkheimian sociological method, or, more accurately, the structural-functionalist model, which Durkheim inherited from Auguste Comte and Herbert Spencer. During the time of the latter two thinkers, "rationality, utility or functional value, order and progress were guiding principles of bourgeois society. These were both an affirmation of its achievements and a justification of its existence."[46] They conceived of society as an integrated social whole based on a utilitarian philosophy of order and progressiveness. Comte's specific contribution was in instituting positivism as a general theory of bourgeois science; Spencer's contribution was the specifically functionalist paradigm in the social sciences. According to the latter, society adapted to changing circumstances through increased division of functions. It was this functionalist paradigm and its attendant notion of the division of labor that constituted the starting point for Durkheim's sociological functionalism. As Mafeje ably asserts,

45. Robert Wilson, *Prophecy and Society* (Philadelphia: Fortress, 1980), 133.
46. Mafeje, "The Problem of Anthropology," 311.

Worst of all he [Durkheim] was not able to escape from Spencer's basic idea of the integrative function of division of labour in society. Nor was he able to overcome Spencer's organic conception of social progress as a movement from homogeneous to heterogeneous systems. In actual fact, he achieved the same effect by equating the former with "mechanical solidarity" and the latter with "organic solidarity."[47]

Gerhard Theissen employs the structural functionalist-sociological model in biblical studies most systematically. According to Theissen, three procedures may be distinguished in a sociology of the Jesus movement. The first he calls "constructive conclusions." This procedure is applicable to sociographic statements, which have to do with descriptions of groups, institutions, organizations, and so forth, and to prosographic statements, which concern individuals, their background, status, and roles.[48] The second procedure he calls "analytical conclusions"; these "are drawn from texts that afford an indirect approach to sociological information. Statements about recurring events, conflicts between groups or over ethical and legal norms, literary forms and poetic modes of expression (e.g., parables) are illuminating in this respect."[49] The third procedure involves what he terms "comparative conclusions"; these derive from "analogous movements to be found in the world of the time."[50]

Having delineated the Jesus movement by using these three procedures, Theissen proceeds to locate the movement structurally, employing what he calls "Analysis of Factors: The Effects of Society on the Jesus Movement." Theissen identifies four major social-structural factors: 1) Socioeconomic factors are at the basis of the "social rootlessness" of the movement. "Socioeconomic factors are the organization of work and the distribution of its products between productive workers and those who enjoy the benefits."[51] 2) The socioecological factors concern the contradictions between town and country. They "are the results

47. Ibid., 312.
48. Gottwald, ed., *Bible and Liberation* (New York: Orbis, 1983), 40.
49. Gerhard Theissen, *Sociology of Early Palestinian Christianity* (Philadelphia: Fortress, 1978), 3.
50. Ibid.
51. Ibid., 31.

of an interplay between man and nature,"[52] and they involve issues like the trading patterns of a country. 3) Sociopolitical factors relate to the institutionalization of oppression and exploitation through government machinery in Palestine. 4) "Sociocultural factors include all values, norms and traditions which give a group self-awareness and identity."[53]

According to Theissen, the Jesus movement was a failure on Palestinian soil because the Palestinian Jewish society of that time was reaching back to its traditional patterns of behavior: it was intensifying its dissociation from anything alien and giving currency to fanatical slogans. "This development, of course, diminished the chances of the Jesus movement, which encroached on the taboos of society with its criticism of the temple and the law."[54] The Hellenistic society, by contrast, positively welcomed the Jesus movement. And its characteristic atmosphere of peace, stability, and prosperity formed the basis for the success of Christianity in its society. "Consequently a sociological theory of integration is a more appropriate perspective from which to approach an analysis of earliest Hellenistic Christianity and from which to assess and co-ordinate the relevant sociological data."[55]

Theissen makes two contentions: first, "a sociological theory of conflict" is applicable to the Palestinian version of the Jesus movement; and second, "a sociological theory of integration" is appropriate for an analysis of earliest Hellenistic Christianity. These proposals, however, are based on a fundamental flaw that characterizes a large number of biblical sociological works. The distinction presupposes the accessibility of one set of data in a way that is independent of the use of another set of data. In other words, they suppose that Palestinian "Christianity" is accessible as an object of study independently of the Hellenistic texts that inform us about it. While some of the biblical texts of the New Testament may have a Palestinian regional focus, it is doubtful whether too much can be made of this, given

52. Ibid.
53. Ibid.
54. Ibid., 113.
55. Ibid., 115.

the pervasiveness of the so-called Hellenistic culture by the time of their composition.

More importantly, Theissen fails to provide an adequate systematic structural location of the Jesus movement within the political economy of the Roman Empire and its specific form within the Provinces. What, for instance, was the mode of integration of the Palestinian economy into the wider and dominant economy of Rome? What contradictions did this occasion in the social life of Palestine, and how? What were the cultural effects on the Jesus movement? More adequate attention to the complexity of class contradictions in the context of the wider Roman Empire might have led Theissen to a more adequate account of the Jesus movement.

Further, Mansueto is correct in charging that Theissen does not deal with the real ecological, economic, or political contradictions in Palestine, but only with the ideological conflicts occasioned by such contradictions. Mansueto writes:

> Thus we hear of a sense of relative deprivation (a term which concerns the subjective state of individuals) and of a conflict between a theocratic *ideal* and the reality of priestly practice, rather than of the relative power of classes, nations, etc. As a result, Theissen is unable to correctly assess the diverse class stands of the various renewal movements and ends up confusing Jesus' opposition to the political program of the Zealot movement—which reflected the interests of urban middle strata and displaced clerical elements—with a generalised pacifism or "love patriarchalism."[56]

Structural functionalism, a product of nineteenth-century Western European bourgeois society, came into being as a theoretical rationalization of an epoch fraught with contradictions and conflicts. Its ideological status was to serve as an instrument of integration for the disintegrating bourgeois social system that threatened the progress of science and technology. Whether its scientific value can prove greater than its ideological function is a matter that must still be demonstrated by its proponents.

In biblical study, functionalist sociology has remained recognizable by its ideological status. As Mansueto puts it,

56. Mansueto, "From Historical Criticism to Historical Materialism," 11.

Functionalist sociology, even where its political agenda is a benign pacifism (Theissen), is fundamentally a study of social phenomena from the point of view of conflict management: i.e. how to contain, defuse, even resolve the economic, political and ideological conflicts generated by capitalism. . . . Thus Theissen's reduction of objective contradictions—which may or may not challenge the prevailing social order—to conflict, tension, aggression which poses a threat to order, or at least to the full integration of individuals into the prevailing system. For these reasons biblical studies joined with functionalist sociology must also be considered ideological rather than scientific in character.[57]

The disappointing character of much of the sociological approach to the Bible derives from precisely this ideological—rather than scientific—orientation. While the sociological approach has advanced biblical study by drawing attention to the sociological basis of many of its objects of analysis, it has taken us two steps back by adopting some of the subtle ideological maneuvers of modern society, lending an academic aura to what is essentially an ideological political method. More significantly, it conceals its ideological and political agenda by using recognized and respected academic methods within bourgeois society, such as the Weberian interpretive sociology and the Durkheimian structural-functionalist sociology.

The essence of my objection is not that the sociological approaches employed by biblical scholars should not have had an ideological and political agenda. On the contrary, my plea is for an open acknowledgment of the class interests that are being represented and thus an acknowledgment of at least the social limitation of the methods. More importantly, like the historical-critical methods before it, biblical sociology tries to be scientific by identifying with the intellectual projects of secular methods on the one side. On the other, it maintains the social and political agenda of the ruling class by not taking seriously the issues of class, ideology, and political economy of not only the societies of the Bible but the societies of the biblical sociologists themselves. For this reason, it seems that an appropriate way to bring this section of our study to a close is to reiterate Terry Eagleton's

57. Ibid., 13.

words, quoted at the beginning of this chapter: "Unless modern criticism defines its future as a struggle against the bourgeois state, it might have no future at all."

In the context of the Azanian/South African black struggle for liberation, the working-class subversion of the normal criteria of biblical interpretation in favor of an organically black working-class hermeneutics—as shown, for example, in their preaching—represents at least an ideological break with biblical criticism. The challenge of the black biblical critic in that situation is to give discursive articulation and theoretical refinement to this black biblical hermeneutics. In the chapters that follow I will attempt to lay the foundations for the development of such a biblical hermeneutics. The point of departure of such a biblical criticism/hermeneutics is the black working-class struggle against an apartheid bourgeois state.

PART II

3

The Historical and Cultural Struggles of the Black People as a Hermeneutical Starting Point for Black Theology

IN SEEKING TO IDENTIFY AND EXAMINE THE SALIENT FEATURES OF the black struggle for liberation, we should understand *liberation* in Amilcar Cabral's sense:

> Liberation of the people means the liberation of the productive forces of our country, the liquidation of all kinds of imperialist or colonial domination of our country, and the taking of every measure to avoid any new exploitation of our people. . . . We want equality, social justice and freedom. . . . Liberation for us is to take back our destiny and our history."[1]

What is important in this definition of the struggle for liberation is the linking of a people's destiny, history, and freedom to the liberation of their *productive forces.* That is to say, a people's liberation is not purely moral or spiritual; it is *material.* "Productive forces" means the articulated combination of the means of production available to a people — for example, land, cattle, machinery, raw materials, and so forth—with human labor. It is the liberation of these elements of social and material life that makes for freedom—spiritual and material.

---

1. Amilcar Cabral, *Revolution in Guinea* (Kent, Eng.: Stage 1, 1979), 83.

Any attempt, therefore, to reconstruct the salient moments of the black struggle will have to focus on the dialectic not only between groups of people but also between people and their productive forces. More specifically, this chapter will attempt to give an account of the struggles of those whom Regis Debray describes as follows:

> An aristocracy of absence—and the highest title of all is conferred by death, by murder or execution. Death gives its noblemen their names and even their facial features. Unlike the more vulgar class of ministers and heads of state, the most eminent people in these secret military ranks only come to life by being put to death. Politicians shine when present and go out like lights when they leave the scene; they, on the other hand, pass directly from obscurity to immortality.[2]

A recovery of this "aristocracy of absence" in the black struggle and an assessment of its concerns and aspirations constitute important heuristic tools in the effort to evolve a black biblical hermeneutics of liberation. This is true because within the biblical text itself an "aristocracy of absence" is characterized by its passing "directly from obscurity to immortality."

I propose to divide the black struggle into epochs. These are characterized by the dominance of a particular mode of production as the fundamental feature of a social formation. Thus a study of black history and culture in South Africa points to the existence, at one point or another (not necessarily unilinearly), of three stages of struggle: the communal, the tributary, and the capitalist stages. These modes of production sometimes precede one another; at other times they coexist, with one dominating. Susan M. Brown's concept of periodization provides a model here:

> Rather than attempting to pinpoint a series of dates of "watershed events," as though dividing the "line" of history into separate segments, periodisation consists in distinguishing qualitatively distinct shifts in social relations. Another mistaken approach to periodisation is the attempt to posit some general sequence of events (e.g. "stages of economic growth") which

2. Regis Debray, *Undesirable Alien* (New York: The Viking Press, 1978), 1.

serves as an historical recipe, or a model which all social formations may be expected to follow. This denies the specificity and
uniqueness of the combinations of structures and contradictions
of a given social formation. The attempt to understand these is
part of periodisation.[3]

In fact, there is a sense in which what follows is an attempt to *periodize* the black struggle in order more usefully to
appropriate it as a biblical hermeneutical factor for liberation.
Periodizing the struggle in this way will enable black theologians to avoid the traditional danger of not being able to find
a way between the Scylla of cultural reedification and the
Charybdis of ahistoricism. Uncritical appropriations of historically diverse features of black history and culture have
often led to either a romanticization or an incorrect dismissal
of the black traditional past. I see a periodizing perspective as
useful in avoiding these dangers, particularly in an effort to
develop a critical biblical hermeneutics of liberation that seeks
to be rooted in the black struggle against oppression and exploitation.

THE COMMUNAL MODE OF PRODUCTION

No direct information or evidence exists about the communal
stages of African development and struggle in South Africa. A
great deal of what is known has to be deduced from cultural and
historical vestiges that persisted into later modes of production.
Nevertheless, enough is known about the fundamental features
of these modes from other parts of the world, either from the
same period or from other periods in history, to enable us to
make a reasonable reconstruction of the black struggle at this
stage. Like other communal modes of production elsewhere, the
African communal stage is distinguishable by the fact that property is communally owned and the products of labor are communally appropriated. It is important to remember, however,

3. Susan M. Brown, "Toward a Periodisation of the South African Social
Formation," in *Conference on the History of Opposition in Southern Africa* (Jan. 1978,
Development Studies Group, University of Witwatersrand, Johannesburg): 21.

that this *communalism* was a function of the low level of development of the forces of production. As Ross Gandy so aptly describes, with regard to the very early stages of the communal mode,

> Life in the primeval forest was hard and dangerous, so people formed groups and stayed together. Food was scarce. When men and women found it they must have shared, for that was the way to survive. Hunting was cooperatively organized. Everyone had to work and to work for the group. There was no surplus and no hoarding: the struggle for life drove primitives into communism.[4]

The key feature, therefore, of this stage — in its early (hunting and gathering) and later (tribal, settled, agricultural, pastoral, and handcraft) forms — is the low level of development of the forces of production. Land and cattle in the later stage of this mode were the fundamental means of production. Members of households contributed their labor on family fields and shared equally in the pastoral and agricultural activities of the community. Egalitarian control over the means of production ensured egalitarian appropriation of the products of social labor.

Production in this society was production strictly of use-value; that is, production was based fundamentally on human needs. Because of the low level of development of the forces of production, which was itself a function of an undeveloped division of labor, the human needs that controlled production were structured around the household as a unit of economic production. There was, therefore, no permanent collective or communal labor organization on a national level. Cooperative productive activity was confined to the basic unit of production, the family. Consequently, not enough surplus

4. See D. Ross Gandy, *Marx and History* (Austin and London: University of Texas Press, 1979); Barry Hindess and Paul Q. Hirst, *Pre-Capitalist Modes of Production* (London: Routledge and Kegan Paul, 1975); Emmanuel Terray, *Marxism and "Primitive" Societies* (New York: Emmanuel Monthly Review, 1972); Samir Amin, *Class and Nation, Historically and in the Current Crisis* (London: Heinemann, 1980); Kwesi K. Prah, *Notes and Comments on Tswana Feudalism in the Precolonial Period* (Working Paper No. 15, National Institute for Research, Gaborone, Botswana, 1977).

production was generated at this stage of African society to enable a further development of the technological capability of the tribe or group that would itself necessitate new methods of labor organization.

There is a dialectical relationship between the forms of labor organization in production and the technological forms this labor sets in motion. On the one hand, what forms of labor organization there are depend on the nature of the technology available to this labor; on the other hand, the technological capabilities of a society have a structuring effect on the labor organizational possibilities. The point is a simple one: peasant production at the communal stage of black history did not permit a further development and progress of its society. This is because it confined its best form of labor organization, cooperative activity in production, to too small a unit of economic production, the peasant household. Nevertheless, the egalitarianism of the communal mode of production has not been paralleled in subsequent history. Instead, contemporary black people take a nostalgic launch now and again into this distant past to seek weapons of struggle from it. For, as Marx has so astutely observed,

> Men make their own history, but they do not make it just as they please; they do not make it under circumstances chosen by themselves, but under circumstances directly encountered, given and transmitted from the past. The tradition of all the dead generations weighs like a nightmare on the brain of the living. And just as they seemed engaged in revolutionising themselves and things, in creating something that has never yet existed, precisely in such periods of revolutionary crisis they conjure up the spirits of the past to their service and borrow from them names, battle cries and costumes in order to present the new scene of world history in this time-honoured disguise and this borrowed language.[5]

Often we borrow from the past, as have other people in other histories and cultures at other times, as a way of finding "the ideals and art forms, [and] the self deceptions that [we] need in

5. Marx, "The Eighteenth Brumaire of Louis Bonaparte," in Marx and Engels, *Selected Works* (London: Lawrence and Wishart, 1968), 96.

order to conceal from [ourselves] the . . . limitations of the content of our struggles."[6]

We must avoid this danger in our attempts to root black theology in black history and black culture. When we reappropriate the economic systems of black history, we must show the intellectual integrity that Friedrich Engels did in his assessment of primitive communism. Gandy has this to say about it:

> Engels speaks well of early communism, but he is not guilty of primitivism. He argues that this stage was inferior to civilization. He notes the war between tribes, the cruelty of the warfare, the stunted productive forces, the religious superstition, and the power of nature over people. Primitive communism, he thinks, was better than civilization in only one way, its morality.[7]

Morality is the fundamental strength of this mode of production, or economic system. And this morality is not abstract, not tagged on from the outside. The ethics of the communal mode of economic production is its condition of existence. It consists in the fact that production is for meeting perceived human needs. The starting point and the goal of production is human beings and their well-being. *People* are the basis and the content of the morality of this economic system.

Thus, when black theology speaks of being critically and firmly based within the black history of struggle, it has in mind the conflicts and harmonies between people and nature and between people and people that revolve around the morality of production for humans needs — the production of *use-values*. Economic investment in the communal mode of production took the well-being of people as a point of departure and structured the goals of economic production and development around that issue. Black theology seeks to base itself on this economic morality in its attempt to become a liberating weapon of struggle, and its biblical hermeneutics must draw especially from the values of a culture that came out of this stage.

In the absence of institutional superstructural processes, which presuppose a fairly developed social division of labor, the African communal stage structured its relationships

6. Ibid., 97.
7. Gandy, *Marx and History*, 17.

primarily through ideology. They ideologized kinship relations to serve as a regulatory mechanism of the necessary socio-economic processes that households undertook in order to survive. Thus Africans theorized about and expressed in ideological terms their struggles with natural and other external forces, which they could not win, as well as the successes they did achieve. I use *ideology* in this regard to mean the nuances pointed to by David Miller: theories, belief systems, and practices involving the use of ideas. Theories involve propositions that purport to explain things; belief systems involve commonsense ideas used by ordinary people to categorize things around them; and practices take more institutional expression.[8]

Even more accurately, it is the notion of *ideology* as described by Louis Althusser:

> In ideology men do indeed express, not the relation between them and their conditions of existence, but *the way* they live the relation between them and their conditions of existence: this presupposes both a real relation and an *"imaginary,"* "lived" relation. Ideology, then, is the expression of the relation between men and their "world," that is the (overdetermined) unity of the real relation and the imaginary relation between them and their real conditions of existence. In ideology the real relation is inevitably invested in the imaginary relation, a relation that *expresses a will* (conservative, conformist, reformist or revolutionary), a hope or a nostalgia, rather than describing a reality. [italics Eagleton's][9]

Some effects of the way Africans "lived the relation between them and their conditions of existence" persisted in the subsequent history and culture of black South Africans, pointing to the struggles they have waged in history. These cultural and ideological products have been attacked, suppressed, prostituted, reappropriated, marginalized, and even co-opted by the variegated forces of subsequent history. It is the Africans' capacity as purveyors of "struggle contexts" that a black theology of liberation is interested in. Within the context of this discussion of the

8. David Miller, "Ideology and the Problem of False Consciousness," *Political Studies* 20 (No. 4, 1972): 433.

9. Quoted in Terry Eagleton, "Ideology, Fiction, Narrative," *Social Text* (Summer, 1979): 62.

communal mode of production, we will identify these cultural vestiges, will briefly discuss their "struggle contexts," and then will follow them up in their reappearance in other black South African modes of production.

*   *   *

Perhaps the most dominant of these cultural vestiges is the "sphere of the ancestor." Gabriel M. Setiloane, who calls the ancestors "the living dead," describes them as follows:

> At biological death, all initiated Sotho-Tswana become "badimo." Babies are the gift of "badimo." Through childhood they grow until they are initiated as adults. At death they again change their state. . . . As the immediate agents of Modimo [God], the function of "badimo" is to ensure the good ordering of social relationships among the biologically living, and the fertility and well-being of men, their crops and stocks. In return they expect "tirelo" [service]. Their attitude to the living is basically parental—protective, corrective and aimed at the welfare of the whole group.[10]

Since at this stage the household remained the basic unit of production, the contradictions that the members of these households—individually or collectively—encountered, especially in relation to the natural forces, were resolved by being projected into the ideological sphere of the ancestors *(badimo)*. At this stage the ancestors were the ancestors of the household. There being only an embryonic social division of labor characterized by the sex- and age-based differentiation of functions, the father in the household officiated ritually with the ancestors on behalf of his household. The equality of social relations of production and reproduction that existed among households existed correspondingly among the ancestors of each household. One must remember that in the communal mode of production human beings are related to nature and to one another in a twofold manner: to the extent that nature provides human beings with the raw materials from which they can fashion their means of livelihood, their relationship with nature is harmonious; to the extent that at

10. Gabriel M. Setiloane, *The Image of God Among the Sotho-Tswana* (Rotterdam: A. A. Balkema, 1976), 64f.

some point the forces of production are undeveloped, thus preventing human beings from taming nature and subjecting it to their needs, their relationship with nature is contradictory. This same twofold mode characterizes the relationships of production and reproduction that exist between and among people within this mode. Depending on the nature of their ability to relate to the natural forces, human can relate to one another in either a harmonious or a hostile way.

It is true regarding the communal mode of production, however, that relationships between people remained harmonious on the whole. The contradictions they encountered were with nature. The ideology of "ancestors" articulated within this mode expresses the "struggle contexts" encountered by blacks during this time. Describing a typical Tanzanian ritual occasion, in which the ancestors are being invoked to intervene —in a manner almost identical to the black South African ritual —J. L. Lebulu says of the Pare of Tanzania's practice:

> The "protective charms" were the technico-symbolical devices whose purpose was to canalize the power of the supranatural forces. The invocations in the form of prayers were addressed to these supranatural forces with the intention of influencing their will and intention. The Pare acknowledged the superior position of these forces (personalized) by offering sacrifices to them. The sacrifice (mtaso) consisted in immolating a bull or a cow, a sheep or a goat, depending upon the gravity of the matter or the circumstances which necessitated the offering of the sacrifice. It was the duty of the head of the family unit to preside over the ritual and all the kinsmen were obliged to participate in the sacrificial performance. Allowing the blood of the sacrificial victim to flow and soak the ground, the officiating person would offer the victim to the ancestry by mentioning their names in ascending order insofar as his memory could carry him. He would tell them that he was giving t'iem their share in the social product of the family unit and would also thank them for their protection and ask them to remain favourable to their descendants and to protect them from any subsequent danger. After the prayer the meat would be shared by the members of the family unit.[11]

11. J. L. Lebulu, "Religion as the Dominant Element of the Superstructure Among the Pare of Tanzania," *Social Compass* 26 (No. 4, 1979): 424; Francois Houtart and Genevieve Lemercinier, "Religion et mode de production tributaire," *Social Compass* 24 (2-3, 1977): *passim*.

The ideological function of the communal mode of production was to reproduce the social relationships of cooperation in addition to providing symbolic mechanisms for living the relationships of contradiction between members of households and the natural forces. The significance of an all-pervasive ideological structure, in a society where an organized military, political, and economic ruling class that could coerce people into cooperation was absent, is underscored by Karl Marx when he says of this cooperation under other modes of production:

> The non-agricultural labourers of an Asiatic monarchy have little but their individual bodily exertions to bring to the task, but their number is their strength, and the power of directing these masses gave rise to the palaces and temples, the pyramids, and the armies of gigantic statues of which the remains astonish and perplex us. It is that confinement of the revenues which feed them, to one or a few hands, which makes such undertakings possible. This power of Asiatic and Egyptian kings, Etruscan theocrats, etc., has in modern society been transferred to the capitalist, whether he be an isolated, or as in joint-stock companies, a collective capitalist.[12]

Under the communal mode of production, "the power of directing the masses" resided in a strong ideological domain. One of the key aspects of this domain among black people in South Africa was, and still is, the role of "the living dead," the "ancestors"—"badimo," "Amadlozi," and "Sinyanya," as they are variously called among the different black linguistic groups. The ideology of the ancestors is first and foremost an ideology of a pastoral and agricultural economy at the *communal stage of development*, which is reflected in the communal character of its values and its crisis-oriented nature. More importantly, the ideology of the ancestors has a structuring effect on all other aspects of that stage's general ideological practices. Thus the struggle for the liberation of the community's productive forces is structured by the communal values of the ideology of "the ancestors."

The other vestige of the communal mode of production is the institution of *bogadi* (bride price). The ideological practice of *bogadi*, or *lobola*, is closely linked to the importance of the labor

12. Marx, *Capital* (New York: International Publishers, 1967), I, 333f.

76

composition of households. Because any individual is an important part of the productive forces of a household, the receiving
household in a marriage will offset the other's loss of such a con-
stituent part by making an exchange of another part of the productive force. This is necessary for maintaining equality between households. The ideology of "the ancestors" is involved
at every stage of the negotiations and arrangements in this exchange. In addition, the *bogadi* serves as a symbolic glue that
binds the ancestors of the one household to the ancestors of the
other, thus ensuring a relationship of solidarity for productive,
protective, and social purposes and enabling otherwise puny individual households to confront the sometimes hostile natural
forces as a strengthened unit.

The other institution that originates from the communal
mode of production is the initiation, or *bogwera,* practice. Here
also the ideology of the ancestors is pervasive. This practice,
however, represents a progressive development in the evolution
of cooperative or solidarity social relationships as an important
force of production in the communal mode. Here household
boundaries are transgressed on the grounds that those who are
more or less the same age can belong together by virtue of
having been initiated together. Setiloane describes the initiation
process well, albeit without distinguishing elements that come
from other modes of production:

> This (initiation) can be achieved, by boys and girls alike, only
> through a long and arduous process of initiation which, starting
> at puberty, may last for two or three years before the final inten-
> sive period of between two and six months' training in the
> "mophato" (initiation school). One aspect of the initiation period
> is an intensification of the training of the girls around the home.
> It takes a more communal nature, being done in groups accord-
> ing to age, the whole community taking the initiative and decid-
> ing the direction. The young men still spending much time with
> the cattle, but now as senior herd-boys, may be put to communal
> tasks by the "kgotla" of the "morafe"—to gathering firewood for
> some feast, to catching stray cattle which destroy the crops, to
> weeding the chief's fields. . . . They may be called as a group to
> the "kgotla" to be whipped, for a flimsy reason. . . .[13]

13. Setiloane, *The Image of God,* p. 36.

The community could call on the initiation groups or age sets to defend them together, to plow, harvest, or weed fields together, to compete with other community age sets in communal practices like *letsema* (labor gangs) by cooperatively undertaking a task on behalf of some household. The solidarity bonds formed during the initiation period were often the strongest cooperative relationships among members of the different households. The importance of the initiation practice as an ideological reproduction mechanism is underscored by Setiloane:

> Propriety with regard to sexual relationship and practice in and outside the home is given a very prominent place in the "mophato" teaching. During this period, people of opposite sex are not allowed even to come near. . . . Any disregard of this taboo . . . is punished by the initiands themselves, of whatever sex, by inflicting a thorough thrashing on the offender there and then. Socially "mophato" separates youths from the life of childhood and brings them to the threshold of adulthood. It conditions them emotionally to the mores of the group and moulds them into unified age-sets. . . . At the same time it introduces them to the supreme right of adults — that of communicating directly with "badimo," who play such an integral part in their lives. In contrast, a "man" who has not been initiated is a perpetual boy, Moshimane, and the woman a Lethisa. . . . No such one could marry, nor partake in the councils of men or women. Uninitiated men were spurned by women as incomplete beings and uninitiated women despised by men and other women.[14]

In the context of the communal mode of production, health care — physical and psychological — was the responsibility of whole households, especially of the father in the home. Knowledge of herbs, mixtures, and divinations by lot or by dreams was a social property. Each man in the household was at once a priest, a medicine man, a lawyer. That is to say, each man was a *Ngaka, Nyanga, Nganga* of his own household. Michael Gelfand, although concerned about the *Ngaka* under other modes of production, describes his functions for all time in the black community:

14. Ibid., 38.

European society has no one quite like the *nganga*, an individual to whom people can turn in every kind of difficulty. He is a doctor in sickness, a priest in religious matters, a lawyer in legal issues, a policeman in the detection of crime, a possessor of magical preparations which can increase crops and instill special skills and talents into his clients. He fills a great need in society, his presence gives assurance in the whole community.[15]

In the communal mode this function was not a specialist activity; it was one of the tasks of each household. In other words, households or combinations of households carried out the struggle for liberation from disease, ignorance, disasters, and dependence on natural forces—*as households.*

Households devised various kinds of survival strategies, technical and cultural. Many of these reappear in other modes of production reflecting the barbaric nature of oppressed people's position within the social relationships of these supposedly more advanced modes. The enormous technological advances that have been made in these other modes benefit certain classes only. The reappearance of the communal mode's cultural practices of survival reflects new forms under the domination practices of, especially, monopoly capitalism. They reappear as cultural weapons of struggle as opposed to mere survival strategies. This is necessitated by the nature of the encounter between colonized oppressed people and the colonizing oppressing culture of capitalism. John Brenkman has aptly characterized this process:

> The capitalist mode of production has evolved by transforming, in two phases, the relation between the *economic* and the *symbolic* dimensions of social life. In its first phase, it severed the economic from the symbolic, dissolving earlier social formations and producing the social conditions that Marx analyzed. But this process, which was always incomplete and contradictory, had consequences which have led to the second phase of capitalism. Now the economy, moving for itself, attempts to subsume the symbolic. . . .
>
> Wage labor reconstitutes labor as an expenditure of energy productive of exchange value. It separates from this activity all

15. Michael Gelfand, *Witch Doctor: Traditional Medicine Man in Rhodesia* (London: 1964), 55.

other expenditures of the body's energy, which, having been designated unproductive, manifest themselves in forms of erotic, aesthetic, and religious experience. These then stand in a completely eccentric relation to the dominant structuring force of society, namely, the economy.[16]

The point, then, of resituating black theology within the cultural struggles of the communal mode of production is to save it from the kind of historical amnesia that disables a liberation movement from recognizing its own weapons of struggle when they resurface under different conditions. Stanley Aronowitz recognizes that this was the problem of the New Left movement in the struggles of the 1960s in the United States of America:

Much of the new left was guilty of a kind of collective amnesia, having rejected the idea that historical knowledge and living traditions could prevent repetition of past errors. Action/experience was to take precedence over history and memory. In this respect, one cannot but be impressed by the naiveté of the widely disseminated notion "Don't trust anybody over thirty," the proposition that older people are somehow a priori plagued by memories and beliefs, habits of thought and action, that ought to be buried.[17]

THE TRIBUTARY MODE OF PRODUCTION

Like all other histories and cultures, black history and black culture are not static. The communal mode of economic production was altered and replaced by another mode during the fourteenth and fifteenth centuries, Common Era. The new mode was based on the *tributary* social relationships of production, an economic system in which tribute paying was a basic means of surplus extraction. It was under this mode of production that the chieftainship developed as the dominant political structure. In this system of production, ownership of the means of livelihood (land, cattle, and implements) is still largely communal; but the genera-

16. John Brenkman, "Mass Media: From Collective Experience to the Culture of Privatization," *Social Text* (Winter, 1979): 94.

17. Stanley Aronowitz, "When the New Left was New," in *The 60s Without Apology,* ed. Sohnya Sayres et al. (Minneapolis: University of Minnesota Press, in co-operation with *Social Text,* 1984), 22.

tion of a surplus in economic production has already allowed the beginnings of class and state formation. The relative development of technology and labor organization in this mode

> necessitates the end of the dominance of kinship (which can continue to exist but only as a vestige dominated by another rationality). The forms of property corresponding to this second step are those which enable the dominant class to control access to the land and by means of this to extract tribute from the peasant producers. The extraction of this tribute is controlled by the dominance of ideology, which always takes the same forms: state religion or quasi religion.[18]

Under the influence of this mode, therefore, the chief, rather than the fathers of the households, becomes the priest; medical and psychiatric activities are also removed from the household to a specialist group of *ngangas/dingaka*, who are now responsible first of all to the chief. Military service is no longer a cooperative activity of the able-bodied persons of each household but the drafting and mobilization of age regiments *(mephato)* under the control of the chief or the chief's deputies. The ancestors of the chief become the chief ancestors in a hierarchical structure of ancestors. While under the communal system "the central contradictions were between elders and juniors and between elders and women,"[19] under the tributary system the contradictions are between the chief, nobility, and retainers on the one side, and the elders, commoners, foreigners, and slaves on the other side.

At this early stage of the development of tributary relations in Africa, production was, however, still the production of use-values and not exchange-values. As Samir Amin puts it,

> The product kept by the producer is itself directly a use value meant for consumption, in general, for the producer's own consumption. But the product extracted by the exploiting class is also directly a use-value for this class. The essence of this tributary

18. Samir Amin, *Class and Nation, Historically and in the Current Crisis* (London: Heinemann, 1980), 49.

19. David M. Cooper, "An Interpretation of the Emergent Urban Class Structure in Botswana: A Case Study of Selebi-Phikwe Miners" (Ph.D. diss., University of Birmingham, 1982), 65.

mode then is a natural economy, without exchange but not without transfers (tribute is one) and redistributions.[20]

The contradictions of this social-economic system consist in its practice of the social relations of dominance, which were sealed by social and religious ideology. Amin is correct when he asserts:

> It is worth recalling that this domination aids in the extraction of the surplus, while the ideology of kinship in the communal mode, where ideology is also dominant, aids in the reproduction of relations of cooperation and domination but not of exploitation.[21]

The early stages of the tributary economic system remain characterized by the persistence of communal values and practices. These exist side by side with new practices peculiar to the tributary mode. Incipient economic exploitation in the form of transfers is offset by the redistributive economic justice. Jean Comaroff captures the irony and inherent contradiction of this setup when she writes:

> The encompassment of the household within the political economy was actually conceived of in terms of the "natural" progression of kin groups into the nation *(morafe)*; and chiefly extraction was couched in the terms of agnatic seniority, a relationship idealized as one of paternal responsibility as well as authoritative licence. The chief, after all, was the "father of the people."[22]

Cooper has identified the material basis that formed the backdrop of the black struggle in the tributary mode of production. Criticizing Schapera's theoretically inadequate description of the Ngwato Kingdom in Botswana, David Cooper points out that "the allocation of grazing, arable, hunting and residential land" constituted the "fulcrum around which this whole structure revolved."[23]

The precise moment at which the transition from the

20. Amin, *Class and Nation*, 51.

21. Ibid., 52.

22. Jean Comaroff, *Body of Power, Spirit of Resistance: The Culture and History of a South African People* (Chicago and London: University of Chicago Press, 1985), 60f.

23. Cooper, "An Interpretation," p. 66; see also Jack Lewis, "An Economic History of the Ciskei, 1848-1900" (Ph.D. diss., University of Cape Town, 1984), 11f.

communal to the tributary mode took place is not known: it can only be deduced theoretically. The change in the control over the means of production—and, concomitantly, the forces of production—indicates wherein the change consists. This is true especially since it is these relationships of power over the forces of production that dialectically structure and are structured by the relations of production, resulting in specific patterns of appropriation of the products of labor.

In line with this development, the ideological and political power base shifts from households and homesteads to wards and the nation. Cooper articulates this clearly:

> It must be stressed that within the kingdoms the ward was more fundamental than the family group, which was a residue from an earlier mode. It was to the ward headman that arable land was distributed and he in turn distributed it, via the family group senior, to the different homesteads.[24]

Jack Lewis has identified the fundamental problematic in the study of social struggles in the tributary mode as the relationship between homestead-based units of production and the chief. However, it would be more theoretically and empirically accurate to add that the "chief" here must be seen as a symbol of a class, a tribute-exacting ruling class.

Thus many of the ideological functions that pertained to the ancestors in the communal mode also shifted to the chief and the chief's ancestors. As Jack Lewis puts the matter,

> The Xhosa economy depended on the availability of land to absorb the conflicts generated by the struggle to control the two most important resources—cattle and people. Both of these were highly mobile. . . . The primary function of the Xhosa chief was to symbolise the attachment of the people to their cattle and their lands. Land, however, is a fixed resource and ensuring the availability of adequate land (both qualitatively and quantitatively) was the most immediate problem confronting the chief in maintaining the political unity of chiefdom.[25]

In the tributary mode the ideology of the chief and the chieftain-

---

24. Cooper, 71; Lewis, 11f.
25. Lewis, 14.

ship replaces the ideology of the ancestors. The ideology of the ancestors is "royalized" in such a way that its basic character as a symbol of how a communally structured society lived its relation to its material conditions is fundamentally eroded. Instead, what emerges is a new ideology (called by an old name) whereby the contradictions between people and nature are overdetermined by a hierarchically structured social system. Lewis summarizes the nature of the black struggle within the tributary mode when he writes the following about the Xhosa:

> The history of the Xhosa may, in large measure, be viewed as the process of the creation of chiefdoms in response to the intensification of the contradiction between the chief and the mass of households. More specifically, it may be viewed as the outcome of the contradiction between the chief (and his supporters amongst the rich heads of households, who enjoyed a close political relationship with him) and the poor indebted members of these households and young men who wished to marry and establish households of their own.[26]

Thus, whereas in the communal mode of production the black struggle took the form of developing the technological and ideological instruments to mediate between producers and the natural environment, in the tributary mode—in addition to the ongoing struggle to tame nature for meeting human needs—the black struggle became a political and ideological resistance to a ruling class that forever imposed its will on the rest of the populace. A black theology of liberation, therefore, must of necessity trace the trajectory of the struggle in which it seeks to participate to the fate of the "aristocracy of absence" in this mode and in the mode that predates this one.[27] This is necessary in order to avoid neocolonial pitfalls that have characterized most African struggles. It is also important to be aware that many of these pitfalls result from theoretical errors inherent in the different "readings" of the black struggle. Some readings of this struggle, especially within black theology, tend to bracket out black history and culture as the basis of the

26. Ibid., 17.

27. Stuart Hall, et al., *Policing the Crisis* (London: Macmillan Press, 1978), 379.

struggle. The black struggle, however, tends to falter wherever and whenever it ceases to be informed by a critical reading of its own history and culture.

THE CAPITALIST MODE OF PRODUCTION

In South Africa, as in other parts of the world, the advent of the capitalist mode of production was preceded by a historically and logically prior phase, which Marx has called "the primitive accumulation phase." This is the historical process in which the original producers and owners of the means of production are dispossessed and transformed into the possessors of marketable labor power. As Marx describes it,

> The capitalist system pre-supposes the complete separation of the labourers from all property in the means by which they can re-alise their labour. . . . The process, therefore, that clears the way for the capitalist system, can be none other than the process which takes away from the labourer the possession of his means of pro-duction; a process that transforms, on the one hand, the social means of subsistence and of production into capital, on the other, the immediate producers into wage-labourers.[28]

In this paragraph Marx encapsulates a theoretical point with great significance for understanding the black struggle within capitalist South Africa. The importance of this theoretical per-spective is that it indicates a historical starting point (the primi-tive accumulation process) for a completely restructured black struggle. Nevertheless, the contemporary character of this struggle cannot be fully understood without bearing in mind its precapitalist history, as outlined above.

Jeff Guy has studied the process whereby the black struggle was restructured within Zulu society—in Natal at the time of the advent of capitalism. The forces of "primitive accu-mulation" against which the black struggle was redirected in-troduced new dimensions and fostered new responses by black people. Guy calls this entire process "the destruction and recon-

28. Marx, *Capital*, 715.

struction of Zulu society."[29] According to him, attempts by colonial capital to separate the Zulu producers from their means of production by direct assault failed in 1879, when the British and colonial troops suffered severe reverses on the battlefield. Having thus failed to impose a direct military siege on black people in Zululand, the British colonialists sought other means. The history of the destruction of Zulu society by means other than military obliteration vindicates Cabral's words:

> The ideal of foreign domination, whether imperialist or not, lies in this alternative: either to eliminate practically all the popula- tion of the dominated country, thereby excluding the possibilities of a cultural resistance; or to succeed in imposing itself without damage to the culture of the dominated people, that is, to har- monize economic and political domination of these people with their cultural personality.[30]

Guy argues that the British colonialists chose the second of Ca- bral's alternatives in their attempts to destroy and reconstitute Zulu society. According to Guy, they rationalized this choice in the following manner:

> The reorganisation of the existing chiefly stratum and the tradi- tional production system would free the people of Zululand from the tyranny of the Zulu dynasty and they would gladly accept the restoration of the "natural" Nguni system of homestead produc- tion under chiefly rule. At the same time, it was said, progress would be ensured by the overall authority of white magistrates and the right of appeal to their courts. The imposition of the hut- tax would substitute the civilising influence of wage labour for the barbaric demands of Zulu military service and would have the added advantage of covering the administrative costs of the colony.[31]

The retention and recognition, however, of precolonial black culture was more apparent than real. Guy points out that while the chieftainship, for instance, was a precolonial feature,

29. Jeff Guy, "The Destruction and Reconstruction of Zulu Society," in *Industrialisation and Social Change in South Africa,* ed. S. Marks and R. Rathbone (London & New York: Longman, 1982), 167ff.
30. Amilcar Cabral, *Unity and Struggle* (London: Heinemann, 1980), 140.
31. Guy, "Deconstruction and Reconstruction of Zulu Society," 173.

"chiefs and their duties had to be altered substantially before they could become a feature of the colonial system."[32] Cabral corroborates this observation when he points out that there is no historical evidence to support the supposition that foreign domination can be imposed without damage to the culture of the dominated people.[33]

The culture of the colonized people, being both the outcome and a determinant of their history, represents a contradiction to the mode of production of the colonizing forces. It has to be distorted first before it can be used against the history and people of which it is a product. But even this process of attempting to distort or subjugate black culture represents an arena of fierce struggles, as the history of the missionaries attests.

In a study of missionary penetration of the Tswana group in South Africa, Anthony Dachs demonstrates how culture became the terrain of struggle by black people against colonialism. He writes of how Mothibi, the chief of the Batlhaping section of the Tswana, refused to allow the missionaries to settle among his people during the nineteenth century:

> Worse than that, "the things which [missionaries] teach are contrary to all our customs, which the people will not give up." Obviously here Mothibe [sic], knowing of the missionary effects upon the neighbouring Griquas, particularly in the reform of dress and attack on polygamy, feared that the missionaries would

---

32. Ibid., 180. See also Stuart Hall's comment on the "typical form" of mating and marital arrangement among the black, African group in the Caribbean society: "The typical form of mating and marital arrangement in the third (black) section is, of course, radically distinct. It is, predominantly and typically, the preferred mating pattern of the most numerous, black, 'African' group. But few historians would make the case that this is a mating form preserved and transmitted, with little or no modification, from the African tribal past. It is clearly the product and legacy of the slave period and the subsequent history of this group within plantation society. Thus, though the 'black' variant is highly distinctive, it has been formed and shaped in relation to the dominant (white) institutions: its persistence cannot be accounted for outside the complex and differentiated 'unity' of the society as a whole, as a historical formation." "Pluralism, Race and Class in Caribbean Society," *Race and Class in Post-Colonial Society: A Study of Ethnic Group Relations in English-speaking Caribbean, Bolivia, Chile and Mexico* (Paris: UNESCO, 1977), 157.

33. Cabral, *Unity and Struggle*, 140.

subvert tribal religion and custom on which his own authority is based.[34]

The black struggle against colonialism assumed a double form. There was a level of the struggle characterized by the resistance of the precolonial ruling classes, the chiefs, and their retainers against foreign domination, in order to protect their authority. This aspect of the black struggle tended to vacillate between support for the general values and customs of black people and collusion with those aspects of colonialism that appeared as though they might buttress the power of the traditional ruling classes. The other level consisted of the struggles waged by those members of the black communities who were traditionally oppressed and exploited by the precolonial rulers themselves and were now also about to be subjected to oppression and exploitation by the colonial rulers.

The importance of distinguishing between these two forms of the cultural struggle becomes clear when one considers how inimical the view of a homogeneous (classless) African culture can be to the contemporary struggle for liberation. This is true because black people have often appropriated oppressive aspects of the culture whose class origins and functions relate to the struggles of the ruling classes.

The black people of South Africa understood better than did the missionaries the subversive nature of foreign religion to the society and culture of the people where it was preached. For this reason the Tswana, for example, held strongly that "the missionaries could, if they wished, reside at the Kuruman and come to Lattakoo *'to trade but not to teach.'*" [italics mine][35] But the missionaries understood the subversive character of class on culture better than did the black people of South Africa. For as Cabral writes,

> Knowing this reality, colonialism, which represses or inhibits significant cultural expression at the grass roots on the part of the mass of the people, supports and protects the prestige and cultural influence of the ruling class at the summit. It installs chiefs

34. Anthony J. Dachs, "Missionary Imperialism in Bechuanaland, 1813-1896 (Ph.D. diss., Cambridge University, 1972), 22.
35. Ibid., 27.

whom it trusts and who are more or less accepted by the population, gives them various material privileges including education for their eldest children, creates chiefdoms where they did not exist, establishes and develops cordial relations with religious leaders. . . . Above all, by means of the repressive organs of colonial administration, it ensures the economic and social privileges of the ruling class in relation to the mass of the people.[36]

And Dachs has shown that Mothibi and his retainers, having initially resisted the missionaries in support of their people and their culture, finally yielded to their class tastes:

Playing on Mothibe's appetite for sharing in the missionaries' wealth and skills, Read gradually won over the chief, by showing him "favors" and making him gifts. By March 1817 he could claim that "the King is my friend." Read dealt similarly with the Tlhaping headmen, particularly those who opposed missionary settlement most strongly. Thus he won over Maklak, "the next chief" to Mothibe and "the chief opposer of Missionaries." Politically the shower of gifts and favours paid off for when Read's presence at Lattakoo was challenged in *pitso* (people's assembly), Mothibe, his brother Molala and many headmen, including Maklak, who were all sharing in the material benefits of missionary settlement, *sprang stoutly to his defence.* [italics mine][37]

* * *

The primitive accumulation process, however, is usually—historically—unable to overcome the cultural resistance of the indigenous people by using purely cultural mechanisms. More repressive measures, such as a military and legal siege on the indigenous people, are a precondition for this process to be successfully set in motion. Thus the first phase of the South African blacks' forceful subjugation and separation from their means of production had to do with the wars of conquest/resistance between the colonizers and the indigenous people. Lebamang Sebidi, in his summary of this phase, concludes that both with respect to the seventeenth-century struggles of the Khoisan and the eighteenth- and nineteenth-century struggles

36. Cabral, *Unity and Struggle*, 146f.
37. Dachs, "Missionary Imperialism," 29.

of the "African" tribes, the issue was the forceful separation of the indigenous producers from their means of production.

> There are two points that one would wish to make here, namely, that the Khoisan did not willingly submit to their systematic incorporation into foreign, white rule; and that the Khoisan base—land and cattle—was the bone of contention between these indigenous people and their white foreigners, right from the onset. . . . The land had been foundational to the lives of the indigenous people. When they lost the land, they lost their independence and their ability to shape and determine their history. The natives lost the land, but not without struggling valiantly to keep it. This is what we would refer to as the tribalistic phase of the struggle. It was characterised by the individual African tribes struggling to hold on to their land. . . . The beginning of the twentieth century saw almost every tribe or clan in South Africa virtually incorporated into the socio-political and economic system of the white settlers. The conquest was all but complete at the turn of the present century.[38]

The period of transition from precapitalist to capitalist societies in South Africa, following the forcible destruction of the material bases of precapitalist formation, took place between the 1880s and 1940s. The different forms that this took in the various parts of the country have been well documented by historians.[39] The black struggle in this period is characterized by a life that "represented a transitional stage between servitude and independence, between pre-capitalist and capitalist societies and between potential for stock accumulation and the likelihood of poverty or wage labour."[40] The point of the onslaught on black agricultural producers and stock owners at every stage was to create a class of wage laborers to be the basis on which capitalist production could gain its foothold. But as Susan M. Brown has pointed out,

> . . . most inimical to the development of productive capitalism proper in South Africa was the structural limitations of the state

38. Lebamang Sebidi, "The Dynamics of the Black Struggle and its Implications for Black Theology," in *The Unquestionable Right to be Free,* ed. Itumeleng J. Mosala and Buti Tlhagale (Johannesburg: Skotaville, 1986), 4ff.
39. See bibliography in Saul Dubow, *Land, Labour and Merchant Capital* (Centre for African Studies, University of Cape Town, 1982), 63.
40. Ibid., 64.

in the Transvaal, and of the division of South Africa into separate states; both of these impeded the large-scale creation and control of a wage labour force. This last constituted the *sine qua non* of the emergent CMP [Capitalist Mode of Production].[41]

Until this period of transition, the dominant form of capitalist penetration in South Africa had been mercantile capitalism, which is characterized by the dominance of exchange relations as opposed to the productive relations that are the key feature of industrial capitalism. In order to establish an industrial capitalist political economy, South Africa needed a state that could restructure the entire country in such a way as to establish a single political economy.

The British imperial military intervention in South Africa in the form of the Anglo-Boer War (1899-1902) represents an attempt on the part of capital to extend the industrial capitalist *productive* relations over the whole of South Africa. This entire process has its landmark in the creation of the South African state in 1910. Marks and Trapido make the point well:

> The goal of British policy in Southern Africa—whatever the rhetoric of the war years—had little to do with granting Africans political rights, or with "freedom and justice." Imperial goals are determined by imperial ends: in the case of southern Africa, there was no intention to change the property relations already existing in the region, though the war and the reconstruction which followed it were intended to transform the nature of the class structure of the territory by hastening the development of a capitalist state which would be more fully capable of fulfilling the demands of the mining industry.[42]

Thus the Anglo-Boer War, while representing the British finance capital's program of seeking to establish a political state that could oversee the general development of capitalism in South Africa, also sought to create conducive conditions for large-scale proletarianization. The contradictions of this period —in terms of the black struggle—have been brilliantly captured

---

41. Susan M. Brown, "South African Social Formation," 30.
42. Shula Marks and Stanley Trapido, "Lord Milner and the South African State," in *Working Papers in Southern African Studies,* ed. P. Bonner (Johannesburg: Ravan Press, 1981), 2:54.

by Jeremy Krikler, who points out how black peasant under-classes in the Transvaal attempted to take advantage of the war to advance their own class interests.[43] They spied on the Boers for the British, they plundered the livestock of the Boers, and they occupied for themselves the land that had been occupied by the Boers. Krikler makes the point that the black peasant un-derclasses understood what was happening as a reversal of what had happened to them:

> In the aftermath of the war, they were said to be "preparing to approach" the Government "on the subject of additional land being given to them in consideration of the services they rendered during the war." In the north-western Transvaal, tenants evi-dently "expected great things in the way of free grants of land after the war." And, as has already been noted, in the northern Transvaal, rural blacks expected the return of ancestral lands ap-propriated by the Boers. In the eastern reaches of the colony, the Pedi peasantry sought the extension of its lands at the expense of the property of land companies to whom land had been alienated before the war. . . .[44]

The black peasant underclasses totally misread the in-tentions of the British imperialists in declaring war against the Boers. The war was not fought against private property, nor was it an intervention on behalf of Africans in order to reverse their dispossession. On the contrary, the war was fought in order to subjugate and integrate both the Boer landlords and the black proletariat into the newly created capitalist social formation. This process culminated in the formulation of the Union of South Africa in 1910.

In order to reverse the gains that the black peasant un-derclasses had made during the war, the British capitalist colonial state gave over power to a settler capitalist state, whose responsi-bility it was to take necessary political and legal actions to guarantee the functioning of the new social formation. But even before this time, mechanisms for reconstituting the Boer land-

43. Jeremy Krikler, "A class destroyed, a class restored: The relation-ship of agrarian class struggle to the destruction of the Boer landowning class during the South African War and its reconstitution thereafter" (Africa Seminar, Centre for African Studies, University of Cape Town, 1986).
44. Ibid., 12.

lords had been set in motion by the British administration. As Krikler points out, however, the restored class was also a mutated class:

> But if the world of the landowners was restored in the aftermath of the Boer War, it was not quite the same world. A series of mutations were engineered within it. The local NC (Native Commissioner), whilst crucial to landlord authority, was no longer simply synonymous with the prominent landowners of a particular area: local policies were now meshed into the much wider programme by which the full development of capitalism in the Transvaal was to be achieved. Within class relations themselves, changes were wrought of momentous importance for the future. The post-war NCs knew well-enough the archaic nature of the regime of the landlords, its dependence upon various forms of unfree labour.[45]

Krikler concludes that there are at least three reasons why the objectives of "the class war of 1899-1902" failed to come to fruition for the agragrian workers. First, the British administration, by means of coercive measures, did not allow the former black agricultural and pastoral peasants to be reunited with their means of production by retaining the land and stock they had repossessed from the Boers. Second, the two-level nature of the black struggle — compromising the traditional rulers and the traditionally oppressed classes—undermined the ability of the blacks to maintain their resistance to proletarianization:

> It was no accident that the British bribed the village elders with gun-licences to spur them into encouraging their followers to surrender their arms; Stanley Trapido has suggestively argued that one of the reasons for the rapid re-establishment of the rural order in the Transvaal after the war was the re-introduction of labour-recruiting which made "chiefs more willing to collaborate once more."[46]

Krikler's third reason why the black struggle failed in its objectives during the war is worth citing at length, because it also represents an indication of why subsequent struggles changed — particularly because it was only about a decade after the war.

> Third, rural workers were unable to ensure a final expropriation

45. Ibid., 32.
46. Ibid., 37f.

of their exploiters because their struggle was overwhelmingly unco-ordinated and spontaneous in nature. It was, in fact, this factor which rendered them unable to vault over the two conditions of their failure mentioned above. The underclasses lacked revolutionary organisation and strategy. Only these would have given Agrarian workers—whether on farms or on communal lands—the weapons with which to continue fighting for a world without landlords. That world they temporarily achieved, but often simply by following in the direction that their alienation and spontaneous acts of resistance led them. They could not hold on to that world, or prevent its retreat, without an idea of a new society and the organisation requisite to materialise that idea.[47]

After 1910 the legal and political apparatus existed for further eroding what successes the black struggle might have achieved during the Anglo-Boer War. One monumental legislative intervention of the new capitalist state was the Natives' Land Act of 1913. The act was doubtless aimed at intensifying the process of primitive accumulation, which, as noted earlier, is the precondition of capitalist production proper. The act was to strengthen the position of the capitalist landlords and to dispossess the independent black peasantry, turning them into holders of labor power only. Tim Keegan, however, has warned against overstating the significance of legislative intervention in the restructuring of class relations:

> If the history of South Africa's countryside demonstrated anything, it is that legislative edict and administrative fiat have little force in shaping the substance and context of class struggle unless the material conditions are also propitious. The struggle was conducted in the countryside, not in parliament. State intervention did, however, alter the power relations implicit in that struggle.[48]

*   *   *

The onslaught of the national state and economy on the black

---

47. Ibid., 38.
48. Tim Keegan, "The sharecropping economy, African class formation and the 1913 Natives' Land Act in the highveld maize belt," in *Industrialisation and Social Change in South Africa*, ed. Shula Marks and Richard Rathbone (London & New York: Longman, 1982), 207f.

indigenous peoples of South Africa during the post-Boer War period provoked the need for a national response to oppression and exploitation. This response crystallized and consolidated in the formation of the African National Congress in 1912. The black response, as an expression of the new form of the black struggle, however, was heavily framed by the historical defeat of black people by the forces of capitalist expansion. Admittedly, "the struggle was not over, it had only shifted from physical to intellectual plane."[49] Be that as it may, the formation of the African National Congress heralded an era of black political discourse by means of which the present and future black political practice would be guided. From this time on, the struggle against colonization would be waged, as was the struggle in pre-colonial times, at the level both of practice and of deliberate discursive articulation.

The black struggle in the context of the capitalist mode of production is, however, more complex, if only because it is waged against more complex ideologies and practices. The complications and contradictions of the black struggle itself were already evident in the motivations of the early proponents of a national response to capitalist colonialism. Pixley Ka Isaka Seme combined, in a curious way, his covetousness of the capitalist civilization with his hatred of its dispossession of his people when he motivated the formation of the National Congress in this way:

> There is today among all races and men a general desire for progress, and for cooperation, because cooperation will facilitate and secure that progress. This spirit is due no doubt to the great triumph of Christianity which teaches men everywhere that in this world they have a common duty to perform both towards God and towards one another. It is natural, therefore, that there should arise even among us this striving, this self-conscious movement, and sighing for Union. We are the last among all the nations of the earth to discover the priceless jewels of cooperation, and for this reason the great gifts of civilisation are least known among us today. I repeat, cooperation is the key and the watchword which opens the door, the everlasting door which leads into prog-

49. Daniel Kunene, "Deculturation—The African Writer's Response," quoted in Bernard M. Magubane, *The Political Economy of Race and Class in South Africa* (New York: Monthly Review, 1979), 278.

ress and all national success. The greatest success shall come when man shall have learned to cooperate, not only with his own kin but with all peoples and with all life.[50]

The middle-class origins and character of the early black political discourse have been well documented.[51] This discourse constituted the theoretical weapons for fighting oppression and exploitation; but it also represented a specific mode of appropriating black history and black culture. The black political discourse is a product of class struggles, a record of class struggles, and an arena and a weapon of class struggles. This fundamental class character of the liberation struggle and of the culture of the people waging it has been aptly captured by Amilcar Cabral:

> The experience of colonial domination shows that, in an attempt to perpetuate exploitation, the colonizer not only creates a whole system of repression of the cultural life of the colonized people, but also provokes and develops the cultural alienation of a part of the population, either by supposed assimilation of indigenous persons, or by the creation of a social gulf between the aboriginal elites and the mass of the people. As a result of this process of division or of deepening the divisions within the society, it follows that a considerable part of the population, notably the urban or peasant "petty bourgeoisie," assimilate the colonizer's mentality, and regards itself as culturally superior to the people to which it belongs and whose cultural values it ignores or despises. . . . A spiritual reconversion—of mentalities—is thus seen to be vital for their true integration in the liberation movement. Such reconversion—*re-Africanization* in our case—may take place before the struggle, but is completed only during the course of the struggle, through daily contact with the mass of the people and the communion of sacrifices which the struggle demands.[52]

All black political and cultural discourses and practices since the complete defeat of black resistance to colonialism at the turn of the century have displayed one or the other of the

50. Pixley Ka Isaka Seme, Document 21, in Thomas Karis and Gwendolen M. Carter, *From Protest to Challenge: Documents of African Politics in South Africa, 1881-1964* (Stanford: Hoover Institution Press, 1973), I:72.
51. B. M. Magubane, *The Political Economy*, Ch. 3; Walter Rodney, *How Europe Underdeveloped Africa* (Washington: Howard University Press, 1974), 203ff.
52. Cabral, *Unity and Struggle*, 145.

class choices described by Cabral. In fact, the African National Congress represented and continues to represent a particular class discourse. The Pan Africanist Congress, which broke away from the African National Congress in 1959, also represents its own brand of class discourse and practice. Similarly, the Black Consciousness Movement, which came into being under the objective and subjective conditions of the late 1960s and the early 1970s, constitutes a particular articulation of class political and cultural discourse. In the case of the latter political movement, this point becomes clear in item *(b)(iv)* of the preamble of its constitution:

> Since class oppression manifests itself in colour terms, the philosophy of Black Consciousness, a dynamic product of objective conditions, has and shall continue to galvanise the people towards our liberation and as such constitutes an indispensable mobilising force in the struggle for self-determination.[53]

Earlier in this chapter I argue that the black struggle manifested itself in a twofold form during the tributary stage: the one level of the struggle was represented by the efforts and desires of the tributary ruling class and its retainers; the other level expressed itself in terms of the attempts of the "commoners" in the African communities to wrest a living from nature and to resist the impositions of the ruling classes. The post-1910 political and cultural discourses of the black struggle, especially as represented by the ANC, the PAC, the BCM, and, most recently, the United Democratic Front and the Azanian People's Organization, have expressed the various permutations of the first level of the struggle—the ruling-class level—and only very mildly some elements of the second level. It is also true that the various political movements have contained in their discourses, more or less, one or the other elements of both levels of the struggle.

The black consciousness philosophy has been able to give birth to a black theology of liberation because of its identification with the concerns and aspirations of the "commoners" in the black community since precolonial times. It is for this rea-

---

53. *B.C.M.(A) Constitution* (London: Black Consciousness Movement of Azania, 1980), 1.

son that Takatso Mofokeng can argue that black consciousness is the philosophy whereby the creation of a new black subject is made possible and by which conformist action is critiqued:

> Here we are concerned with Black Consciousness as a positive negation of any action of the oppressed that is determined by values, culture and history that causes, and perpetuates suffering. The new black subjects undertake concrete action that will open up the future. The discarded history of the oppressed . . . provides symbols that inform and transform their consciousness and dynamize their action. For this to happen this history is interpreted no longer in the light of the value system of the oppressor but in the light of this new Black Consciousness. . . . The new subjects reappropriate this history, translate its lessons into appropriate and effective actions, thereby continuing it.[54]

*　　*　　*

The point of raising the question of the class and ideological commitments of the political and cultural discourses of the various liberation movements is to demonstrate that the appropriation of the black struggle as a biblical hermeneutical starting point is not unproblematical. Class and ideological choices have to be made because the black struggle is not a homogeneous phenomenon. But whatever choices are made between the various discourses of the struggle, those choices will at least root the struggle to some measure in black history and culture, and doing so will provide the weapons for reading the Bible in genuinely liberating terms for black people in South Africa.

As for black theology, in order to be genuinely liberating in its use of the Bible, it will have to identify for itself contemporary forms of black history and culture that will better situate it so that it can reappropriate past struggles of black people in a critical and hermeneutically fruitful way.

This chapter has highlighted some of the features of the black struggle that must be presupposed and must inform any attempt to develop a black biblical hermeneutics of liberation. The various forms of appropriating this struggle determine the

---

54. Mofokeng, "The Crucified among the Crossbearers," 14f.

various uses of the Bible by black theologians. That is, how black theologians are located within the longer and wider black history and culture influences the biblical hermeneutical lenses they develop. The process of a liberating biblical hermeneutical appropriation, however, is a long one that begins with a critical appreciation of the history and culture of the hermeneuticians. It then moves on to an appreciation of the historical and cultural struggles of the biblical communities before finally confronting the signified expressions of those struggles in the texts. The following chapters, therefore, represent an attempt at a materialist reading of the biblical texts as an integral part of the process of using the Bible in the black struggle for liberation.

And the rest of this study must keep in mind the "struggle" contexts of the various phases and forms of black history and culture. The communal, tributary, colonial, and modern capitalist modes of production represent the struggle contexts that inform the contemporary discourses of the black struggle. The class and ideological choices made vis-à-vis these contexts will determine the specific hermeneutical tools for reading and using the Bible.

PART III

4
A Materialist Reading of Micah

BIBLICAL SCHOLARS HAVE ALWAYS BEEN AWARE OF THE TENDENCY IN biblical literature for older traditions to be reused to address the needs of new situations. The whole question of the reappearance of themes and motifs in different contexts at different times exemplifies this process. This practice has, in fact, been seen as a natural order of things in the internal hermeneutics of the Bible. As Ferdinand Deist has put it, "It is the primary function of tradition to explain the new in terms of the old and in that way to authorize the new."[1] Von Rad has gone further and drawn attention to the fact that, in the biblical literature, not only do we have a reapplication of old themes and motifs, but we are confronted with what are in fact historical data alongside a "spiritualizing interpretation of these data."[2] According to him, there is a unifying principle that keeps the various traditions together:

In the process the old disassociated traditions have been given a

1. Ferdinand Deist, "Idealistic *Theologiegeschichte,* ideology critique and the dating of oracles of salvation," *Ou Testamentiese Werkgemeenskap van Suid Afrika* 22, 23 (1980): 65.
2. Gerhard von Rad, *Old Testament Theology* (London: SCM Press, 1975), 118.

reference and interpretation which in most cases was foreign to their original meaning. . . . Only the reader is not aware of the tremendous process of unification lying behind the picture given in the source documents.[3]

Until recently, however, the historical-ideological significance of the "unified diversity" of biblical literature seems to have eluded biblical scholars. By this I mean that, although scholars have noticed the disparate character of the material and the manner in which it has been precariously held together by what they have called "theological interpretative themes," they have nevertheless failed to see the ideological unity that prevails in most of the Bible. In recent times new directions have emerged. Norman K. Gottwald's monumental work *The Tribes of Yahweh* breaks new ground in a radical way. Among other things, Gottwald argues convincingly for the cultic-ideological origins of the texts of the Bible.[4] A number of other scholars follow, *mutatis mutandis*, a procedure similar to Gottwald's.[5]

We should note, however, that the ideological unity of a text, notwithstanding its literary and other disparities, is not discernible as a matter of *natural* course to every reader. On the contrary, specific kinds of ideological questions put to the text as a result of particular kinds of ideological commitments and practices are necessary to detect the text's own practices. My use of a historical-materialist method to reconstruct the social system and practices behind the text of Micah in this chapter is a result of a theoretical commitment that issues out of a concurrent commitment to the black struggle for liberation from capitalism, racism, sexism, and imperialism in South Africa. It is only right to ob-

3. Ibid., 118.
4. Gottwald, *Tribes of Yahweh*, 63ff.
5. Michel Clevenot, *Een Materialistische Benadering van de Bijbel* (Bazarn: Ten Have, 1979); Fernando Belo, *A Materialist Reading of the Gospel of Mark* (New York: Orbis Books, 1981); Walter Brueggemann, *The Prophetic Imagination* (Philadelphia: Fortress Press, 1978); George Pixley, *God's Kingdom* (New York: Orbis Books, 1981); see also the journals *Opstand* (Christene v/h Socialisme, Amsterdam, The Netherlands) and *Radical Religion* (Community for Religious Research and Education, Berkeley, CA).

serve that most, if not all, of the materialist-exegetical and hermeneutical studies of the Bible that we have seen in recent times share this ideological orientation to real political struggles.

I used a materialist method to delineate the struggles inherent in black history and culture; I will use a similar method to connect us with the struggles behind and in the text of the Bible. It is, therefore, worth recalling the following points in this regard. How a society produces and reproduces its life is fundamentally conditioned by its mode of production. The legal, religious, political, and philosophical spheres of society develop on the basis of the production mode and refer back to it. Thus any approach seeking to employ a materialist method must inquire into 1) the nature of the mode of production; 2) the constellation of classes necessitated by that mode; and 3) the nature of the ideological manifestations arising out of and referring back to that mode of production.

THE MATERIAL CONDITIONS
OF THE BOOK OF MICAH

The Mode of Production. Given a proper theoretical framework, we can discern quite readily that the Israelite monarchical system was based on a tributary mode of production. However, since the concept of a production mode is a theoretical abstraction, it is important to give historical specificity to the form of such a mode in the Israelite monarchy.

The Forces of Production. The most fundamental means of production in Palestine throughout all ancient historical epochs was the land. People needed land to settle in as families *(beth 'a voth)* and as associations of extended families *(mishpahoth)*. But whatever land they settled in was determined not only by historical factors but also by ecological characteristics. Both agriculture and pastoralism depended for their form on the nature of the land as determined by demographic, climatological, and topographical factors. We can appreciate the significance of land as a fundamental means of production even more if we keep in mind that "environmentally, Palestine is a conglomerate of many different ecological zones of dramatic contrast. These essentially geographical differences in the sub-regions of Palestine are reflected in the patterns of settlement, as well as in economic and historical development."[6] Thus the struggle for the occupation and indeed possession of the more favorable portions of the land of Palestine was one of the key motors of historical development in ancient times.

Both demographic and historical factors, however, led to situations in which innumerable communities had to make do with naturally unfavorable parts of the land. Settlements have been uncovered by archaeologists in arid and hilly desert areas that are often long distances away from sources of water. These parts of the land required particular kinds of technological means to mediate between human labor and the means of production as a way of setting the forces of production in motion. The question of tools, therefore, as part of the means of production indicates another level at which the historical struggles of ancient Palestine were waged.

The Israelite community of the period before the monarchy, faced with the oppressive reality of the feudal dictatorships of the city-states of Canaan, was forced to retribalize and regroup as an alternative egalitarian society. This process took place in the hill country of Palestine under extremely adverse natural conditions. The basic requirements for good agriculture, namely, soil and water, were for them particularly problematical. C. H. de Geus summarizes the situation as follows:

> The tremendous efforts of the terracing of the mountain-slopes were undertaken in order:
>
> (a) To transform a continuous slope into a series of level surfaces of terraced planes.
> (b) To prevent the fun-off erosion and enhance the accumulation of soil and water. ʳ
> (c) To get rid of the stones and to form a flat upper layer of cultivatable soil. The stones are used for building the terrace-walls and other structures accompanying the terraces.

6. Thomas L. Thompson, "The Background of the Patriarchs: A Reply to William Dever and Malcolm Clark," *JSOT* 9 (1978): 13.

(d) To facilitate the transport and distribution of irrigation water in the case of (spring) irrigated terraces.[7]

Gottwald has recently reconstructed the specific combination of the relationships and forces of production, that is, the mode of production of premonarchical Israel. He points among other things to the way in which an egalitarian communal society, arranged in large extended families that were relatively self-contained socioeconomic units and political equals, took advantage of the recent introduction of iron implements for clearing and tilling the land and of slake lime plaster for waterproofing cisterns in order to keeps reserve water during the annual dry season.[8]

Despite the technological breakthrough that the use of iron implements represented for the Israelite communities of the hill country, we should remember that technical difficulties in the local production of iron imposed a slowness in the general adoption of iron for practical use. There were, for instance, not yet any local smiths by the time of the beginning of the monarchy (I Sam. 13:19ff.). As Jane Waldbaum has put it,

> In 11th century contexts agricultural use of iron appears for the first time. Though most tool types continue to be made exclusively in bronze, such objects as a ploughshare for Gibeah, a sickle for Beth Shemesh, and a hafted axe-head for Tell-el-Far'ah South—all for occupation levels—testify to the advent of iron for practical use in Palestine, though it is still far less commonly used than bronze.[9]

Archaeological evidence from some Iron Age sites in Palestine indicates that by the tenth century B.C.E. there was not only a good supply of iron in Palestine but that some conscious manufacturing of steel was taking place in the area. Stech-Wheeler and friends make the point that

7. C. H. de Geus, "The Importance of Archaeological Research into the Palestinian Agricultural Terraces, with an Excursus on the Hebrew Word *gbi*," *PEQ* 107 (1975): 67.

8. Gottwald, "Domain Assumptions and Societal Models in the Study of Premonarchic Israel," *VT Supp.* 28 (1974): 95.

9. Jane Waldbaum, "The First Archaeological Appearance of Iron," in *The Coming of the Age of Iron* (New Haven and London: Yale University Press, 1980), 86.

The evidence presented by the Tel Qiri axe tends to confirm observations drawn from the Taanach iron. Although an isolated object from a single site is not sufficient to permit the characterization of a regional industry, it does lend support to the contention that steel was being regularly used in the Jezreel Valley by the tenth century B.C.E.[10]

There is, therefore, no doubt that agricultural production, which was the basis of the ancient Israelite economy, was greatly improved by the generalized use of iron technology. But since "the seasonal character of the climate that sets the boundaries of the agricultural year contrasts with the seasonal demand for food which knows no boundaries,"[11] it is necessary in a discussion of the forces of production to identify patterns of labor use to get a complete picture of the nature of the forces of production.

In premonarchical Israel the basic economic unit was the *beth-'av,* or father's house. The labor of the family was differentiated on the basis of age and sex to accomplish the process of producing the basic means of subsistence. Grain and fruits were grown, and limited animal husbandry was practiced if the *beth-'av* owned some sheep and goats and a few cattle. "The staple crops were barley and wheat, wine and olive oil, which were produced alone or in combinations depending on the variable climate and soil from region to region."[12] Cooperation between the *beth-'avoth,* which made up the *mishpaha* (extended families networks: II Sam. 6:6; I Sam. 23:1; Ruth 3:2, I Kgs. 22:10), helped to disperse risk and to increase productivity, particularly in view of "the great diversity of the agricultural environment created especially by a variegated landscape overlaid by variations in rainfall, soil and vegetation."[13]

The forces of production that took shape on the hill

10. T. Stech-Wheeler, et al., "Iron at Taanach and Early Iron Metallurgy in the Eastern Mediterranean," *American Journal of Archaeology* 85 (1981): 255.

11. David C. Hopkins, "The Dynamics of Agriculture in Monarchical Israel," *SBL Seminar Papers* (1983): 187.

12. Gottwald, *Tribes of Yahweh,* 292; Leon Marfoe, "The Integrative Transformation: Patterns of Sociopolitical Organization in Southern Syria," *BASOR* 234 (1979): 5.

13. Hopkins, "The Dynamics of Agriculture," 188.

country of Palestine remained fundamentally the same during the period of the monarchy, with differences in the degree of their development. However, since the area occupied by Israelites during the monarchy was far wider, covering some of the plains and valleys formerly belonging to the Canaanite city-states, we must refer to the changes brought about by this expansion in the forces.

Marvin Chaney has suggested—and I concur—that the expansion of the Israelite land by David's conquest of the alluvial plains and valleys brought about a change in the relationship between production and ideology in premonarchical Israel.[14] The starting point, however, for understanding a change in the social relations and ideology of a social formation is seeing how the alterations in the forces of production necessitate such a change.

The availability of crown lands in the plains and valleys gave King David the political power to install a system of land tenure there that conflicted with the older communally owned and communally tilled land of the hill country. The land in the plains and valleys was more fertile, less vulnerable to soil erosion, and because it was on a flat surface, more retentive of water. This situation already represented an advantage over land in the hill country. Thus, since "rain agriculture in Palestine was subject to the vicissitudes of periodic drought, blight, and pestilence," the incorporation of the valleys and plains into Israel meant that there were inherent inequalities in the means of production.

But, however fertile the lands were, wealth was—then as now—a function of human labor. In themselves the crown lands of the plains and valleys could not produce the wealth that the Davidic monarchy required as a material basis of its state power. For this, the incipient kingdom required a system of surplus extraction whose presupposition is *unrewarded* human labor. To be sure, the crown lands were tilled and they yielded surpluses, but the mode of integrating human labor to those

14. Marvin Chaney, "Systemic Study of the Sociology of the Israelite Monarchy" (paper presented to the SBL Seminar on "Sociology of the Monarchy," Annual Meeting, Dec. 1981), 12.

means of production must be discussed together with the question of the relations of production in the united monarchy of Israel. To this we shall turn shortly. First, however, we must specify in some detail the level of development of the forces of production during the eighth century B.C.E., that being the original sociotemporal context of the book of Micah.

THE EIGHTH-CENTURY B.C.E. CONJUNCTURE IN JUDAH

Historians and archaeologists of the Old Testament period agree that the eighth century was for Israel and Judah a time of considerable growth, development, and prosperity. From the perspective that dominates the analysis in this study, this growth and development must be seen as an expansion of the forces of production. It is important to keep this in mind because a study of the relations of production will reveal the converse side of this development: the underdevelopment of the majority of the populations of Israel and Judah. This specific look at the eighth-century conjuncture seeks to examine the expansion in the forces of production evident in Judah, the geographical context of the prophetic text of Micah.

The expansion and development of the production forces in eighth-century Judah was due to advances and changes in at least three areas: the geopolitical arrangements; regional specialization of productive activities; and labor availability and utilization.

The first half of the eighth century saw the rise of Assyrian imperialism and the decline of the hegemony of the Aramean states, especially Damascus. Internal problems in Assyria and threats from elsewhere in the imperial terrain, however, weakened the expansionist designs of Assyria. Meanwhile, Damascus's attempts to recover from the battering it had incurred at the hands of the Asssyrians were frustrated by rivalry with Hamoth. With the ascendancy to power of Uzziah the son of Amaziah, Judah seems to have been able to reverse some of its military losses to Syria and Israel by imposing control over the Edomite lands (II Chron. 26:1-8), which allowed for favorable geopolitical conditions. John Bright describes the situation as follows:

> By the mid-eighth century the dimensions of Israel and Judah together lacked but little of being as great as those of the empire of Solomon. Since full advantage seems to have been taken of the favourable position in which the country found itself, a prosperity unknown since Solomon ensues. The two states being at peace with each other, and the major trade routes—up and down Transjordan, into northern Arabia, along the coastal plain, into the hinterland from the Phoenician ports — all once more passing through Israelite-held territory, tolls from caravans, together with the free interchange of goods, poured wealth into both countries. There was probably a revival of Red Sea trade, as there was of the copper industry of the Arabah. It is almost certain that Tyre—not yet at the end of her great period of commercial expansion—was again drawn into the program by treaty, as in the days of Solomon and the Omrides.[15]

It was, however, the regional specialization of productive activities that allowed a boost in the economy of Judah in eighth century. Marvin Chaney and Anson Rainey—independent of each other—have argued that II Chronicles 26:10 yields biblical textual evidence of this specialization "translated according to the known facts of Hebrew syntax and economic geography." The text is translated:

> He [Uzziah] built guard towers in the steppe and hewed out many cisterns, for he had large herds; and in the Shephelah and in the Plain [he had] plowmen; and vineyard and orchard workers in the Hill and in the Carmel. . . .[16]

Devadasan N. Premnath suggests that a distinction be maintained between royal and private enterprises in the regionally specialized economic activities of the eighth-century monarchy—a distinction that will keep us aware of some of the factors that would promote specialization.[17] Be that as it may,

---

15. John Bright, *A History of Israel* (London: SCM Press Ltd., 1977), 255.

16. Marvin Chaney, "Latifundialization and Prophetic Diction in Eighth-Century Israel and Judah," SBL / ASOR Sociology of the Monarchy Seminar (Anaheim, CA, Nov. 1985), 4.

17. Devadasan N. Premnath, "The Process of Latifundialization mirrored in the Oracles pertaining to 8th century B.C.E. in the Books of Amos, Hosea,

we should not lose sight of Chaney's way of connecting specialization with the luxury trade as necessitated by the tastes of the
ruling classes. He writes:

> Here we learn that under royal tutelage, herding was increased
> in the steppe by means of guard towers and cisterns, plowing—
> the cultivation of cereal crops, the predominant of which was
> wheat—was intensified in the plain and piedmont region, and
> viticulture and orcharding were pressed in the uplands. In each
> case, the economic exploitation of a given region was specialized
> to the one or two products by whose production that region could
> contribute maximally to the *export trade and/or to the conspicuous
> consumption of the local elite*. [italics mine][18]

Premnath argues that the wine industry at Gibeon was a private
enterprise; I take him to mean that it was a *latifundia* (large
estate). His argument is based on the fact that the stamped handles from this area bore the name Gibeon as well as the name of
the producer, unlike the royal connections implied by the *Imik*
handles.[19] The Samaria *ostraca* have also been shown to point to
the existence of large latifundiary estates for the production of
wine and oil in the eighth century. Premnath holds that there are
also indications from the Samaria *ostraca* concerning the existence of royal vineyards.

The eighth century B.C.E. also witnessed a proliferation
of centers of oil production. Oil was, of course, an important ex-
port commodity. Of particular significance in the eighth century was the introduction of beam presses in the oil industry.[20]
About oil Premnath concludes:

> What was said about the increased production of wine is also true
> of oil production. The increase in the references to oil in the epi-
> graphic sources, the proliferation of oil presses during this time,
> and the incidence of storage jars for wine and oil point to the in-
> creased production of oil. Moreover, the invention of the beam

---

Isaiah and Micah" (Th.D. diss., Graduate Theological Union, Berkeley, CA,
1984), 57.

18. Chaney, "Latifundialization," 5.
19. Premnath, "The Process of Latifundialization," 58.
20. Ibid., 65.

press in the eighth century was a technological innovation which facilitated the production of large quantities of oil.[21]

As to the nature of the state/royal involvement in this expansion of the forces of production, Chaney says:

> If the processing installations for oil and wine give little hint of who initiated their proliferation, 2 Chron 26:10, when corroborated by the inscriptional evidence for royal vineyards and olive orchards, strongly suggests elements of a "command economy."[22]

Specialized use of agricultural land was also a feature of the eighth century B.C.E. A case in point is the agricultural intensification exemplified by the building of terraces. There is archaeological evidence to suggest that this form of agriculture may have become a significant development in the period under consideration. In this regard, David C. Hopkins writes:

> The most trustworthy determination of terrace age has been made by Edelstein and Kislev at Mevasseret Yerushalayim where 8th century pottery from the terraces is plentiful. Another team headed by Edelstein has investigated "farms" in Jerusalem's Rephaim Valley and found one of them, Khirbet er-Ras, complete with terraces, buildings, and assorted agricultural installations, to date from between the 8th and 6th centuries B.C.E. Taken together, the terraced sites of Khirbet er-Ras and Mevasseret Yerushalayim demonstrate the presence of terraced culture in the hills surrounding Jerusalem as early as the 8th century.[23]

Further developments in productive forces were in the areas of metallurgy, as evidenced by the copper and iron mines in the "Arabah South of the Dead Sea"; pottery, indicated by its mass production in response to the need to store and transport wine and oil in large quantities; wool industry, attested at Tell en-Nasbeh, south of Bethel on the border of Judah, and at Lachish, which was located in the Shephelah; perfume industry, about which there is evidence of state sponsorship at places like En-Gedi.

---

21. Ibid., 69.
22. Chaney, "Latifundialization," 6.
23. Hopkins, "The Dynamics of Agriculture," 199.

En-Gedi was one of the settlements which was consciously developed by the Judean kings. The welfare of the settlement depended upon a strong central administration capable of providing adequate irrigation facilities, economic organization and protection. . . . Correspondingly, the site showed decline during periods of weak governments.[24]

The various means of production enumerated up to this point as an index of expansion are not in themselves the forces of production. They only become productive forces when the specifically human dimension is added to them. As I have noted above, the articulated combination of the means of production and human labor constitutes the forces of production. Thus a discussion of the development in production forces is adequate only if it accompanies an indication of arrangements in the area of labor.

The most pervasive form of labor use during the period of the monarchy was the *corvee* system, a form of forced labor. Major building projects such as the temple, palaces, fortifications, and roads were accomplished by the *corvee* system. Premnath says about this form of labor use in the eighth century B.C.E.:

> The building of palatial mansions, storage silos and administrative centres under Jeroboam II implies the use of a large labor force. In the south, the building of the network of fortresses and system of highways in the Negev and establishment of administrative centres again reflects the employment of a tremendous amount of forced labor force. It is not possible to conceive how else such projects could have been carried out except by the imposition of corvee.[25]

The fighting of wars, as well as the preparations for wars, consumed enormous amounts of labor. This meant that the labor that would otherwise have been expended in productive activities, especially among peasants, was instead mobilized as a military/destructive force. This was particularly the case in the prosperous period of the eighth century, when the ruling classes engaged in war exercises and preparations as a luxury. In this way resources, human and material, were diverted from pro-

24. Premnath, "The Process of Latifundialization," 76.
25. Ibid., 115.

ductive uses and spent on ruling-class luxuries such as weapons, horses, chariots, and the maintenance of professional as well as conscript armies (II Chron. 25:5-9; 26:11-15; Mic. 4:3-4; 5:10-11). Premnath says:

> These professional troops consisting of mercenaries formed a special contingent and were distinct from the troops which the citizens furnished in times of emergency. . . . The conscript army consisted of "men of war" . . . who were called for military service in times of war and would return home after it.[26]

THE RELATIONS OF PRODUCTION

King David had incurred debts and obligations to the military mercenaries who had fought by his side during his rise to power. Scholars generally agree that the capture of the Canaanite lowlands made it possible for him to make grants of land there, rather than from the village lands in the hill country, by way of meeting obligations to those mercenaries. What is more, the surplus derived from the lowlands helped him to avoid the imposition of heavy demands on the villages in order to finance the new state bureaucracy.

Hopkins has isolated four advantages made possible by the economic situation of the period of the monarchy. First, the expansion of the Israelite borders brought about the much-needed geopolitical security "conducive to the smooth operations of agricultural systems." Second, the monarchical tax base was expanded, thus lightening the burden on village agriculturalists. In addition, the possession of newly acquired lands "fueled international trade such as that developed with Tyre to supply the court with costly timber." Third, the expansion of borders made the agriculturalists less vulnerable to the vicissitudes of the Palestinian environment. Fourth, "the expansion of borders not only meant an increase in sources of income and produce for import/export trade, but also could lead, given propitious geopolitical conditions, to an expansion of transit trade."[27]

---

26. Ibid., 115f.
27. Hopkins, "The Dynamics of Agriculture," 194f.

Notwithstanding the above, Hopkins argues further that historically agrarian states depend more on surpluses extracted from the agricultural base on profits from trade.

> Maintaining secure borders and participating in export/import and transit trade were decisive determinants of the extent of the burden imposed by the monarchy upon the village-based agricultural systems. The literary and archaeological record evidences plentitudinous royal-sponsored construction relating to these areas of its concern. The fiscal apparatus which supported these and other activities of the monarchy, with its facilities and personnel expenses, must have required an even greater imposition of taxes. On top of taxes of agricultural produce, Chaney is right to emphasize the pernicious effect of royal enterprise on the availability of tools and labour both of which it siphoned away from possible involvement in the agricultural sector.[28]

There are, therefore, three main factors that precipitated changes in the social relations of production during the monarchy. First, the unpredictable nature of the environment and climate of Palestine on the one hand, and the availability of surplus-producing alluvial crown lands on the other, created a situation in which people incurred debts in times of crisis.[29] Second, as Gottwald argues, the question of the military "call up on rotation to supplement David's professional army on the basis of a twelve tribe-system (I Chron. 27:1-21)" would have had an impact on the labor needs of the village agricultural systems. This state of affairs, whatever its extent, would surely have "contributed to the neglect of crops and falling of surpluses."[30] On the basis of exegesis of a number of texts in the books of Samuel and Kings, I have argued elsewhere that the political murders and rebellions during the reign of David were a function of the dislocations brought about by structural changes in the political economy of the monarchy.[31] Third, the imposition of taxes on

28. Ibid., 195.

29. Chaney, "Latifundialization."

30. Gottwald, "Social History of the United Monarchy . . ." (paper presented to the SBL Seminar on "Sociology of the Monarchy," Annual Meeting, Dec. 20, 1983), 5.

31. Itumeleng J. Mosala, "Social Justice in the Early Israelite Monarchy as Illustrated by the Reign of David" (unpublished M. A. thesis, University of Manchester, 1980), *passim*.

agriculturalists, especially under Solomon, marked the dominance of a new mode of production: the tributary mode of production. Gottwald superbly summarizes the fundamental character of this mode:

> We can identify the quantum leap in pressure on free agrarians by noting the officers that Solomon added to those of David's administration:
>
> (1) a chief administrator over the twelve regional areas for the provisioning of an enlarged court establishment with accelerated tastes . . .
>
> (2) a large network of officers supervising forced labour operation . . .
>
> (3) a head steward who managed the royal household, probably including royal holdings and estates not granted to retainers . . . .
>
> These added officers indicate a more thorough administration of the court proper, and especially a smoother, more regular, and far more abundant flow of resources *from the Israelite cultivators* to the court and royal bureaucracy, both at Jerusalem and wherever officials were installed throughout the land. In this way Solomon "rationalized," not "modernized," the agricultural base of the economy, for his basic strategy was not to improve the means of production but to improve the flow of as much agricultural surplus as possible into the control of his regime. [italics Gottwald's][32]

Thus the stage was set for the development of a tributary social formation. The class structure of this formation was characterized by a social division of labor resulting in antagonistic social relations of production, exchange, and distribution. At the top of the class structure of the monarchy was the royal aristocracy made up of the king and nobility, which consisted of the king's sons and their wives. Next to the royal aristocracy, but within the ruling class, were the *sarim* (chiefs or governors); the *horim* (nonroyal nobility); the *nedibim* (members of the houses of assembly by virtue of their wealth and power, which derived from their land properties and their control of pools of landless labor); the *qibbore hayil* (valiant men, brave warrior, etc.); and the *zeqenim* (heads of influential families most probably on the basis

32. Gottwald, "Social History," 6.

of their property).[33] There can be little doubt that the author of the book of Micah has the behavior of this ruling class in mind when he writes: "How terrible it will be for those who lie awake and plan evil! When morning comes, as soon as they have the chance, they do the evil they planned. When they want fields, they seize them; when they want houses they take them. No man's family or property is safe" (Mic. 2:1f.).

Next to the ruling aristocratic and propertied class was the middle class, made up of the bureaucratic and state ideologist's sectors; merchants (mainly foreigners); and artisans or craftsmen. II Samuel 20:23ff. describes some of the elements of this class: "Joab was in command of the army of Israel; Benaiah son of Jehoiada was in charge of David's bodyguard; Adoniram was in charge of the forced labor; Jehoshaphat son of Ahilud was in charge of the records; Sheva was the court secretary; Zadok and Abiathar were the priests, and Ira from the town of Jair was also one of David's priests."

Chaney has estimated that the ruling class, together with the middle class, made up 2 percent or less of the population yet controlled half or more of the total goods and services produced in the society.[34] The rest of the Israelite population was made up of the oppressed and exploited class: poor peasants, debtor slaves, captured slaves, prostitutes, and criminals. Micah has this group in mind when he declares against the rulers of Israel: "You skin my people alive and tear the flesh off their bones. You eat my people up. You strip off their skin, break their bones, and chop them up like meat for the pot" (Mic. 3:2f.).

Premnath and Chaney have impressively assembled scattered bits of evidence from biblical and extrabiblical sources about the different forms of surplus extraction by the ruling classes of the Israelite and Judean monarchies.[35] Gottwald has provided more nuanced and systemic articulation of the mechanisms of surplus extraction in the monarchical period. He identifies especially three forms of extraction:

33. See Roland de Vaux, *Ancient Israel* (London: Darton, Longman and Todd, 1961), 68ff.; Mosala, "Social Justice," 94ff.
34. Chaney, "Latifundialization."
35. Premnath, "The Process of Latifundialization," 106ff.; Chaney, "Latifundialization," *passim.*

(a) taxes and tithes imposed by the indigenous Israelite monarchy and priesthood;

(b) tributes imposed on the Israelite ruling classes by foreign oppressors . . . both during the period of dependent monarchy and provincial administration;

(c) rents extracted by the growing numbers of latifundiaries, who further stood in diverse and complex relations with the various Israelite dynasties, foreign states, trading partners, etc.[36]

Numerous biblical texts intimate these various forms of surplus extraction directly or indirectly, provided one applies a deliberately socioeconomic perspective in their study. Such a perspective must also include a class analysis component in order to bring out a more holistic picture of the network of social relations. In this respect also, Gottwald provides a more nuanced class analysis of the Israelite monarchical social formation than has been given above. The following is a picture of the social classes and fractions of classes as he sees it:

(a) ruling class groups: the Israelite royal houses, during the monarchic period, together with priestly sectors, dependent on taxes and corvees from the peasant communities; the metropolitan ruling classes of the various empires which dominated Israel, dependent on tributes levied on the population and collected by the indigenous ruling classes or imperial administrators; and latifundiaries, dependent on rents from more or less private estates;

(b) middle layers: craftsmen, functionaries, and lower clergy dependent on benefices which do not provide income sufficient to maintain an aristocratic style of life, and independent craftsmen and merchants;

(c) exploited classes: two principal kinds of peasantry —peasants protected by redistributional land tenure and other community guarantees—tenant farmers on the estates of latifundiaries, and marginated rural people who have no regular access to the land.[37]

36. Norman K. Gottwald, "Contemporary Studies of Social Class and Social Stratification and a Hypothesis about Social Class in Monarchic Israel" (Seminar on the Sociology of the Monarchy, ASOR-SBL, Anaheim, CA, 1985), 18.
37. Ibid., 18.

These forms of surplus extraction, together with the social classes and class factions of Israelite society, appear in the biblical text in a signified form that needs to be decoded by an appropriate exegetical and hermeneutical method. They necessarily appear in this form in the Bible because the biblical text was not written as a sociological manual whose purpose would have been to provide straightforward and explicit sociological information.[38]

The book of Micah, therefore, arises out of the tributary mode of production represented by the Israelite monarchy, and the structural elements of this mode are inscribed in a signified form in its text. David inaugurated this social formation, Solomon pushed it to its logical conclusion, and the rest of the Israelites and Judean rulers took it to its grave. We find in Micah, as in other prophetic texts, some of the evidence pointing to the material conditions out of which these biblical texts came. The route to this point has been a long one, but a reconstruction of the material conditions of the text is a necessary first step before we can develop an analysis of the ideological conditions.

CLASS ORIGINS AND INTERESTS OF THE TEXT: GENERAL REMARKS

While the text of Micah offers sufficient indications concerning the nature of the material conditions, the configuration of class forces, and the effects of class rule, it is nevertheless itself cast within an ideological framework that at the same time creates contradictions within the book and distorts the usefulness of its text for struggling classes today. The ideological character of the text has much to do with this.

Ideology is not a lie. It is rather a harmonization of con-

---

38. Stuart Hall makes this point exquisitely in relation to television discourse: "The raw historical event cannot in that form be transmitted by, say, a television newscast. It can only be signified within the aural-visual forms of the television language. In the moment when the historical event passes under the sign of language, it is subject to all the complex formal 'rules,' by which language signifies. To put it paradoxically, the event must become a 'story' before it can become a *communicative event*." In Hall, *Encoding and Decoding,* 2ff.

tradictions in such a way that the class interests of one group are universalized and made acceptable to other classes. Also, ideology is not a selection process or filter through which only certain facts pass. On the contrary, it is a process by which the presence of certain facts is constituted by their absence. Therefore, making scientific sense of the ideological condition of a text means knowing that text in a way in which it is incapable of knowing itself. Eagleton makes this point when he says:

> The task of criticism, then, is not to situate itself within the same space as the text, allowing it to speak or completing what it necessarily leaves unsaid. On the contrary, its function is to install itself in the very incompleteness of the work in order to *theorise* it —to explain the ideological necessity of those "not-saids" which constitute the very principle of its identity. Its object is the *unconsciousness* of the work—that of which it is not, and cannot be, aware. [italics Eagleton's][39]

The text of Micah is eloquent about certain issues by being silent about them. Biblical scholars have long been aware of the literary disjunction between Micah 1–3 and Micah 4–7. Broadly speaking, they have designated the first three chapters as genuinely Micah passages and have considered the following three chapters later additions. The issue that has not been faced squarely is: What kind of additions are they?

Viewed ideologically, these chapters fit well into the royal Zion ideology that started during the time of David, was made more sophisticated and began to be the dominant self-consciousness of the nation in the later reigns, and culminated in the ideological activity of the priestly class during the Babylonian exile. Bourgeois biblical scholarship has long been aware of this development but has been unwilling or unable to perceive the political significance of such an ideological setup. Walter Brueggemann was among the first biblical scholars to grasp the political and ideological character of the Bible. He has isolated two different covenant traditions representing two different social, political, and ideological tendencies in the Bible: the Mosaic covenant tradition, which is revolutionary, and the

---

39. Terry Eagleton, *Criticism and Ideology* (London: Verso, 1980), 89f.

Davidic covenant tradition, which is status-quo-oriented. According to him, the "Davidic tradition . . . is situated among the established and secure."[40] Brueggemann summarizes the tension in the biblical traditions in this way:

> The David-Solomonic tradition with its roots in Abrahamic memory provides an important alternative theological trajectory. We may identify two theological elements which are surely linked to this movement and which are important to the subsequent faith and literature of the Bible. First, it is generally agreed that the emergence of creation faith in Israel has its setting in Jerusalem and its context in the royal consciousness. The shift of social vision is accompanied with a shifted theological method which embraces more of the imperial myths of the ancient Near East and breaks with the scandalous historical particularity of the Moses tradition. The result is a universal and comprehensive world-view which is more inclined toward social stability than toward social transformation and liberation.[41]

The central themes of this monarchical ideology are stability, grace, restoration, creation, universal peace, compassion, and salvation; they contrast radically with the ideology of premonarchical Israel, which would have themes such as justice, solidarity, struggle, and vigilance.

The book of Micah, therefore, is eloquent in its silence on the ideological struggle waged by the oppressed and exploited class of monarchical Israel. Apart from making available an otherwise unsuppressible body of information about the material situation of oppression, it simply luxuriates in an elaborate ideological statement of self-comfort by dwelling on issues like the Lord's universal reign of peace (4:1ff.); the promise of return from exile (4:6ff.); God's promise of a ruler from Bethlehem (5:2ff.); the Lord's salvation (7:8ff.), and so forth. These are the dominant ideological themes of the book.

It is little wonder that dominant, traditional theology has found the Bible in general politically and ideologically com-

---

40. Brueggemann, "Trajectories in Old Testament Literature and the Sociology of Ancient Israel," in *The Bible and Liberation* (New York: Orbis Books, 1983), 308.

41. Ibid., 314.

fortable, notwithstanding the unsuppressible evidence of a morally distorted material situation. Micah itself, as is true of most of the Bible, offers no certain starting point for a theology of liberation. There is simply too much de-ideologization to be made before it can be hermeneutically usable in the struggle for liberation. In short, viewed as a whole and ideologically, it is a ruling-class document. However, enough contradictions within Micah enable eyes hermeneutically trained in the struggle for liberation today to observe the kindred struggles of the oppressed and exploited of the biblical communities in the very absence of those struggles in the text.

I will undertake a hermeneutical appropriation of the biblical texts of Micah further in the next chapter by exploiting more specifically the contradictions inherent in the text. The presupposition of such an activity will be the black struggle—historically and in its contemporary form—as outlined in Chapter Three. I will approach this more nuanced analysis of the text with Archie Mafeje's counsel for theoretical precision in mind: that "identification of the issues is as important as fighting in the streets or in the mountains."[42] In point of fact, any fighting in the streets or in the mountains that does not presuppose a clear identification of the issues is inimical to the very goals of such fighting. The experience of the so-called "black-on-black violence" in South Africa recently, together with the destruction of KTC squatter communities in Cape Town, represents a tragic case in point. (KTC is the name of a squatter place adjacent to Cross Roads in Cape Town where many black poor and unemployed people have engaged the government forces in bitter struggles that have claimed many lives. During the last two states of emergency it has been permanently militarily occupied.) Stuart Hall underscores this fundamental need for a rigorous theoretical response in addition to activist involvement when he comments on the black revolt in Tottenham, England:

> Exactly what are the forms in which the black political response can be made remains extremely difficult to forecast. But it seems to me undeniable that the crisis of Tottenham is now also a crisis

42. Archie Mafeje, "The Problem of Anthropology," 332.

of and for black politics. Keeping faith with the people who, in the teeth of relentless oppression, spontaneously resist, is all right on the night. But it is not enough when the next day dawns, since all it means is that, sooner or later, the frontline troops, with their superior weapons and sophisticated responses, will corner some of our young people on some dark night along one of these walkways and take their revenge for Tottenham. There has never, in my view, been so urgent a need for the most radical and searching black political response as there is now, as the kick-back on the Broadwater Farm estate begins and the "law and order" juggernaut rolls back into place.[43]

A radical and searching black theological response, like the political response Hall is calling for, must not simply venture out into the streets and mountains to fight without being clear about which biblical ideologies and struggles it is hermeneutically connecting with.

43. Hall, "Cold Comfort Farm," *New Socialist* 32 (Nov. 1985): 12.

5
The Case of Micah

How is the troubled passage between text and reader to be smoothed,
so that literary consumption may be facilitated?

—Terry Eagleton

EAGLETON'S WORDS APTLY EXPRESS THE NATURE OF THE HERME-
neutical exercise. They refer to the space between the reader and
the text as an arena for a hermeneutical engagement. I would
argue, however, that the cultural, historical, and ideological bag-
gage from both the text's side and the reader's side provides the
hermeneutical weapons for battling through that "troubled passage." They also provide the hermeneutical lens for reading
one's way through it. I contend in this study, therefore, that the
social-ideological location and commitment of the reader must
be accorded ~~methodological~~ priority. And for this reason I see the
category of "the black struggle," from precolonial times to the
present, as representing an important hermeneutical factor.

This is why I have attempted in Chapter Three to locate
the biblical hermeneutics of liberation within a particular discourse of the black struggle. And the light of the theoretical presuppositions inscribed in that discourse of the black struggle, I

subjected the text of Micah to a critical reading in Chapter Four. In this way I have tried to draw out the cultural and ideological presuppositions inherent in the texts in order to bounce them off those of the history, culture, and class of the reader. This specific activity takes place in that space between the text and the reader. The best way to smooth the "troubled passage" between text and reader is to unleash the forces of struggle that each brings in the encounter with the other. In this way one can relive the struggle of the communities behind the texts as well as that of the communities this side of the texts as a new *practice*.

However, it is important to realize that the struggles of the biblical communities do not appear in the Bible as mirror reflections of the real. Rather, they have been produced as new textual practices: they come to us as *signified practices*. This understanding is crucial to our circumventing the empiricism that has bogged down the historical-critical method for many years. The biblical texts, therefore, do not represent an unproblematical record of historical events and struggles. On the contrary, they represent particular *productions* of historical and social events and relations. In this chapter we will examine the nature of the productions that the text of Micah represents.

No biblical scholar illustrates and provides the clues for understanding this process of *signification* of reality in the prophetic texts better than does Robert Coote. In his monumental book entitled *Amos Among The Prophets: Composition and Theology*, Coote undertakes an illuminating analysis of the nature of the text of Amos and the process of its production. According to him, however, "it is important to remember that Amos is just an example. To understand the process by which the book of Amos came into being is to learn an approach that will be useful with *all* prophetic literature."[1]

---

1. Robert B. Coote, *Amos Among the Prophets: Composition and Theology* (Philadelphia: Fortress Press, 1981), 2. I will not attempt in this study to rehearse the traditional studies on Micah. Many of these have been debated and adequately assessed by scholars like James Luther Mays in his commentary on Micah quoted below. Suffice it to simply make reference to some of the most useful: Siegfried J. Schwartes, "Critical Notes on Micah 1:10-16," *Vetus Testamentum* 14 (1964):454-461; E. Cannawurf, "The Authenticity of Micah IV:1-4," *Vetus Testamentum* 13 (1963):26-33; B. Stade, "Bemerkungen über das Buch Micha," *BZAW*:

More importantly, Coote has given intelligibility to what has thus far been an elusive trait of scriptural texts: their class and ideological nature. This quality of the biblical texts has tended to hide behind what appeared to be purely logical, historical, and literary inconsistencies and contradictions. The recent use of sociological and ideological analyses of the Bible has re-posed the question of the nature of the biblical literature and opened up new possibilities of understanding and appropriation.

Coote correctly warns, however, against the danger of creating the notion of an original prophet surrounded by secondary additions. This is the danger of an empiricist-historicist approach, which leads to the inference that the original words are truer than those of subsequent editions or recompositions. Such an approach would be inadequate because it would imply a hermeneutics of "selection" by which certain parts of the Bible would be chosen as appropriate and others simply dismissed.

Coote has raised the fundamental question of the class nature and commitments of the various editions or recompositions of the prophetic texts—especially by his division of Amos into Amos A, B, and C. He falls short, however, of providing an adequate hermeneutical *appropriation* of these texts in class and ideological terms. Such appropriation would seek to avoid a selectivity that amounts to an ideological avoidance tactic, and it would be an appropriate and adequate biblical hermeneutics of liberation because it would raise the question of "struggle" as a fundamental hermeneutical factor in the text, as indeed in the communities behind the text and those appropriating the text presently.

Thus Coote's isolation of the different editions or recompositions of the text put in a framework of biblical hermeneutics of liberation has as its purpose not the selection of one edition and the dismissal of others. On the contrary, the aim is to resurrect and identify the forces of struggle inherent and dominant in each edi-

---

Zeitschrift für die alttestamentliche Wissenschaft (1881):161ff.; A. S. van der Woude, "Micah in Dispute with the Pseudo-Prophets," Vetus Testamentum 19 (1969):245-260; and an even more useful study, Knud Jeppesen's article "New Aspects of Micah Research," Journal for the Study of the Old Testament 8 (1978):3-32; D. R. Hillers, Micah: A Commentary (Philadelphia: Fortress Press, 1984).

tion. This process then leads to an engagement with these texts that would be framed by the class interests and commitments of the readers. Put simply, it acknowledges the value of all the editions of the texts. But it must be argued forcefully that such value is variable: it could be positive or negative. It is fundamentally framed by the nature of the social and ideological struggles in the text as well as of similar struggles in the life of the readers.

Explaining his method of identifying the various editions of the text, Coote says:

> Suppose author A composed some separate short works (oracles, for example), which we can call 2, 4, and 6. Later editor B, to some extent making use of prophetic tradition (perhaps even some of other A material), composed a similar group—let's call them 3, 5, and 7—to express the concerns of his own person and time. Appropriating A's 2, 4, and 6, B preserved them (possibly modifying them slightly) by joining them to his own words, and composed a new work, 2b - 3 - 4b - 5 - 6b - 7, in which 2b stands for A's 2 as preserved or modified by B, 3 for B's 3, and so forth. Then came editor C, who rewrote this work with the addition of an opening and closing, which we'll call 1 and 8. . . . This new work gives a third slant to the words of A and another to the words of B. It can be schematized as 1 - 2bc - 3c - 4bc - 5c - 6bc - 7c - 8, in which 1 stands for C's 1, 2bc for B's 2b as preserved or modified by C, 3c for B's 3 as preserved or modified by C, and so forth.[2]

The following, therefore, is a structural reclassification of the text of Micah on the basis of the criteria suggested by Coote and on historical-materialist exegetical considerations being proposed in this study:[3]

Micah A	Micah A B	Micah B	Micah C
1:10-16	1:8-9	1:5b-7	1:1-5a
2:1-5, 8-9		2:6-7, 10-11	2:12-13
3:8-12		3:1-7	
	4:3-4		4:1-2, 5-13
5:9-14		5:1, 4-6	5:2-3, 7-8
6:9-15		6:1-8, 16	
		7:1-7	7:8-20

2. Coote, *Amos Among the Prophets*, 5.
3. Ibid.

THE BLACK STRUGGLE AND THE SIGNIFIED PRACTICE OF MICAH C-TEXTS

Micah C-Texts [Bible translations are the author's, except where otherwise indicated.]

Micah 1:1-5(a)

1. The word of Yahweh which came to Micah the Moreshite in the days of Jotham, Ahaz, and Hezekiah, kings of Judah, which he saw concerning Samaria and Jerusalem.
2. Hear, O peoples, every one;
   listen, O earth, and all who are in it;
   that Lord Yahweh may be a witness against you,
   the Lord from his holy temple (palace).
3. For, behold! Yahweh comes forth from his place;
   he descends and treads upon the high places.
4. The mountains melt under him,
   the valleys burst open
   like wax before fire,
   like water pouring down a slope.
5. All this because of the crime of Jacob,
   because of the sins of the house of Israel.

Micah 2:12-13

12. I will surely assemble, O Jacob, all of you;
    I will surely gather the remnant of Israel.
    I will unite him like a flock in the fold,
    like a herd in the midst of a pasture;
    and that will cause a disturbance.
13. The breaker will ascend,
    they will break out before them,
    they will cross the gate and go out of it.
    Their king will cross before them,
    Yahweh in front of them, at their head.

Micah 4:1-2

1. And it shall come to pass in the latter days,
   the mountain on which the house of Yahweh stands
   will be established at the top of the mountains,

be exalted above the hills.
Peoples will stream to it,

2.   and many nations will come.
They will say,
"Come, let us go up to Yahweh's mountain,
to the house of the God of Jacob,
that he may instruct us about his ways,
and we shall walk in his paths."
For from Zion instruction goes out,
the word of Yahweh from Jerusalem.

Micah 4:5-13

5.   For all the peoples walk,
each in the name of its God;
but we will walk in the name of Yahweh our God
   forever and ever.

6.   "On that day,"
oracle of Yahweh declares,
"I will assemble the lame;
I will gather the banished,
those whom I have caused evil to fall on.

7.   I will make the lame into a remnant,
and those who are scattered afar (beyond) into
      a mighty nation.
Yahweh will reign over them in Mount Zion
from now on and forever.

8.   But you, Migdal-'eder,
Ophel of Zion's daughter,
to you shall come
the former realm,
the kingdom to Jerusalem's daughter.

9.   Now, why do you cry alarm?
Is there no king with you?
Or has your counselor perished
that you should writhe and twist like a woman in labor?

10. Writhe and twist, daughter of Zion,
like a woman in labor,
for now you shall go forth from the city
and dwell in open country.

You shall go to Babylon,
   there to be delivered.
There Yahweh shall redeem you
   from the grip of your enemies.

11. And now many nations assemble against you.
   They say: "Let her be desecrated,
   let our eyes gaze on Zion."

12. But they do not know
   what Yahweh is contemplating,
   nor do they discern his plan.
   For he will gather them like sheaves to the threshing floor.

13. Rise up and trample/thresh, daughter of Zion,
   for I will make your horn into iron;
   for I will make your hoofs into bronze,
   and you shall crush many peoples.
   You shall devote their booty to Yahweh,
   their wealth to the Lord of all the earth.

Micah 5:3-4, 8-9

3. Therefore they shall be handed over until the time
   when she who is in labor has given birth
   and the rest of his brothers return
   to the children of Israel.

4. He shall stand and pasture in the safety of Yahweh,
   in the exaltation of the name of Yahweh his God.
   They shall dwell (safely), for now he will be great
   to the ends of the earth.

8. The remnant of Jacob shall be in the midst of many peoples
   like a lion among the beasts of the forest,
   like a young lion among flocks of sheep,
   which claws when it passes,
   when it tears there is no rescue.

9. May your hand be lifted against your enemies,
   and may all your enemies be cut off.

Micah 7:8-20

8. Rejoice not over me, my enemy!
   Though I have fallen, I shall arise.

129

Though I sit in darkness,
Yahweh will be my light.

9. Yahweh's anger I bear
because I have sinned against him,
until he pleads my case
and gets me acquitted.
He will bring me out to the light;
I shall see his righteousness.

10. My enemy shall see,
and shame shall cover her who says to me,
"Where is Yahweh your God?"
My eyes shall see her;
now she will be trampled like mud in the street.

11. A day of building your walls!
That day the boundaries will be extended.

12. The day when they shall come to you
from Assyria and Egypt and from Egypt to the river,
from sea to sea and mountain to mountain.

13. The earth will become desolate
because of its inhabitants as a result of their deeds.

14. Shepherd your people with your staff,
the flock of your inheritance,
who dwells alone in the forest,
in the midst of the fertile slopes.
Let them graze in Bashan and Gilead
as in ancient days.

15. As in the days when you went forth from the land
of Egypt,
let us see wonders.

16. May the nations see
and refrain from all their power.
Let them lay their hand on their mouths,
their ears be deaf.

17. Let them lick dust like a snake,
like things that crawl on the earth.
Let them come trembling from their strongholds
to Yahweh our God;
let them dread and fear you.

18. Who is God like you,

taking away guilt
and passing over crime
for the remnant of his inheritance?
He does not persist forever in his anger,
for he delights in mercy.
19. He will again have compassion on us,
will subdue our iniquities;
he will cast into the depths of the sea
all our sins.
20. He will show faithfulness to Jacob,
mercy to Abraham,
as he has sworn to our fathers
from days of old.

These texts, scattered throughout and interspersed with others in the book of Micah, have been isolated and grouped together here so that they may be read together. I hold that in this way they give a coherent flavor of their concerns and rhetorical structures. We will follow a similar approach with respect to the other editions of the text of Micah: Micah B, A, and A/B.

A black biblical hermeneutics of liberation should interrogate the Micah C-texts in more or less the following way: What is the nature of the challenge of these texts? Whose class, gender, and race interests does this challenge exist to serve? Who is making the challenge? Where and when? What are the ideological and literary mechanisms whereby the challenge is formulated? And more fundamentally, what effects, then and now, are these texts having on the social classes, genders, and races on whose behalf they were *not* produced?

The C-stage texts provide the dominant ideology of the Micah prophetic discourse. The perspective of these texts frames the various other layers of meaning of the discourse in such a way as to relegate these layers of meaning to a secondary position. In fact, the ideology of Micah-C represents a new production of the discursive practice of Micah. The C-editor of Micah is surely of the same class and ideology as the C-editor of Amos. for here, as in Amos,

Having already said, through the inclusion of the A and B stages, if you do wrong you will die and I urge you to do right, the C-

131

editor looks to the future, asking, who will hear the message? Who *will* obey God's stipulations?

For the C-editor and his readers, the world of meaningful action lies in the future, not the past or the present. With a view to the future, God judges attitude, not action. God is looking for what people today might call "readiness for justice."[4]

Thus Micah 1:2-5a describes the impending action of Yahweh by which he will create a new community. This textual unit can only have the effect of engendering an attitude whose presence or absence will be the basis of God's judgment. The text represents an important part of the core of the ideology of Micah-C material: the shift on the part of God's demands from action to attitude, from concrete relations to abstract principles.

The God of the C-stage material is the God of restoration (2:12-13). Thus this God reconstructs the citadel of power of the former ruling classes of Judah and transforms it into an international meeting place (4:1-2). The theology of the C-stage material feeds on the Zion ideology of the Davidic empire.[5] It is fundamentally imperialist in character (7:11-12).

In this edition of the Micah text Babylon is the new Egypt. The former oppressors of peasants and casual laborers and underclasses in Judah are now seeing themselves as the oppressed in relation to their captors. More importantly, they rewrite the traditions of struggle of ancient Israel to apply to their situation. Thus, instead of the rich and the powerful, it is the nations and the pagans who become targets of Yahweh's judgment. In this tradition the enemy changes:

> My enemy shall see,
> and shame shall cover her
> who says to me,
> "Where is Yahweh your God?"
> My eyes shall see her;
> now she will be trampled like mud in the street. (7:10)

By the time the text of Micah reaches this edition, this production, this signification of reality, vague and generalized descrip-

---

4. Ibid., 120.
5. J. J. M. Roberts, "The Davidic Origin of the Zion Tradition," *Journal of Biblical Literature* 92 (1973): 340ff.

tions have replaced concrete and specific references to evil. Consequently, this articulation of the enemy in the sight of God does not resonate with the contemporary oppressed and exploited people's knowledge of evil in their situations.

The black working-class people of South Africa do not recognize this enemy. It is not an enemy that their badges of slavery—the passbooks—epitomize; it is not an enemy that torture and death in their detention cells reminds them of; it is not the enemy of ignorance, meaninglessness, and abject poverty in their country's various squatter camps, which they have to deal with daily. This enemy is too abstract and too religiously defined. The enemy in this text, as well as the God who is at war with it, are not trappable.

The hermeneutical code with which black working-class Christians operate—which issues out of the struggle for survival in the black ghettos—refuses to appropriate the text of Micah in the code in which it is cast. Micah-C represents the dominant code in which the whole prophetic practice of Micah is cast. It fits the description of dominant definitions provided by Stuart Hall:

> The dominant definitions . . . are hegemonic precisely because they represent definitions of situations and events which are "in dominance," and which are *global*. Dominant definitions connect events, implicitly or explicitly, to grand totallizations, to the great syntagmatic views of the world: they take "large views" of issues; they relate events to "the national interest" or to the level of geopolitics, even if they make these connections in truncated, inverted or mystified ways. The definition of a "hegemonic" viewpoint is (a) that it defines within its terms the mental horizon, the universe of possible meaning of a whole society or culture; and (b) that it carries with it the stamp of legitimacy—it appears coterminous with what is "natural," "inevitable," "taken for granted," about the social order.[6]

The process of "grand totallization" and "syntagmatic viewing" of the world is nowhere more evident than in the theology of restoration that pervades the C-stage ideological practice:

6. Hall, *Encoding and Decoding*, 23.

And it shall come to pass in the latter days,
the mountain on which the house of Yahweh stands
will be established at the top of the mountains,
be exalted above the hills.
Peoples will stream to it,
and many nations will come. (4:1)

This imperialist theology is more suited to the interests of a formerly powerful class whose pride has been hurt by exile than to a previously oppressed class whose real interests lie in the building of democratic structures to guarantee its protection and liberation. C-stage theology cannot provide inspiration to oppressed peoples because it is inherently a theology of domination and control. The practice of the oppressed cannot draw its hermeneutical weapons of struggle from this theology. On the contrary, the practice of the oppressed must engage in struggle with it for a recovery of the suppressed traditions of liberation in the Bible.

THE BLACK STRUGGLE AND THE SIGNIFIED PRACTICE OF MICAH *B*-TEXTS

Micah 1:5(b)-9

5(b).Whose is the transgression of Jacob?
Is it not Samaria's?
And whose is the sin [following LXX] of Judah?
Is it not Jerusalem's?
6. "I will mete out punishment to Samaria.
I will make her into a vineyard field for planting;
I will pour her stones into the valley,
and I will roll away her foundations.
7. All her idols will be crushed;
all her takings [wages] from prostitution will be burned
by fire;
all her idols I will put to desolation.
For she collected them as fee for prostitution.
So to the fee of a prostitute they shall revert."

134

Micah 2:6-7, 10-11

6. "Stop dripping [prophesying].
   They *drip*. Let them [the prophets] not *drip* about
      these things.
   Disgrace shall not overtake us."
7. "Is the house of Jacob accursed?
   Is Yahweh impatient?
   Or are these things his deeds?
   Do his acts not benefit
   the one who walks uprightly?"
10. "Arise and go,
    for this is no place of rest.
    Because of uncleanness you shall be destroyed
    by ruinous destruction.
11. If a man came in the spirit [inspired/intoxicated]
    and lied deceptions—'I drip for you in
    wine and beer [intoxicating drink]!'—*he* would
    be the "dripper" [prophet] for *this* people."

Micah 3:1-7
[Translation follows James Luther Mays, pp. 76f.]

1. And I said,
   "Hear, you chiefs of Jacob
   and magistrates of the house of Israel.
   Is it not your duty to know justice,
2(a).O haters of good and lovers of evil?
3. They eat the flesh of my people,
   and strip their skin off them,
   and break their bones.
   They chop [them] up as if for the pot,
   like meat to put in the cauldron.
2(b).Their skin will be torn off them,
    their flesh off their bones."
4. Then they will cry out to Yahweh,
   but he will not answer them.
   He will hide his face from them in that time,
   since they've turned their deeds to evil.

5. This is what Yahweh said against the prophets:
   "Who mislead my people
   when they have something to chew on,
   they proclaim 'Peace.'
   Let a man fail to put something in their mouth,
   and they sanctify war against him.
6. Therefore it will be night for you without vision,
   darkness for you without divination.
   The sun shall set for the prophets,
   the day go dark for them.
7. The seers shall be confounded,
   and the diviners in consternation.
   All of them will cover their beard
   because there is no answer from God."

Micah 5:2, 5-7

2. "But you, Bethlehem of Ephratha,
   small among the clans of Judah,
   from you shall come forth for me
   one to be ruler in Israel.
   His origins are from old times,
   from ancient days."
5. This shall be peace from Assyria,
   because he came into our land
   and marched against our fortified palaces.
   We will raise against him seven shepherds
   and eight human chieftains.
6. They shall shepherd the land of Assyria with the sword,
   the land of Nimrod with a drawn sword.
   He will deliver us from the Assyrians
   when he comes into our land,
   and when he walks within our borders.
7. The remnant of Jacob shall be in the midst of many peoples
   like dew from Yahweh,
   like raindrops upon grass,
   which does not wait for a man
   nor await the sons of humankind.

Micah 6:1-8 [For textual emendation, see Mays, p. 128.]

1. Hear what Yahweh is saying:
   "Arise! Make a case with the mountains;
   let the hills hear your voice.
2. Hear, O mountains, Yahweh's case,
   and listen, O foundations of the earth.
   For Yahweh has a case with his people,
   with Israel he argues.
3. My people, what have I done to you?
   How have I wearied you? Testify against me!
4. For I brought you out from the land of Egypt;
   from the house of slavery I ransomed you.
   I sent Moses before you,
   Aaron and Miriam [5] with him.
   Remember what Balak, king of Moab, advised
   and how Balaam, son of Beor, answered him.
   . . . from Shittim to Gilgal
   in order to know the righteousness of Yahweh."
6. With what shall I meet Yahweh,
   humble myself before God above?
   Shall I meet him with burnt offerings,
   with year-old calves?
7. Would Yahweh be pleased with thousands of rams,
   with innumerable streams of oil?
   Shall I give my first-born for my crime,
   the fruit of my body for the sin of my soul?
8. He has told you, man, what is good.
   What Yahweh requires from you is
   nothing but to do justice, to love mercy,
   and humbly to walk with your God.

Micah 6:16

16. "You have followed the practices of Omri,
    every deed of Ahab's house;
    you have walked in their counsels.
    So I will turn you into a cause of horror,
    and your residents into an object of derision.
    You shall bear the scorn of the peoples."

Micah 7:1-5

1. How I sorrow!
   For I am like the gatherer of summer fruit,
   like the gleaners of the vintage,
   when there are no grapes to eat,
   none of the early figs I crave.
2. The faithful have vanished from the earth;
   not one human being is upright.
   All lie in wait to shed blood;
   each hunts his brother with a net.
3. Their hands are good at doing evil:
   the official demands a favorable decision,
   and the judge decides to get the reward;
   the great speak only of what they want.
4. They twist their good like a brier bush,
   their uprightness like a thorn hedge.
   The day of their punishment has come;
   now their confusion is at hand.
5. Don't rely on a neighbor;
   don't trust a friend.
   Even with her who lies in your bosom,
   be guarded in what you say.

This group of texts is cast in what Stuart Hall calls the "negotiated code": they represent a mixture of adaptive and oppositional elements. In line with the social-class practices of its proponents, the negotiated code is shot through with contradictions. As Hall puts it,

> Negotiated codes operate through what we might call particular
> or situated logics: and these logics arise from the differential posi-
> tion of those who occupy this position in the spectrum, and from
> their differential and unequal relation to power.[7]

This assessment of the *B*-stage prophetic material is supported by Coote's similar study of Amos. According to Coote, the *B*-stage material—or material cast in a "negotiated code," as Hall would put it—exhibits certain distinctive features:

7. Ibid.

1) It addresses a general audience. In the case of Micah, this means all the people associated with Jacob or Judah, or Samaria or Jerusalem (1:5b-9). The closest *specific* description of the *B*-stage addressees in Micah is in 3:1; but this concrete description is quickly neutralized by a more general and vague description in a parallel line in 3:2a. The tendency to speak in general terms on the part of this code is congruent with its blending of adaptive and oppositional elements within the same discourse. In fact, this is a structural trait, with ideological roots in the middle classes of all social formations. It is the contradictory tendency inherent in a historically marginal but spiritually central class position. Eagleton describes the historical and ideological dilemma of this group within a capitalist social formation when he asserts:

> Committed by its nuclear social and economic conditions to a framework of overarching authority, to "standards" and "leadership," the petty bourgeoisie rejects at once the democratic "anarchy" it discerns below it and the ineffectualness of the actual authority posed above it. . . . Through *empirically* decentred, largely excluded from the ruling academic caste, it nevertheless laid claim to *be*, spiritually, the "real" elite. [italics Eagleton's][8]

Thus the nonspecific description of the addressees is a function of the historical and class contradictions attendant on the proponents of the *B*-stage material. Because of their differential relationship to power, especially in the historical context of Josiah's reform and of the Babylonian siege of Jerusalem, the *B*-stage ideologists broadened the indictment against the Jerusalemite and Judean ruling classes "to include a comprehensive notion of cultic and political idolatry—the practice of pagan religion and trust in military security."[9] It is from this that the material derives its feature of generality concerning its addressees.

2) On the basis of Micah 3:2, 4-7 and 6:8, it seems reasonable to argue, with Coote, that the basic message of *B*-stage prophetic oracles is: "Perform justice or else."[10] This means that the

---

8. Eagleton, *Criticism and Ideology,* 14.
9. James Luther Mays, *Micah: A Commentary* (Philadelphia: The Westminster Press, 1976), 25.
10. Coote, *Amos Among the Prophets,* 62.

bearers of tradition of this stage offer the ruling classes of Judah a chance to survive. But even if the survival option were not available, the fate of these classes seems bearable, and they are not beyond redemption: their vision will be darkened, and they will be confounded. There will be no answer from Yahweh (3:4-7).

3) The *B*-stage material is characterized by a propensity for abstract rather than concrete description. Coote says:

> B-stage phrases tend to be *wordy* rather than terse, *vague* rather than specific, *abstract* rather than concrete, and *stereotyped* rather than fresh. . . . In the B stage one does not "sell the needy into debt slavery for a pair of sandals"; instead one "does wrong." There is ultimately no specific authoritative rationale for the pro-Jerusalemite stance; so the B editor calls it, in effect, "good." [italics Coote's][11]

4) Ambiguity is another feature of the *B*-stage prophetic oracles. This quality is certainly present in 1:5b-7 and 2:6-7, 10-11; but in 3:1 and 6:6-8 it comes through more clearly. Here the text avoids clarity of statement by posing rhetorical questions on issues that are unambiguously asserted in the *A*-editions of the prophetic material. The effect is to give the appearance of addressing similar issues as the *A*-edition, while the concern is weakened by the language structure in which it is cast.

5) The prophetic *rib*, the suit or litigation, with its implication of open-endedness, defines another set of *B*-stage oracles. "Other forms found in the *B*-stage include chastisement, exhortation, call to worship, the narrative describing the commissioning of the prophet, the speech in the divine council, prophetic visions, and theophanies."[12] Certainly Micah 6:1-4 represents a perfect example of this feature of the *B*-stage material. The confidence of the *B*-stage editors in the justice of the legal system's open-endedness is betrayed in this text. The politics and the sociology of the law courts as well as those of the cultic systems are not an issue for the *B*-editors.

6) The *B*-stage text offers an open future. In the case of Micah, it is represented unambiguously by 5:1, 4, 5b-6. The method of "exhortation" is used to communicate this future.

11. Ibid., 63.
12. Ibid., 64.

According to Coote, the *B*-stage material is largely the product of a scribe or scribes who are at the service of a ruling elite;[13] and the features of the oracles of this stage are a function of the class and ideology of this scribal group. I have already pointed out that the discursive productions of this group reflect, unavoidably, its different and unequal relationship to power. The vagueness of the *B*-stage material, its generality in terms of its addresses, its abstractions and ambiguity, and the open-endedness of the future it offers, represent the extent and nature of the ideology of the class that put it together.

The *B*-stage oracles derive their identity from a certain kind of incompleteness: they are eloquent by their silence on the struggles of poor and exploited peasants in the Israelite monarchy. Although these oracles condemn evil and injustice and exhort people to good and justice, they do not name the actual actions of oppressors, except vaguely, and the resistance of the oppressed is present only by its absence. The task of a biblical hermeneutics of liberation is to theorize the ideological necessity of this incompleteness, this absence. Black theology as a discursive practice that is rooted in the progressive dimensions of black history and culture should provide the basis for a critical appropriation of these texts.

The first point to make is that this part of the prophetic text of Micah, as seen from the perspective of the hermeneutics of liberation, has a negative identification with the concerns of the poor and the oppressed. It helps to point to the behavior and ideology of a social class that needs careful watching in the liberation struggle. The *B*-stage prophetic texts, by virtue of their class character, appeal more to their counterparts in modern society, the petite bourgeoisie, than to the working-class people — the really poor and exploited members of contemporary societies. Modern middle-class people, who are similarly differentially and unequally related to power structures, display a similar vagueness, abstractness, generality, and ambiguity as the proponents of the *B*-stage texts in relation to oppression and justice. Cabral has this in mind when he says in regard to this class:

13. Ibid., 74.

We must, however, take into consideration the fact that, faced with the prospect of political independence, the ambition and opportunism from which the liberation movement generally suffers may draw into the struggle individuals who have not been reconverted. The latter, on the basis of their level of education, their scientific or technical knowledge, and without losing any class cultural prejudices, may attain the highest positions in the liberation movement. On the cultural as well as the political level vigilance is therefore vital. For in the specific and highly complex circumstances of the process of the phenomenon of the liberation movements, all that glitters is not necessarily gold: political leaders—even the most famous—may be culturally alienated.[14]

A similar dynamic seems to have taken place in the *B*-stage texts. There seems to have occurred a cultural alienation of a concrete, direct, specific, and clear message. The original message of Micah against the ruling classes of Judah has been reified, in the *B*-stage, which Henri Mottu describes as, among other things, a process of recurrence and a process of stealing. Concerning the conflict between Hananiah and Jeremiah, he writes:

> To the degree that reification as a general phenomenon is "grounded in historically recurrent circumstances of human existence in society," one can say that Hananiah operates upon the belief that God's fidelity is simply a recurrent fact. "Recurrence" is a procedure of demonstration that consists in extending to all terms of a series what is valid only for the first two terms. This is exactly what he does: he extends the events of 701 under Sennacherib to the events of 594/3 under Nebuchadnezzar without seeing those events in terms of the historical activity of Babylon and Judah.[15]

The nature and orientation of the *B*-stage prophetic oracles indicates that Hananiah symbolized a whole tradition with firm ideological and social-class roots. Concerning reification as "stealing," Mottu says:

> Reification occurs when certain people "steal" the praxis of others, which is the case when Hananiah "steals" [Isa. 9:4] from

14. Cabral, *Unity and Struggles*, 145.
15. Henri Mottu, "Jeremiah vs. Hananiah: Ideology and Truth in Old Testament Prophecy," *The Bible and Liberation*, ed. N. K. Gottwald (New York: Orbis Books, 1983), 242.

Isaiah and simply transfers a word said in a given situation into a quite different one. This process of "stealing" is a far-reaching one and covers many different situations, as illustrated by the German peasants who saw their praxis being "stolen" from their hands by the princes of Luther. . . . So the text of Isaiah 9 becomes a "thing," even a commodity, at the disposal of anyone at any time. Jer. 23:30 speaks pointedly against this "reification" of the words of God.[16]

Thus, while black theology shares the sentiments expressed in the message about justice in the *B*-stage texts, it cannot identify with the abstract context in which this message now appears. In these texts both oppression and justice have been "thingified," appearing now as vaguely good and evil. The original message of Micah, which was directed at the ruling classes of Judah during the eighth century B.C.E., has now been stolen from its concrete situation, where it concerned the condition of the poor and exploited, and is being applied to the Judean ruling class in their relationship with their foreign oppressors. The more basic contradiction between exploited peasants and exploiting latifundiaries in Judah has now been replaced by the secondary contradiction between Babylon and Judah or other nations and Israel.

THE BLACK STRUGGLE AND THE SIGNIFIED PRACTICE OF MICAH *A*-TEXTS

Micah 1:10-15(a)

10. Declare it not in Gath;
    weep, only weep.
    In the streets of Beth-aphrah
    roll in the dust.
11. The Shophar they sound for you,
    rulers of Shaphir.
    From her city she comes not out,
    nobilities/rulers of Zaanan.

16. Ibid.

I will make a lamentation, Beth-ezel,
I will take from you your standing place.

12. Who can hope for good,
    nobilities/rulers of Maroth?
    For evil has come down from Yahweh,
    to the gate of Jerusalem.

13. You harness the chariot to the team,
    nobilities/rulers of Lachish.
    That was the chief sin for the daughter of Zion,
    that in you were found the crimes of Israel.

14. To you they give parting gifts,
    Moresheth-Gath.
    Nobilities/rulers of Achzib have become a failing brook
    to the kings of Israel.

15 (a). Shall still the heir come to you,
    nobilities/rulers of Mareshah?

Micah 2:1-5, 8-9

1. Woe to those who contemplate wickedness,
   who do evil upon their couches/beds.
   At morning's light they carry it out
   because they wield power.

2. They covet fields and expropriate them,
   houses and carry them away.
   They oppress a man and his household,
   a producer and his fundamental means of production.

3. Therefore, thus says Yahweh,
   "Behold, I devise evil against these homesteads,
   an evil from which they cannot withdraw their necks,
   and in relation to which they cannot walk upright,
   for it shall be an evil time.

4. In that day a taunt-song shall be raised over you;
   a lament shall be sung, saying:
   'We are utterly ruined.
   The property of my people is exchanged/moved to and fro.
   There is none to remove it, to return our field through
      redistribution.'"

5. Therefore there will be no one to divide property by lot
   in the assembly of Yahweh.

8. But you! against my people
   you arise as enemy. [Following Mays, p. 67]
   From them [in front of them] their garment,
   [their cloak] you strip off [taking away security].
   Causing those who return from war
   to bring over security.
9. The women of my people you drive out,
   from the houses they delight in.
   From their children you take their
   honor forever.

Micah 3:8-12

8. But indeed, I am filled with the spirit of the Lord,
   with justice and power,
   to declare to Jacob his crime,
   to Israel his sin.
9. Hear this, chiefs of the house of Jacob,
   and magistrates of the house of Israel—
   the ones who pervert justice
   and twist the straight thing,
10. building Zion with bloodshed/murder,
    Jerusalem with violence.
11. Her chiefs judge for a bribe,
    her priests give instruction for a price,
    her prophets divine for money.
    And they still trust in Yahweh, saying,
    "Is not Yahweh near us?
    Evil will not come upon us!"
12. Therefore because of you,
    Zion shall become a plowed field,
    Jerusalem will be a ruin,
    and the mount of the house a wooded height.

Micah 5:10-15

10. "It shall be in that day," says the Lord,
    "I will cut off your horses from your midst.
11. I will cut off the cities of your land,
    and I will tear down all your fortresses.

12. I will cut off sorceries from your hand,
    and you will have no soothsayers.
13. I will cut off your idols
    and your sacred pillars from your midst.
    You shall not fetishize again
    the works of your own hands.
14. I will root out the Asherim from your midst
    and will exterminate your cities.
15. I will take vengeance in anger and in wrath
    upon the [nations] that have not heard."

Micah 6:9-15

9. The voice of Yahweh calls to the city
    (and he who hears your name is well-advised),
    "Hear, O tribe and those who assemble in the city.
10. Shall I forget the house of wickedness,
    where treasures of wickedness are stored,
    and the despicable use of an ephah that is too small?
11. Shall I approve anyone with false scales,
    with cheating weights in his pouch?
12. The rich ones are full of violence;
    the rulers speak with deception,
    all their speech is treachery.
13. So I have begun to smite you,
    to lay you waste because of your sins.
14(a). You shall eat and not be satisfied.
14(b). Semen into your womb you will take
    and not bring forth;
    and the ones you bring forth
    I will give to the sword.
15. You shall sow and not reap.
    You shall tread olives and not anoint yourself with oil,
    grapes, and not drink wine.

This group of texts is specific about the class of people
it addresses. In 1:10-16 the addressees of the *A*-stage material are
described as the "rulers/nobilities/landlords/authorities" of
the various cities listed in the lament. The translation of *yoshev*
as "ruler/authority" in contexts such as the one in this text has

been cogently argued by Gottwald, who builds on the arguments of Albrecht Alt as well as Frank M. Cross and David Noel Freedman. Concluding his study of the use of *yoshev* as referring to political and/or socioeconomic rule, Gottwald writes:

> When referring to the leaders of a region which we otherwise know to have been divided into several political sovereignties, such as Canaan with its independent city-states, the plural views all the heads of state in those several political units as a collectivity sharing similar values, attitudes, policies, or strategies. Therefore, while I incline to view most of the enemy leaders called *yoshev/yoshevim* in the premonarchic sources as kings or princes, I do not agree with Cross and Freedman in restricting the meaning of the term to "reigning princes." The functional import of the general designation is something like this: *yoshev/yoshevim* are leaders in the imperial-feudal statist system of social organization, with primary reference to enemy kings but embracing other functionaries in the statist system. As Israel developed statist sociopolitical organization of its own, the term was increasingly applied to Israelite functionaries in the state apparatus and, on occasion, referred to persons of power in the upper socioeconomic strata irrespective of their political office.[17]

Understood in this way, the lament in 1:10-16 addresses rulers of town or cities who may or may not have held political power in a specific office. They do, however, wield power (economic or social), and this text laments the behavior and practices that are commensurate with their position as the cause of the disaster that has beset Judah. Mays argues that the historical context for this lament of Micah is the destruction and suffering that descended on Judah following Sennacherib's military campaign along the eastern Mediterranean coast in 701 B.C.E. Mays writes further that

> Sennacherib moved against Judah from the west, overwhelmed Lachish and other "strong cities," according to his count forty-six in all. The defense system of fortified cities in the Shephelah was certainly a focus of his attack. He also claimed countless villages. Two hundred thousand of the population were said to have been deported. Hezekiah was driven inside Jerusalem, held there as

17. Gottwald, *Tribes of Yahweh*, 532.

though in prison, and finally was spared only by submission and the payment of an impoverishing tribute.[18]

In this lament, however, Micah does not simply bewail the destruction the Assyrians inflicted but, more importantly, the pain the population of Judah has been caused as a result of the practices of the powerful classes of Judah's cities. They were the ones who were exacting tribute from the peasants and squandering it in luxurious lifestyles. It is they for whom the *shophar* has been sounded (1:11), much as it is sounded for the propertied classes and the slave masters on the day of atonement (repossession, restitution, restoration) in the jubilee year (Lev. 25:8ff.).

The *A*-stage oracles are unambiguous about the crimes of the ruling classes. They are economic exploiters who accumulate wealth by treacherous means: "They covet fields and expropriate them, houses and take them; they oppress a man and his household; a producer and his fundamental means of production" (2:2, 8-9). This class also consists of judicial authorities (communal leaders and magistrates) and religious functionaries (priests and prophets) who participate in the injustices of the ruling classes by perverting the judicial system in the one case and commodifying religious services while invoking the egalitarian religious ideology of Yahwism in the other (3:8-11).

The message of the *A*-stage oracles is equally direct: Yahweh devises evil for this class. The ruling classes' positions of power, together with their pride, will be destroyed (2:3-5). Similarly, all the symbols of oppression and exploitation will fall prey to the wrath of Yahweh: "Zion shall become a plowed field, Jerusalem will be a ruin" (3:12). The oracles in 5:9-14 and 6:9-15 represent a vivid and dramatic depiction of the forms and instruments of oppression and exploitation against which Micah-*A* speaks.

Thus the class or group of people on whose behalf the Micah-*A* oracles are speaking is not sympathetic with the economic, political, and ideological interests of the class under attack. It prophesies the destruction of this class and its political and ideological structures. It represents the God who sees fundamental disruption of the status quo as the only solution to the violence

18. Mays, *Micah*, 53.

and corruption of the ruling classes. But radical as the oracles of Micah *A* are, they lack a dimension that would qualify them as revolutionary. The absence of this dimension is discernible only from the perspective of a hermeneutics of liberation that is rooted in the struggles of oppressed and exploited people today.

While identifying fully with the judgment meted out against the ruling classes by the *A*-stage oracles, the black working-class people of South Africa would experience an absence of the voice of the laboring and underclasses of Micah's Judah in these texts. This is so because the Micah text as a whole is a curious mixture of *A*-stage condemnation of injustice with *C*-stage eschatology. There is a glaring absence of an oppressed people's eschatology, which constitutes the incompleteness of the Micah text as a signifying practice. That is, from the perspective of the poor, the text lacks a vision of the future. It does not even summon the poor people to action. Thus there is a serious ideological lacuna in the text that can only be filled from *our* side of history. By this I mean that contemporary struggles for liberation, having encountered a void in terms of the actual struggles of the poor and exploited in the text, must offer their struggles —hermeneutically speaking—to complete the text. In this way the Micah discourse can be liberated to enable contemporary victims of injustice to do what Eagleton has called staging one's "own signifying practices to enrich, modify or transform the effects which others' practices produce."[19]

It is at this point of our thinking about creating alternative discourses and practices that it is appropriate to turn to a minority set of texts in the wider discourse of Micah — the *A/B* texts.

THE BLACK STRUGGLE AND THE SIGNIFIED PRACTICE OF MICAH–*A/B* TEXTS

Micah 1:8-9

8. Against this I will mourn and wail;
   I will go stripped and naked.

19. Eagleton, *Literary Theory,* 212.

I will make a lamentation like jackals,
a grieving like the young of an ostrich.
9. Because I am sick from her wound;
for it has come up to Judah,
it has reached the gate of my people,
right up to Jerusalem.

Micah 4:3-4

3. He will judge between many peoples [see Is. 2:2],
and decide against the strong nations up to a distant one.
They will beat their swords into plowshares,
their spears into pruning knives.
Nation will not raise sword against nation,
nor will they learn war again.
4. Each man shall sit under his vine,
under his fig tree;
and no one will be terrified,
for the mouth of Yahweh of hosts has spoken.

This group of texts occupies a position on the border between *A*-stage and *B*-stage material. In fact, one might say that this group represents the kind of *A*-stage texts that have been none too successfully edited by the *B*-stage signifying practitioner.

The first of these is Micah 1:8-9: this unit of material describes the mourning of the prophet for the state of Judah because of the wrath that Yahweh allows to befall the area. Mays says: "The historical event interpreted by this theological language is Sennacherib's attack on Judah and conquest of many of its cities, leaving King Hezekiah shut in Jerusalem. The situation suggested by the verse [9] is the time when the conquest of the Shephelah and hill country is complete, and only Jerusalem remains."[20] Notwithstanding some vagueness, indirectness, and a certain air of abstractness in this text, there is a concreteness that only the experience of solidarity can signify. It is a concreteness and a directness only tears can express. Walter Brueggemann makes the point succinctly:

20. Mays, *Micah*, 41.

150

Tears are a way of solidarity in pain when no other form of solidarity remains. And when one addresses numbness clearly, anger, abrasiveness, and indignation as forms of address will drive the hurt deeper, add to the numbness, and force people to behaviors not rooted in experience.[21]

Even more important, "grieving" under certain circumstances may constitute a *revolutionary practice*. The funerals of black victims of police and army violence in South Africa are a case in point. The revolutionary effects of the "grieving" of black masses for their daughters and sons who have fallen in the struggle have forced the powers that be to impose legislative, political, and military restrictions on the freedom of blacks to lament for their dead. For as Brueggemann correctly states,

> Such weeping is a radical criticism, a fearful dismantling, because it means the end of all machismo; weeping is something kings rarely do without losing their thrones. Yet the loss of thrones is precisely what is called for in radical criticism.[22]

The second group of Micah-*A/B* texts is 4:3-4. There can be no doubt that verse 3a is a *B* text. It addresses "people" and "nations" in general. This verse has replaced what was originally *A* material, which addressed itself to specific classes within the tributary social formation of monarchical Judah. This *B* material, however, provides a new hermeneutical framework for what must be the most revolutionary part of the entire biblical discourse (3b-4). The latter redirects attention to the sphere of production of material life. Verse 3b points to an aspect of the productive activity that is destructive not only because the technology it produces is for war but because it is a luxury that consumes human and natural resources that might have been usefully invested in activities supporting the life of the entire community. For the first time, a vision of an alternative society is projected as a result of this realigning and redirecting of production processes: "Each man shall sit under his vine, under his fig tree, / And no one will be terrified, / For the mouth of Yahweh of hosts has spoken" (vs. 4).

21. Walter Brueggemann, *The Prophetic Imagination* (Philadelphia: Fortress Press, 1978), 59.

22. Ibid., p. 61.

Thus while the oppressed and exploited peasants, artisans, day laborers, and underclasses of Micah's Judah are entirely absent in the signifying practice that the wider text of Micah represents, something of their project and voice has almost accidentally survived in the form of an *A/B*-stage text. The survival of contradictory texts like these in a discourse that is dominated by contrary perspectives exemplifies the working of ideology. As I have argued in Chapter Four of this study and elsewhere,

> Ideology is not a lie. It is rather a harmonization of contradictions in such a way that the class interests of one group are universalized and made acceptable to other classes. Also, ideology is not a selection process or filter through which certain facts are constituted by their absence.[23]

There are, therefore, aspects of the texts that provide hermeneutical links with the struggles and projects of the oppressed peoples of biblical communities. These aspects of biblical discourses serve also as a critique of present-day cultural and political discourses of the oppressed. The absences in the text of material concerning the experiences of the oppressed in ancient society also reopen the canon of Scripture in some sense, to the extent that they stimulate the production of new liberating religious discourses that enrich, modify, or transform existing practices. Thus black culture and history as hermeneutical factors in black theology in South Africa ask questions of the biblical text that seek to establish ties with struggles for liberation in the biblical communities. Similarly, the liberating aspects of the biblical discourses interrogate black culture and history in the light of the values and goals of struggling classes in biblical communities. A theological hermeneutics that brings out this dialectic in the appropriation of biblical texts operates with a clear recognition of the fact that usually in ideological discourses "only the successful . . . are remembered. The blind alleys, the lost causes, and the losers themselves are forgotten."[24] Differently put, this hermeneutics is informed by a perspective recognizing that

23. Mosala and Tlhagale, eds., *The Unquestionable Right to be Free*, 194.
24. Edward P. Thompson, *The Making of the English Working Class* (Middlesex: Penguin Books, 1963), 13.

The ideas of the ruling class are in every epoch the ruling ideas, i.e. the class which is the ruling *material force* of society is at the same time its ruling *intellectual force*. The class which has the means of material production at its disposal has control at the same time over the areas of mental production, so that thereby, generally speaking, the ideas of those who lack the means of mental production are subject to it. [italics Marx's and Engels']²⁵

The task of a biblical hermeneutics of liberation is to go behind the dominant discourses to the discourses of oppressed communities in order to link up with kindred struggles. In South Africa a common mythological expression of the role of biblical discourses in the dispossession of blacks runs like this: "When the white man came to our country, he had a Bible and we had the land. The white man said to the black man, 'Let us pray.' After the prayer, the white man had the land and the black man had the Bible." The task now facing a black theology of liberation is to enable black people to use the Bible to get the land back and to get the land back without losing the Bible. In order for this to happen, black theology must employ the progressive aspects of black history and culture to liberate the Bible so that the Bible may liberate black people. That is the hermeneutical dialectic.

In order for that to happen, though, a theoretically sound and an ideologically clear approach to the text of the Bible is a prerequisite. The above study of the book of Micah is an example of how this might be done. The point of this textual study has been to confront the class and ideological conditions of production and existence of the text with the class and ideological position and commitment of the reader. In the specific circumstances of the racist and sexist oppression and capitalist exploitation of black people in South Africa, Micah-*A* and *A/B* texts provide a positive hermeneutical connection with the struggles of black workers; but the *B* and *C* texts of Micah serve the struggles of oppressed peoples negatively. These latter texts represent the forms of domination and the interests of dominant social classes that are similar to those of contemporary oppressors and exploiters. We can, through an appropriation of these texts, albeit a negative one, once again bring the category of "struggle" to the fore.

25. Karl Marx and Friedrich Engels, *The German Ideology* (London: Lawrence and Wishart, 1970), 64.

6
A Materialist Reading of
Luke 1 and 2

THE MATERIAL CONDITIONS OF LUKE 1 AND 2

THE SOCIOHISTORICAL CONTEXT OF LUKE 1 AND 2 IS NO DOUBT THE colonial occupation of Palestine by Rome. Palestine is, therefore, characterized by the articulation of two tributary modes of production at this time. The Palestinian tributary mode of production of the first century C.E. was overdetermined by the imperial tributary mode of production of the Roman colonial power. We need to reconstruct briefly these two tributary social formations and their relationship to each other. Such a reconstruction will enable us to see how the social history of that world was constituted ideologically through the discursive practice of the Luke 1 and 2 text.

The Forces of Production of First-Century Palestine. The fundamental means of production in Palestine had been since antiquity, and was during the first century C.E., the land, especially the arable land. G. E. M. de Ste. Croix makes the point succinctly that

> Wealth in the Greek world, in the Archaic, Classical and Hellenistic periods, as in the Roman Empire throughout its history, was always essentially wealth in land, upon which was conducted the

cultivation of cereals . . . and of other agricultural products, especially those of the olive and the vine and also the pasturing of cattle, sheep and horses.[1]

The other key means of production were the lakes and seas and probably rivers of Palestine. With respect to the lakes, Joseph Klausner says:

> The Sea of Galilee contained all manner of fish, including certain very choice varieties. . . . So plentiful were the fish that they were salted and sold in Palestine and abroad; this accounts for the fact that a town on the lakeshore which apparently bore the Hebrew name Migdal . . . was in Greek called by the name "Tarichaea" from the word salted fish. The newly built Tiberias became the fishing centre and fish market of Galilee.[2]

Minerals such as salt, bitumen, phosphorus, and tar were sometimes found in such places as the Dead Sea.[3] Furthermore, during the Hellenistic period the construction of artificial irrigation schemes such as terraces, pools, and canals contributed to the improvement of agriculture. The evidence of rabbinical literature points to even more intensive agriculture, trade, and commerce than in the Old Testament times.[4] However, first-century Palestine seems not to have witnessed any significant development of the forces of production. Sufficient and balanced technological progress is not evident during this time. The setting in motion of the forces of production through the tilling of arable land seems to have followed ancient ways of labor organization. Peasant family labor appears, as in the old times in the absence of slave labor, to have constituted the basic economic production unit in agriculture and in the fishing industry. In fact, the colonial social relations of Palestine, from the Persian through the Ptolemaic, Seleucid, and Roman periods, imposed constraints on the development of the national productive forces.

1. G. E. M. de Ste. Croix, *The Class Struggle in the Ancient Greek World* (Ithaca, NY: Cornell University Press, 1981), 120.
2. Joseph Klausner, *Jesus of Nazareth* (New York: Macmillan Company, 1925), 176.
3. Ibid. See also Michel Clevenot, *Materialist Approaches to the Bible*, 43.
4. Martin Hengel, *Judaism and Hellenism* (London: SCM Press, 1974), 46.

The colonial economy of Palestine was designed primarily to provide tribute for the colonial powers. Thus the Palestinian forces of production remained relatively undeveloped despite the thriving of commerce and trade during the same period. Further, the diversification of agriculture and the introduction of certain technical improvements such as better forms of oil and wine presses, the treadmill, the irrigation wheel, and the plow seem to have failed to propel the overall Palestinian productive development to qualitatively higher levels.[5] There is an area of social and national life, however, that did benefit from the few technical advances of this time. It is instructive to note the connection between this area and the needs and interests of the ruling classes of the period. Writing about the Hellenistic rule under which some developments took place, Martin Hengel says:

> The technical progress of the Hellenistic period accordingly manifested itself above all in the construction of astonishing machines of war, of increasingly large warships and in types of fortification.[6]

The war industry is not, for the majority of the population of a class-stratified society, a constructive development. The situation is worse in a colonial setup such as Palestine was at this time. War industries function to reinforce the internal divisions while at the same time keeping a check on external threats to internal domination. War industries are ruling-class instruments par excellence. I have noted above how in the Old Testament a prophetic critique captured the real nature of this phenomenon (Mic. 4:3). Thus the contribution of this kind of industry to the overall development of an area leaves much to be desired.

The Relations of Production of First-Century Palestine. The specific expression of the forces of production in a society is a function of the existing social division of labor. In Palestine during the first century C.E., the principal social contradiction was between the Roman colonial state and the dependent

5. Ibid., 46f.; Sean Freyne, *Galilee: From Alexander to Hadrian* (Notre Dame: M. Glazier Inc. and University of Notre Dame Press, 1980), 170ff.
6. Hengel, *Judaism and Hellenism*, 13.

colonized Palestinian social formation. By virtue of its colonial domination, Rome extracted a surplus from the population of Palestine through a comprador Palestinian royalty, nobility, and priesthood. This contradiction between Rome and Palestine, however, was overdetermined by an internal social division of labor out of which issued a tributary class formation.

The surplus extracted from the peasants in agriculture and other industries through land taxes, animal taxes, tithes, and so forth, functioned to finance the resident alien armies, the local ruling classes, and the Roman colonial state. There seems to be no indication that the surplus was ever invested in productive activities that could help raise the capital needed for developing the forces of production and consequently increasing productivity for the purpose of meeting the overall human needs. The Roman colonial tributary social formation was a dead end for the majority of the local Palestinian people. It functioned to farm out surpluses for the ruling classes of Rome at the expense of the overall development of Palestine itself.

External trade tended to focus on luxury items such as oil and wine. Internal trade assumed the form of internal regional barter:

> The Palestinian towns exchanged their agricultural produce. Sharon in Judea sold its wines and bought bread. Jericho and the Jordan Valley sold their famous fruits for bread and wine. The Judean Shefela had a superabundance of bread and oil, and Galilee of corn and vegetables. Palestine also exported its surplus of oil, wine, wheat and fruit, while it imported a considerable number of commodities.[7]

First-century Palestine was a complex colonial social formation with a complex class structure. This does not mean that the class forces of this social structure cannot be delineated with reasonable precision. It simply means that the forms of surplus extraction that existed in this society were not confined to the relationships represented by the principal contradiction. There

---

7. Klausner, *Jesus of Nazareth*, 186; see also Fernando Belo, *A Materialist Reading of the Gospel of Mark*, 62ff.; Joachim Jeremias, *Jerusalem in the Time of Jesus: An Investigation into Economic and Social Conditions during the New Testament Period* (Philadelphia: Fortress Press, 1969), 31ff.

were, for instance, historically accrued traditional Palestinian ideological mechanisms of surplus extraction that the Romans did not tamper with; but they certainly benefited from their use on the peasants of Palestine. Clevenot provides a terse characterization of the relationship of production to the social formation that shaped the material conditions of production of the Gospel of Luke:

> In short, First Century Palestine was a class-structured society at every level. At the economic level the masses were fiercely exploited by the privileged. In politics the priestly class, supported by the great landowners, held the mechanism of the state in their hands. Ideologically the ruling class imposed its ideology (essentially the system of purity), which was passed on in diverse ways by the groups, sects, and parties.[8]

Sean Freyne has recently provided an instructive delineation of ownership relations with respect to Galilee. He points out the importance of grasping the principle of "land won by the spear" as a key to understanding the situation of land ownership outside the cities. This principle indicates how private ownership of land was increasingly replaced by the establishment of large holdings of land belonging to the royal house. The power of the royalty was predicated in large measure on the accumulative and distributive control of these *latifundia*, which could be parceled out as "bequests of land."[9] Hengel makes the point more succinctly with regard to Ptolemaic administration:

> The starting point here was the conception that the whole land was the personal possession . . . of the king. The titles of the Ptolemaic administrative officials therefore often derive from the terminology used in large private estates in Greece. The king "managed the State as a plain Macedonian or Greek would manage his own household."[10]

The evidence points to the fact that the royal estates were under the supervision of managers. Among the duties of these managers was the collection of rents and taxes from those

8. Clevenot, *Materialist Approaches*, 50.
9. Freyne, *Galilee*, 156.
10. Hengel, *Judaism and Hellenism*, 10.

peasants who owned their own land.[11] The notion that all the land belonged to the king refers to the political control of an area or village by the king, not necessarily the total absence of private peasant holdings. As Freyne indicates,

> The villagers were certainly free and may even have owned, or at least permanently leased, their own lots, so that the owner of the village was rather a mediator between the villagers and the royal administration, and "the rent" which was paid to him was their share of the . . . *[phoros]* to the central bureaucracy.[12]

Nevertheless, the economic domination of Palestine throughout its colonial period and including the Herodian era is well attested. This domination took the form, on the one hand, of royal monopolies being worked solely to produce for the royalties, foreign and local; on the other hand, the ruling classes imposed heavy taxes and rents on independent lands and industries as a means of extracting tribute for their benefit. The Herodian ruling classes followed the example of the previous regimes in their monopoly and exploitation of the best lands as well as the oppression of peasant labor.[13]

Thus the colonial social formation of Palestine in the Graeco-Roman period is characterized by a complex class structure that may be represented as follows:

1) The ruling classes, comprising the colonial royalty and nobility; the colonial civil servants (*stratēgoi* and *dioiketes*), many of whom would be beneficiaries of royal land bequests; comprador Palestinian royalty and nobility, for example, the Herodians; comprador economic and political ruling classes— Sadducees, some of the Pharisees, scribes, and priests.

2) the dominated classes, consisting of artisans, peasants, lower-stratum priests, lower-stratum Pharisees, and poor peasants. This class Freyne describes as the *laoi* and says that they are "free but dependent, and their condition can deteriorate with the changing economic or agricultural situation which makes it impossible for them to meet the demands of the . . . *[phoros]* or royal tribute."[14]

11. Freyne, *Galilee,* 158.
12. Ibid., 162.
13. Ibid., 165.
14. Ibid., 161.

3) The underclasses, made up of casual laborers, bandits, petty criminals, prostitutes, and beggars. These groups were very exploitable—politically, economically, and ideologically. Politically, they could be drawn into mercenary activities that for the most part were not in their own interests (Mk. 14:10-11). Economically, they could be pitted against one another, as when they complain about one another's wages in Jesus' parable (Mt. 20:1-16). Ideologically, they could be the target of moral and religious hypocrisy (Jn. 8:1-11).

IDEOLOGICAL CONDITIONS OF LUKE 1 AND 2

What, then, is the nature of the movement from history as we have described it above to a reconstitution of that history in a Gospel discourse? In examining Luke's ideological production of the historical situation of first-century Palestine, we shall avoid the empiricist problematic that plagues most biblical historical critics.[15] We shall rather concur with the view that "the notion of a direct, spontaneous relation between text and history . . . belongs to a naive empiricism which is to be discarded."[16] Equally, the idea of a possible neat division between the ideological, which is hard to trap with scientific tools, and the historical, which is accessible through formal quasi-scientific methods, I regard as epistemologically doubtful. Following Eagleton, I shall assume that

> History . . . certainly "enters" the text, not least the "historical" text; but it enters it precisely *as ideology*, as a presence determined and distorted by its measurable absences. This is not to say that real history is present in the text but in disguised form, so that the task of the critic is then to wrench the mask off its face. It is rather that history is present in the text in the form of a double-absence. The text takes as its object, not the real, but certain significations by which the real lives itself—significations which are themselves the product of its partial abolition. . . . History . . . is the ultimate signifier of literature, as it is the ultimate signified. For what else

15. See, for instance, Richard Cassidy, *Jesus, Politics, and Society: A Study of Luke's Gospel* (Maryknoll, NY: Orbis, 1983), 9ff.
16. Eagleton, *Criticism and Ideology,* 70.

in the end could be the source and object of signifying practices but the real social formation which provides its material context? [italics Eagleton's][17]

Luke's Gospel has been described variously as universalist, concerned about the poor and outcasts, and as a social gospel. The reason for such descriptions lies in the subject matter of this Gospel, which covers these areas of social life more extensively than do the other Gospels. No attempt has been made, however, to determine more precisely what the social-class perspective is from which Luke addresses these issues and how it determines the nature of "the historical" in Luke. Such a process of inquiry would lead not only to the class position of Luke but also to the class and ideological interests that frame Luke's discursive practice.

In what follows I will critically evaluate some of the recent literary, political, and social readings of Luke's Gospel. I will then argue that a hermeneutical appropriation of Luke's texts that takes seriously the material and ideological conditions producing them and signified by them leads to very different conclusions about Luke's discourses.

*   *   *

A recent major study of Luke's social and political description of Jesus argues that Luke portrays Jesus as someone who was dangerous to the Roman Empire.[18] Richard Cassidy argues that Luke's Jesus "espouses a concern for persons and groups from all social levels and backgrounds, but especially for the poor and the sick, for women and Gentiles."[19] But he fails to scrutinize the *class character* of a position that would portray Jesus in this way. Cassidy illustrates Luke's description of Jesus as one concerned for groups and persons of all levels by drawing attention especially to his attitude toward the "use of material possessions."[20] According to Cassidy, "Luke indicates that Jesus adopted an ex-

17. Ibid., 72.
18. Cassidy, *Jesus, Politics, and Society*, 77ff.
19. Ibid.
20. Ibid.

tremely strong position against surplus possessions. Jesus himself lived simply and sparingly and he praised others like Zaccheus when they took steps to do likewise."[21] It is difficult not to sense in Cassidy's argument hermeneutical assumptions that derive from contemporary liberal-humanist ideology. We will argue later that a different set of hermeneutical assumptions deriving from not only a different ideology but also a different cultural and political agenda detects a vastly different ideological maneuver on the part of Luke.

Robert J. Karris, in contrast to Cassidy, states more categorically that the "poor and rich" constitute what he calls "the Lukan *Sitz im Leben*":

> Luke's community clearly had both rich and poor members. Luke is primarily taken up with the rich members, their concerns, and the problems which they pose for the community. Their concerns . . . revolve around the question: do our possessions prevent us from being genuine Christians?[22]

Karris is undoubtedly correct in his focus on the rich as Luke's primary preoccupation. But Karris fails to draw the hermeneutical implications of Luke's discursive employment of the Jesus story to address a problem that fundamentally arises out of and concerns a community of rich and powerful people. What happens to Jesus when he is ideologically co-opted into the struggles and concerns of the dominant classes of society? I will suggest later that we have "to read the text, as it were, backwards—to examine the nature of its 'problems' in the light of its 'solutions'" in order to be able to transcend its ideological limitations.[23]

For Wolfgang Stegemann, "the gospel of Luke is a sustained call to repentance—and it is addressed to Christians of wealth and repute."[24] It is absolutely clear to Stegemann that Luke tries to make a virtue for the rich and powerful of what is a necessity for the poor and powerless majority of the Palestin-

21. Ibid., 78.
22. Robert J. Karris, "Poor and Rich: The Lukan *Sitz im Leben*," in *Perspectives on Luke-Acts*, ed. C. H. Talbert (Edinburgh: T. and T. Clark Ltd., 1978), 124.
23. Eagleton, *Criticism and Ideology*, 88.
24. Wolfgang Stegemann and W. Schottroff, *God of the Lowly: Socio-Historical Interpretations of the Bible* (Maryknoll, NY: Orbis Books, 1984), 165.

ian people, namely, their poverty and homelessness. The experiences of starvation, sickness, imprisonment, homelessness, separation from family and friends, persecution by authorities, and, indeed, of being a single mother were inescapable realities for the majority of people in first-century Palestine. In his Gospel, Luke turns this experience into an ethical choice for the rich and powerful men who make up his audience. Stegemann hints at the ideological effects of the kind of discursive practice Luke engages in here in the following:

> What would it mean for us theologically if the historical Jesus movement had in fact drawn its recruits from among the lowly? What if the followers of Jesus, like their master, were from the poor and hungry, not as the result of renunciation of possessions but because in fact they possessed nothing? What if the desired goal of their criticism of the rich was that in the kingdom of God present relationships would be reversed? . . . Would this kind of radicality, which has nothing to lose but much to gain, still win our sympathy?[25]

Luke's ideological production of the story of Jesus within the historical context of first-century Palestine has made available a gospel that is acceptable to the rich and the poor of Luke's community, but in which the struggles and contradictions of the lives of the poor and exploited are conspicuous by their absence. By turning the experiences of the poor into the moral virtues of the rich, Luke has effectively eliminated the poor from his Gospel.

The dominant exegetical practices, however, seem incapable of penetrating the ideological practices of Luke to reach to the radical story of Jesus and his followers, which Luke *produces* in such a way that it is "acceptable" to the rich and the powerful. In a frenzied attempt to defend the ruling-class interests of Luke as revolutionary—of course, "responsibly revolutionary"—recent studies of political issues in Luke have colluded with the ideological interests of the texts at the expense of the oppressed and exploited people of first-century Palestine, as well as their descendants in the contemporary world.[26] The issue

---

25. Ibid., 166.

26. Richard Cassidy and D. Scharper, eds., *Political Issues in Luke-Acts* (Maryknoll, NY: Orbis, 1983), *passim*; J. M. Ford, *My Enemy is My Guest* (Maryknoll, NY: Orbis, 1984), *passim*.

is not that these scholars misunderstand Luke; they do not. Rather, they collude with Luke. This is perfectly understandable in social class terms, even though it is critically indefensible.[27]

By employing the ideological concerns and aspirations of the oppressed and exploited black people of South Africa as a hermeneutical structuring pole, I hope to show how the text of Luke 1 and 2 can yield greater secrets than it has so far. In this I follow Eagleton's cogent argument:

> It is not, in other words, simply by virtue of ideology being forced up against the wall of history by the literary text that it is terrorized into handing over its secrets. Its contradictions may be forced from it by its historically determined encounter with another ideology, or ideological subensemble; indeed it is possible to claim that it is in such historical conjunctures that the moment of genesis of much literature is to be found.[28]

Black theology must attempt to transcend the ideological limits that Luke imposes in his particular production of the Jesus story by using the history, culture, and struggle of the black people as a hermeneutical tool. We must recognize in black theology that the very pretense of political neutrality regarding texts represents in fact the furtherance of certain political ends.[29]

Even more importantly, black theology needs an ideological suspicion in its approach to texts based on the understanding that

> Discourses, sign-systems and signifying practices of all kinds, from film and television to fiction and the languages of natural science, produce effects, shape forms of consciousness and unconsciousness, which are closely related to the maintenance or transformation of our existing systems of power. They are thus closely related to what it means to be a person. Indeed "ideology" can be taken to indicate no more than this connection—the link or nexus between discourses and power.[30]

---

27. See, for instance, Fredric Jameson, *The Political Unconscious: Narrative as a Socially Symbolic Act* (Ithaca, NY: Cornell University Press, 1981), esp. the conclusion, 281ff.

28. Eagleton, *Criticism and Ideology,* 96.

29. Eagleton, *Literary Theory,* 209.

30. Ibid., 210.

Thus, in order to become situated properly within the wider nexus of power relations that Luke signifies ideologically in the stories of chapters 1 and 2, black theology must retreat hermeneutically to black history, black culture, and the black struggle as sources of concepts for decoding the text.

Black theology's point of focus is an economically, politically, culturally, and morally dispossessed people. It carries with it the morality and social assumptions of a people who have suffered at the hands of the hypocrisy of a supposedly superior civilization. One important component of the struggle for the liberation of black people is a relentless resistance to the totalizing hold of modern capitalism. With Marlene Dixon, black theology must begin from an awareness that

> Capital leaves not the tiniest corner of society free of its domination. A simple juridical review of marriage, divorce, custody, bastardy, and welfare laws, and of the laws related to sexuality, prostitution, and moral life in general, amply demonstrates capital's direct concern with marriage, the family, children, sexuality, and so-called "morals." The supervision by the state of the moral life of the working class is directly related to the role of that class in commodity production, including the production of labor power itself, without which the entire capitalist society would cease to exist.[31]

Armed with this understanding of oppression and of struggle against it—and like the Caribbean Rastafarian movement, whose appropriation of the Bible is necessarily selective and partisan—the black people of South Africa must be "mindful of the long and bitter struggles master and slave fought across its [Bible] pages."[32] The question, therefore, of whose side Luke the writer takes in the political and moral struggle found in chapters 1 and 2 is of pivotal importance to black theology.

Viewed from a black theological perspective, the juxtaposition of the story of John the Baptist's birth with Jesus' birth

---

31. Marlene Dixon, *The Future of Women* (San Francisco: Synthesis Publications, 1983), 15.

32. Paul Gilroy, "Steppin' out of Babylon: Race, Class, and Autonomy," in *The Empire Strikes Back* (London: Centre for Contemporary Cultural Studies Publication, 1982), 295.

has far-reaching ideological implications. This juxtaposition is seen as an ideological solution to a fundamental politico-moral problematic facing the religious sector of the comprador Jewish ruling class. The above analysis of the social structure of colonized Palestine has shown that the Roman Empire ruled Palestine by proxy of an indigenous comprador class consisting of the priestly sector, among others. The Lukan discourse, in an attempt to depict Jesus as an acceptable figure to the ruling class, produces a discursive practice in which the priestly class has given its legitimation to the birth and subsequent mission of Jesus. This is not to imply that there were no members of the priestly sector who were ideologically and politically opposed to both the Roman and Palestinian tributary oppression of the nation. It is significant, however, that this class plays no part in the rest of Luke's work outside the birth narratives. I contend, therefore, that the story of Mary's visitation to Zechariah and Elizabeth is intended to deal with the embarrassing social-class origins and position of Mary. Luke's attempt to sell the story of Jesus to the Jewish priestly groups must have floundered on the rocks of Jesus' family background, which was not socially acceptable. Raymond E. Brown hits the nail on the head, even though he does not draw the implications of this, when he writes:

> The marriage situation envisaged in Matthew and (seemingly in Luke where Mary has conceived or will conceive before living with Joseph) implies that Jesus was born at a *noticeably* early period after his parents came to live together. This could have been a historical factor known to Jesus' followers and opponents. . . . The Jewish opponents of Christianity eventually accused Jesus of being illegitimate . . . but Christians rejected any implication of sin in Jesus' origins. . . .[33]

As the custodians and administrators of what Fernando Belo has called the "symbolic order"[34] —comprising the pollution and debt system—the priestly class would have questioned the messiahship of Jesus on specifically priestly-morality-class

33. Raymond E. Brown, "Luke's Method in the Annunciation Narrative of Chapter One," in *Perspectives on Luke-Acts*, ed. C. H. Talbert, 134.
34. Belo, *A Materialist Reading of the Gospel of Mark*, 37ff.

grounds. It is part of the brilliance of Luke as a signifying practitioner to address this aspect of the opposition to Jesus in his writing. Naturally, he must necessarily do it from the perspective of what *he* regards, in class terms, as significant.

The point is not to impute to Luke any conspiratorial motives; rather, it is to recognize that

> Like private property, the literary text . . . appears as a "natural" object, typically denying the determinants of its productive process. The function of criticism is to refuse the spontaneous presence of work—to deny that "naturalness" in order to make its real determinants appear.[35]

Mary, probably a single mother from the ghettos of colonized Galilee, needed the moral clearing of the priestly sector of the ruling class—those who were the target of Luke's Gospel. Essentially, her class origins were too unbecoming for the eyes of the class for which Luke is writing. How can the Savior of the world come from depressed ghetto areas and not from wealthy suburbia, like other prominent societal figures before him? Luke could not sell that kind of messiah to his ruling-class audience. His ruling-class perspectives inscribe themselves even in his choice of places, as Yann Redalie so perceptively observes:

> But to pay attention to locality, land, squares, places, is to be faithful to the way Luke writes his story. For him the writing of the Gospel occurs within a geography that goes "toward Jerusalem" in his Gospel and "from Jerusalem to Rome" in Acts. The story he tells takes shape within a definite route in the heart of the Greco-Roman world.[36]

In the Gospel, where he is dealing more directly with the Jewish colonial comprador ruling class, Judea—and especially Jerusalem—serve the function of legitimation for Luke. The Gospel of Luke moves dialectically from talking about the oppressed and exploited to addressing the concerns of the local ruling class and how they might receive the message and ministry of Jesus. In this he is careful not to contradict their class

35. Eagleton, *Criticism and Ideology,* 101.
36. Yann Redalie, "Conversion or Liberation? Notes on Acts 16:11-40," *Radical Religion* 2 (Nos. 2 and 3, 1975): 103.

position. What is required of them is that they should use their possessions to support the movement. Their class position is de-historicized and turned into a virtue for the benefit of the incipient Christian church. The movement of Mary from Galilee to Judea should be viewed in the same context of ideological legitimations and harmonizations.

Thus Luke is not a mere distorter of facts or traditions; he is a shrewd ideologist who writes for his class in the sense of Antonio Gramsci's "organic intellectuals."[37] He is true to his facts. The only difference is that he presents the facts in his text with a certain incompleteness. Luke's fidelity to history is represented in the birth narratives by this inclusion of nationalistic revolutionary hymns, which reflect the social revolutionary mood of the period he is describing (1:46-56; 67-79). However, he draws on the nationalist revolutionary traditions whose ability to liberate the really poor had already been tested and found wanting during the Hasmonean dynasty. Josephine Massyng-berde Ford aptly illustrates the connection with the traditions of struggle when she says:

> Our examination of the infancy narratives has shown that the war angel, Gabriel, appeared to Zechariah and Mary. John the Baptist was to work in the spirit and power of the zealous prophet Elijah. The names Jesus (Joshua), John, and Simeon are names found among Jewish freedom fighters. The annunciation to Mary and the Magnificat have political and military overtones. The words of Elizabeth and Mary echo the beatitude pronounced over Jael and Judith. The shepherd verses have imperial overtones, and a heavenly army appears to them. . . .[38]

And then, in a strange turn of thought, Ford continues:

> From now on in his Gospel, Luke will take almost every opportunity offered him to show that Jesus, contrary to all expectations as seen in the infancy narratives, is a preacher with an urgent message to his generation and to the generations to come, the powerful message of non-violent resistance and, more strikingly, loving one's enemy in word and deed.[39]

37. Antonio Gramsci, *Selections from the Prison Notebooks* (New York: International Publishers, 1983), 5ff.
38. Ford, *My Enemy is My Guest*, 36.
39. Ibid.

The way the birth narratives have functioned in the churches of Western Christianity, including those geographically situated in the Third World, is an eloquent witness to the success of Luke in his ideological suppression of the social revolutionary-class origins of Mary, the mother of Jesus. She has been appropriated theologically more as the priestly "first lady" than as a key symbol of a revolutionary movement to overthrow the dominant oppressive structures of church and society. The hope that Mary might have inspired in the hearts of millions of single mothers under conditions of modern monopoly capitalism was first dashed by Luke in his Gospel. That hope lingers on in this Gospel only by its effective absence. It remains for the questions of contemporary single mothers, given discursive articulation by a militant black theology of liberation, to reclaim the Gospel's histories, cultures, and moralities of the oppressed.

But Luke needed to integrate not only the priestly apology into the otherwise embarrassing moral background of Jesus, at least from the point of view of the colonial ruling class. He also had to specifically face the problematic of Jesus' class origins. Again, we have to get to this problem by reading the text backwards. For as Eagleton argues:

> It is criticism's task to demonstrate how the text is thus "hollowed" by its relation to ideology—how, in putting that ideology to work, it is driven up against those gaps and limits which are the product of ideology's relation to history. An ideology exists because there are certain things which must not be spoken of. In so putting ideology to work the text begins to illuminate the absences which are the foundation of its articulate discourse. And in so doing it helps to "liberate" us from the ideology of which that discourse is a product.[40]

In the annunciation of Jesus' birth, Luke puts ideology to work in a way that successfully establishes the absences that are the foundation of his discourses. The relevant verses in the text are 1:27: "He had a message for a girl promised in marriage to a man named Joseph, who was a descendant of King David. The girl's name was Mary"; 1:32f.: "He will be great and will be called the Son of the Most High God. The Lord God will make

40. Eagleton, *Criticism and Ideology*, 90.

him a king, as his ancestor David was, and he will be the king of the descendants of Jacob forever; his kingdom will never end!"; and 1:34: "Mary said to the angel, 'I am a virgin. How, then, can this be?'"

The problem underlying this part of Luke's discourse is clearly hinted at in 1:34, where the writer has Mary protest that she is a virgin and that the angel's story does not make sense. Luke has tried to anticipate this contradiction by beginning the annunciation with an explanation that the "girl was promised in marriage to a man named Joseph." It is quite clear, however, that Luke knew the problem was not really solved, since the bounds of historical credulity could not have been stretched beyond asserting a betrothal between Mary and Joseph. As an ideological creation, Joseph could not be made to serve the function of a biological father, because that would be moving beyond ideology to history. The real function of Joseph in this part of the text is to help invoke a royal connection for Jesus. And since the historical context of this story is the national colonization of the Jews, Luke appropriately invokes the Davidic royal connection. Raymond Brown draws attention to the fact that this angelic pronouncement in Luke "clearly echoes the promise of Nathan to David (2 Sam. 7:8-16), the promise that came to serve as the foundation of messianic expectation."[41]

The David connection, therefore, plays a double role in this story. On the one hand, given the national oppression by the Romans, the return of the Davidic kingship, symbolized by the birth of Jesus, could be intended to herald the national liberation that the king whom Robert Coote calls "the early David" brought to ancient Israel. In regard to a similar use of David in the C-stage of the book of Amos, Coote says:

> The reference is to the early David, the folk hero, the protector of the disenfranchised, the David of the byways and caves of the Judean hill country, sprung from the country town of Bethlehem, the ruler who knew his subordination to Yahweh, and who delayed the building of the temple that would serve in folk memory as the functional symbol of despotic royal power.[42]

41. Brown, "Luke's Method," 132.
42. Coote, *Amos Among the Prophets*, 124.

On the other hand, there is the David who was an accomplice in the political murders of the early monarchy; who used his royal power against Uriah because of his adultery with Uriah's wife; who deprived a poor man of his small possession in order to feed his royal visitors; who rationalized his economy by attempting to impose a census—a king who was an instrument of political and economic exploitation.[43] Even more importantly, there is the David who reinterpreted, through his royal ideologues, the Yahwist faith into a political ideology that served as a glue for keeping the interests of the monarchical ruling class together (II Sam. 7:8-16).[44]

Given the fact, therefore, that Luke's audience is undoubtedly composed of the dominant groups of first-century Palestine—even though the subject matter is the conditions and struggles of the poor—there seems little doubt that his invocation of the Davidic royal connection was meant to suppress Jesus' unacceptable low-class origins.

From the point of view of the oppressed and exploited people of the world today, Luke's ideological co-optation of Jesus in the interests of the ruling class is an act of political war against the liberation struggle. Black people and other oppressed groups recognize in Luke's discursive practice a social-class struggle in which Luke has taken a definite side. In their appropriation of Lukan discourse, black people must raise their own class sights beyond what Luke wants to permit them, and they must make, through their own struggle, a hermeneutical connection with the struggles of the poor that Luke compromises so much for his own purposes.

In order to construct a biblical hermeneutics of liberation, black theologians must draw inspiration from the conclusions that Mansueto draws in his proposal of a new exegesis:

> Together the results of a materialist history and of historical criticism allow us to read scripture in the light of the real struggles of those who forged the tradition: to reappropriate the real, *objective* significance of these books which have weighed so heavily in our

43. Mosala, "Social Justice in the Early Israelite Monarchy," chapters 4-6.

44. See Brueggemann, *The Prophetic Imagination*, 308.

cultural heritage. The results of such a reading, which has only begun to take shape [Chaney: oral presentation; Gottwald, 1979], suggest that those who have found an affinity between our present struggles for national liberation and an end to exploitation, domination, and mystification of all kinds, and the struggles which gave birth to the Jewish and Christian traditions have not erred. We speak with justice when we say that the same God who delivered Israel from Pharaoh, and struck Midian at the rock of Oreb, has even now stretched out his right hand over the battlefields of the revolution from Kronstadt to Yenan, and from Mozambique to Morazon.[45]

Oppressed and exploited black people must liberate the gospel so that the gospel may liberate them. An enslaved gospel enslaves, but a liberated gospel liberates.

45. Mansueto, "From Historical Criticism to Historical Materialism," 40.

7
Black Hermeneutical Appropriation of the Signified Practice of Luke 1 and 2

THE LUKAN TEXT DOES NOT HAVE THE SAME LONG HISTORY THAT the Micah text has. Consequently, it does not reflect the process of recompositions that is discernible in Micah. Coote's method of isolating *editions* of the text cannot, therefore, be applied in the study of Luke. But the ideological and theoretical questions put to the Micah text, especially in relation to its hermeneutical use value in the black liberation struggle, remain pertinent. In this sense, then, I will undertake hermeneutical appreciation of Luke 1 and 2 in this chapter similar to that of Micah in Chapter Five.

LUKE 1:1-4

Luke 1:1-4 represents the introduction to the entire Gospel of Luke. It has no particular relationship with the infancy discourse that follows from verse 5. No understanding of any part of Luke-Acts, however, can be wrenched from this introduction without losing an important part of its rhetorical framework. It is this introduction, looked at from the point of view of the struggles of the oppressed, that exposes its social-class base.

The upper-class form, conventionality, and interest of this portion, addressed to "Theophilus, His Excellency," is unmistakable. For, as Anton Mayer writes about the class base and commitment of Luke,

> As historian he acts, irrespective of his personal interest, in the service of the ruling class, which considers history as its domain. He no more has the time and power to withdraw from his reality than does the underclass, which is forced to resign itself to its present plight.[1]

Luke's desire to write "an orderly account" for the consumption of the ruling class in whose service he obviously works reflects the *Ordnungtheologie*[2] that is the ideological framework whereby he is to signify the Jesus movement and practice. Such a theology subjugates and subsumes the cultural discourses of subordinate classes under those of the dominant classes. A black working-class biblical hermeneutics detects this *ab initio*, because it arises itself from the praxis of a people whose movement and struggles have constantly lost their values and symbols.

The black struggle has constantly lost these values and symbols to the dominant signifying political, cultural, and economic practices that steal them under the guise of promoting the interests of black people. Critical analysts have, of course, subsequently found the hidden agenda to have been tied to "law and order" concerns. These concerns amount to the maintaining of the status quo rather than the struggle for liberation and justice. The ideology of apartheid in South Africa, for instance, was inaugurated under the guise of enabling black people not to lose their "culture." The Bantustan system is promoted by its black appointees as an instrument through which black "values and culture" can be promoted, signifying the independence and autonomy of blacks. Monopoly capitalist advertising practices, whereby the black

---

1. Anton Mayer, *Der zensierte Jesus: Soziologie des Neuen Testaments* (Olten: Walter Verlag, 1983), 122f. [author's translation from the original German]

2. Ibid., 137.

working class is further undermined and exploited by capitalists, now uses African culture and experience to universalize the dominance of the commodity form. For example, a current advertisement for Xtra-strong sweets/candy steals a black mineworker's oppositional discourse, which is expressed in the form of a song, and uses it to strengthen capital's dominance over labor. The song in question is the famous "Chocholoza kwezintaba, setimela sivela eRhodesia," which concerns the experiences of migrant mineworkers in South Africa returning from the mines in Rhodesia. It has now been turned into a commercial and retranslated: "Di-Xtra strong, Di-Xtra strong. . . . "

Hegemonic discourses thrive on the theft of the struggles, symbols, and values of the movement or people they seek to contain and eventually subjugate. I am arguing here that this is also true of religious texts such as the Bible. The "stories" recorded in the Bible are as ideologically problematical as those in other secular discourses.

Although Luke, in his Gospel, deals with what can only have been a subversive movement in Palestine and Rome during the first century, his purpose, as inscribed in his introduction, seeks to contain that movement. Thus the "black struggle" as a hermeneutical category of black theology would begin a reading of Luke's discourse by drawing daggers against his ideological intentions. It would refuse to be drawn into an appreciation of an "orderly" presentation of Jesus and his movement. Luke seeks to clean Jesus up—to make him one of the heroes, a cult leader rather than the failure that his death represented in the face of the repressive and murderous state machinery of "law and order."

Biblical scholars have hinted at Luke's tendency to promote Rome and its agents, who were strewn all over the empire, including among Jewish religious and secular nobilities. But the scholars' ideological commitments have often prevented them from drawing out the hermeneutical implications of Luke's tendency. Joseph Fitzmyer, for instance, correctly points out that Luke differs from the other evangelists because of "his desire to relate the story of Jesus not only to the contemporary world and culture, but also to the growth and development of the nascent Christian church."[3] He also locates the writing of Luke's Gospel in the crucial period of 80-85 C.E. Nevertheless, none of these issues seems to evoke any sociohistorical and cultural implications for Fitzmyer. It does not even seem to occur to him that the period of 80-85 C.E. may have been the time of the deepest division between the Jesus movement and the dominant forces of Roman society, as is illustrated by the severity of Christian persecution under Emperor Domitian.[4]

Norman Perrin exhibits a greater sensitivity to the sociopolitical character of Luke's signification of the Jesus movement. He constantly points to Luke's tendency to seek normalization of the relations between the church and the Roman Empire. He adds, however, that we should remember that Luke "also uses the earlier traditions of Hellenistic Jewish Mission Christianity."[5] His point is that Luke wants to ground his message in the religio-cultural traditions of the Jesus movement and within Jewish history and religion. This is the basis on which his message is legitimated.[6] But the real purpose of his message is to accommodate the gospel of Jesus and its movement to the Roman Empire. Nevertheless, while the Jewish origin of the gospel is an important factor in Luke, he also blames the Jews for the death of Jesus, as well as the destruction of Jerusalem. As Perrin aptly describes the situation,

> . . . in Luke-Acts persecution is only part of the whole problem of relations between the Christians and the Empire. . . . As long as Christians expected the world to pass away shortly, they could revile Rome and its Empire in anticipation of its imminent destruction, as John of Patmos does in Revelation 18. . . .
>
> The author of Luke-Acts consistently presents Roman authorities as sympathetic to the Christian movement. . . . The Christians' difficulties are not the hostility of Roman authorities

3. Joseph Fitzmyer, *The Gospel According to Luke I-IX* (New York: Doubleday & Company, Inc., 1981), 35.

4. Williston Walker, *A History of the Christian Church* (Edinburgh: T. & T. Clark, 1959), 30.

5. Norman Perrin, *The New Testament: An Introduction* (New York: Harcourt Brace Jovanovich, 1974), 196.

6. Keith I. Nickle, *The Synoptic Gospels: An Introduction* (London: SCM Press, 1981), 129.

but the machinations of the Jews (Acts 13:28; 14:2, 19; 18:12 etc.)....
Thus the author attempts to present Roman authority to Christians, and the Christians to Roman authorities, in the best possible
light, in the hope of fostering good relations between them.[7]

But Perrin seems unable to draw out the real political
hermeneutical implications of Luke's ideological practice. On
the contrary, he timidly interprets the issue of this practice as a
matter of *realpolitik*.[8] The question that he fails to put is: On
which side in the social-class struggles of the Roman Empire
does Luke's discourse come down? This question raises the
further question of whether it matters to Luke—if it is true that
realpolitik is his concern—whether in the process he destroys the
raison d'etre of the very movement he is trying to save.

A black biblical hermeneutics of liberation, nurtured in
the knowledge that struggles and images of struggles get stolen
—ostensibly to promote the interests of the oppressed but in reality to serve the cause of the ruling classes—departs from Norman Perrin's explanation of the reason for the Lukan practice.
In this respect, the position of a black biblical hermeneutics of
liberation approximates Keith Nickle's position. It is, first, a
polemical appropriation of the text. It seeks to expose the rhetorical structures of the text by which discourses produce politically undesirable effects. In other words, it *joins* the class
struggle of which the biblical text is a signified practice. We
should keep in mind two important points that Keith Nickle argues, for instance, when we deal with Luke 1:1-4. The first is that
Theophilus calls to mind a special category of people in the
Greek society of the time: gentiles who were attracted to the
Jewish religion. According to Nickle, this group would have
been receptive to the gospel because of their acquaintance with
Jewish traditions, especially the traditions of the Messiah. The
second point is that the term "most excellent" was commonly
used to address high officials. Nickle writes:

Possibly Luke was concerned to correct any misunderstanding
Theophilus had about the nature and intent of the Christian

---

7. Perrin, *The New Testament*, 200.
8. Ibid., 197.

movement. . . . He seems to have been sensitive to that segment of the society in which his community lived.[9]

Concerning the first point, Nickle comes close to exposing the ethnic reductionism that characterizes most scholarship of this period. The essence of this reductionism consists of tendencies to artificially separate Jewish ethnicity from Hellenistic Greek or even Roman cultural orientations. It is this separation that posits the non-Jewishness of Luke on the grounds simply that he was culturally Greek and was from Antioch in Syria. (Scholars do not cease, however, to puzzle over Luke's predilection for the Jewish scriptures—albeit the Greek version of the scriptures.)

But more important is the ideological suppression of the hermeneutical significance of the Palestinian persecution of the Jesus movement. As was pointed out earlier, Luke blames the "Jews" for the death of Jesus and the destruction of Jerusalem. But surely the oppressed and exploited Jewish peasants, day laborers, unemployed persons, prostitutes, and members of various other subclasses cannot be made to share in this blame! Rather, it was the Roman ruling classes, in collusion with their Jewish ruling-class agents, who combined to crush the movement in Palestine and in other parts of the Empire.

The persecution of a largely—but probably not exclusively—Jewish movement like the Jesus movement was no new phenomenon. The Maccabean revolt was a consequence of similar repressive measures used against the Jesus movement. Luke, by collapsing all social configurations under the encompassing terms "Jews" and "Gentiles," deliberately obscures the objective class divisions that cut across ethnic cleavages in the Empire. When biblical scholarship continues to use these terms, it colludes ideologically with the Lukan discourse.

The second point Nickle makes raises the possibility that Luke may have been an employed ideologist for a government official in some magisterial area in a province of Rome. While the point cannot be pressed too far, it is plausible. But whether or not it is historically true that Luke worked for such

9. Nickle, *The Synoptic Gospels*, 140.

an official, he in fact wrote for the social class to which such an official would belong. Nickle says:

> Luke made a considerable effort to exonerate the Roman Empire from any direct guilt for the execution of Jesus (Lk. 23:4, 7, 13-16, 22, 47) and for the persecution of the Christian church (a frequent motif in Acts). He was concerned to portray Christianity as an apolitical movement. It was not a subversive sect of revolutionaries intent on overthrowing Imperial Rome. Luke even hinted that since God was at work in the Christian church, governmental authority was incapable ultimately of suppressing the Christian faith.[10]

LUKE 1:5-25

Fitzmyer, following Millar Burrows, makes the point that to call "the infancy narratives 'imitative historiography' means that whatever historical matter has been preserved by the two evangelists has been assimilated by them to other literary accounts. . . . Luke's story of Jesus not only parallels his story of John in part, but has unmistakable resonances of the story of the childhood of Samuel in the Old Testament (I Sam. 1–3)."[11] James A. Sanders, in contrast to Fitzmyer and many other biblical scholars, draws attention to the hermeneutical significance of these story parallels. Although to others these parallels appear to be simple objects of empirical literary discovery, Sanders asserts that "the true shape of the Bible as canon consists of its unrecorded hermeneutics which lie between the lines of most of its literature."[12]

Rooted in the history of struggle that requires it to develop, among other things, a hermeneutics of suspicion, a black theology of liberation recalls in its reading of Luke 1:5-25 what has recently been termed a "war of images." In an article entitled "Images of War, War of Images," Barbara Hilton-Barber describes how black South Africans who are involved in the revolt

---

10. Ibid., 140.

11. Fitzmyer, *Luke I–IX*, 309.

12. James A. Sanders, *Canon and Community* (Philadelphia: Fortress, 1984), 46.

against the apartheid state and society have come to learn what the government knew for much longer: "That once you lose control of the images that have been taken of you, you are open to exploitation on a grand scale."[13] This is true because the subsequent forms of any struggle are shaped and determined, to a very large extent, by the signification of that struggle in extant discourses. As Hilton-Barber points out with regard to South Africa,

> It doesn't help that the world's media are portraying the country as a seething pit of revolutionary and reactionary violence. However, conflict is the staple diet of news, and where there's conflict, there's room for rich trading in images. This has put foreign correspondents at the forefront of the government's ire. Security legislation in the wake of the Emergency is being designed to put a halt to the flow of embarrassing images of human rights violations that are being hung up for all the world to see. Losing control of the image of one's self is tantamount to losing control of one's self altogether.[14]

Thus black theology appropriates Luke 1:5-25, first, in a *political* way. Using the category of "the black struggle," part of whose experience is contesting against the creation of certain images on the one hand, and promoting certain others on the other hand, black theology must interrogate the annunciation of the birth of John the Baptist as part of Luke's discourse on the Jesus movement. In other words, it asks, What is the role of this section of the text in the signification of the Jesus practice? This question takes us back to Fitzmyer's point that that parallel of the Jesus story with John the Baptist and Samuel's childhood is unmistakable. The hermeneutical question, however, must inquire as to the ideological effects intended by Luke in framing the Jesus story on the basis of the discourse concerning John the Baptist.

However, in order to make historical, sociological, and ideological sense of Luke's hermeneutical technique, we should first recall the general sociohistorical context out of which Luke's discourse arises and in which it represents a determinate

---

13. Barbara Hilton-Barber, "Images of War," *Vula!* (June 1986): 33.
14. Ibid., 14.

ideological intervention. Almost all biblical scholars of the early Christian period tend to underplay, if not ignore, the social conflict characteristic of the centuries just preceding the birth of Jesus, consequently losing the significance of this conflict for understanding New Testament discourses. The recent study by Richard Horsley and John Hanson of the popular resistance movements at the time of Jesus promises to provide a real sense of the mood and processes at work. However, it is Norman Gottwald who provides the most illuminating perception of the struggles and conflicts in the period leading up to Jesus' birth. He points out that during the second century B.C.E.

> The national situation that generated sharply defined factions was the major realignment of socioeconomic, political, and religious forces set in unrelenting motion by the abortive attempt to Hellenize Judaism radically and by the reactive emergence of an independent Jewish state that ironically took on a decisive Hellenistic character in spite of its anti-Hellenistic beginnings. The radical minority coup to displace traditional Judaism by submerging it in a syncretistic Syro-Hellenistic cult failed totally. . . . With *Hellenistic religious syncretism* excluded by an overwhelming Jewish consensus, the key question now had to do with whether and how Jewish society and state should appropriate the internationally operative *Hellenistic socioeconomic and political structures and assumptions*. [italics Gottwald's][15]

In order to properly understand the importance for Luke of the priestly traditions he invokes in 1:5-25, we must go back to the situation facing the Jewish population under Hellenistic colonial rule, as described by Gottwald. The Hellenizing program of the Hasmoneans increasingly caused the emergence of factions and parties among the Jews. The Hasidian group of devout Judahites who had supported the Maccabean revolt became progressively dissatisfied with the Jewish rulers, who played the role of Hellenistic princes. This group was the forerunner of the Pharisees. Another faction of devout Judahites who felt even more strongly about a strict practice of the law was the Essenes. This group "decided to pull away from the corrupt society into rural communes where they could live out their

---

15. Gottwald, *The Hebrew Bible* (Philadelphia: Fortress, 1985), 450.

religion uncompromisingly."[16] At the same time, another faction developed out of the commercial opportunities offered by the wars of expansion of the Hasmonean state. Gottwald describes that situation this way:

> The rising commercial sectors formed an aristocracy of "new wealth" that openly vied with "old wealth" aristocrats for political and economic power, for instance for control of seats on the national governing council, for influence on royal policies and appointments, and for control of the temple economy. It was this new aristocracy that came to be known as the Sadducees, stemming largely at first from lay circles, although in time they gained ascendancy in the priesthood at the expense of the old aristocrats. By Herodian times it appears that "old" and "new" aristocracies reached an accommodation based in large part on their common need to block and counterbalance the rising influence of the "populist" Pharisees.[17]

Given this configuration of social, political, and religious forces, how did Luke make his choices, and from which specific tendencies did he pick his images of the Jesus movement? What ideological interest shaped his hermeneutics? Using varying preexisting traditions of struggle from the earlier period of Israelite history (I Sam. 1–3), as well as from the more recent history of resistance under home colonial rule, Luke fashions a discourse whose class and ideological interests are specific. Given the nature of the resistance during the period preceding Jesus' birth, it seems reasonable to argue that the image Luke finds amenable to his purposes from this period is of a tradition of pious priesthood that fully obeyed all the Lord's commands and laws (1:5-7). Out of this tradition will come one to whom the following will apply:

> You are to name him John. How glad and happy many others will be when he is born! He will be a great man in the Lord's sight. He must not drink any wine or strong drink. From his very birth he will be filled with the Holy Spirit, and he will bring back many of the people of Israel to the Lord their God . . . he will turn disobedient people back to the way of thinking of the righteous; he will get the Lord's people ready for him. (1:13-17)

16. Ibid., 451.
17. Ibid.

The Essene-like features of this image of John the Baptist's mission are unmistakable; it is also colored, like that of the Qumran community, by some apocalyptic visions. This image could form a socioreligious discourse in the second century B.C.E. that sought to deal with the cultural-political oppression and economic exploitation of the Jewish population by opting out of what it saw as a corrupt community. That John the Baptist is to be located within this tradition can be seen not only from Luke's identification of him with the pious priestly group here but also by how he is portrayed in Luke 3:1-20, Matthew 3:1-12, Mark 1:1-8, and John 1:19-28. Thus Luke selects the "withdrawal" image of resistance against cultural, political, and economic domination as a hermeneutical lens for appropriating the Jesus movement.

*   *   *

Second, black theology engages the text of Luke 1:5-25 *appropriatively.* By this I mean that black working-class Christians, using the weapon of black theology, must interpret the text against the grain. They must refuse to allow the text to limit the hermeneutical options to Luke's choice of images of struggle. Black working-class Christians, drawing from their own history of struggle against hostile natural forces in the precapitalist mode and against hostile social forces—the chiefs and their entourage in the tributary stage and white capitalists and their lackeys in the capitalist mode—must bounce the Lukan discourses off their own. The significance of this encounter between discourses is underscored by Paul Willis and Philip Corrigan in their study of contemporary working-class cultural forms. They write:

> It is when "discourses" are brought together, or contextualized
> in real situations which always have other bases of meaning, that
> their partiality and contradictoriness is exposed—through the
> very resources of those "discourses" and the complex juxtaposed
> patterns of what each does not say or renders non-contradictory
> through omission.[18]

18. Paul Willis and Philip Corrigan, "Orders of Experience: The Differences of Working Class Cultural Forms," *Social Text* (Spring & Summer 1983): 94.

But the absences in Luke's discourse speak more eloquently to the black theology of liberation. Similarly, the Lukan discourse interrogates the silences of the black working-class struggle, questioning its lack of support for specifically ruling-class values and practices. Of course, Luke can interrogate the black struggle's orientations because he first interrogated and contained the Jesus movement, as evidenced by his Gospel. Thus Willis and Corrigan explain how ideology functions in the texts through discourses bouncing off each other:

> "Ideology" is not only the "content" of these "discourses" but the particular "preferred" relation of their silences to each other as well. It is working class culture, or its cultural praxis, which makes this silence speak—but not in words, or not in words with the verbal "discourse" of its meaning at their centre. The various "discourse" positions which to a greater or lesser extent base themselves on language thus write out working class meaning, destroy the real agency of its subjects, and banish sense and knowledge from all but bourgeois "discourses" — we have the largest social tautology masquerading as science: and its cost is the eradication of the working class from history.[19]

It is through those social forces and processes about which Luke's Gospel is silent, as illustrated by the omission in the text of other responses to Hellenistic and Roman domination, that black working-class Christianity seeks to speak. The "presences" of the black struggle have to interrogate the "absences" in the biblical text. The black struggle, with its broad variety of responses to domination and exploitation, exposes the contradiction between the cognitive and emotive structures of the text. That is to say, through its cognitive structures the text would have us believe that its choice of the priest Zechariah represents an enforcement of historical truth—that the historical situation concerning priests as a social category in first-century Palestine is exhausted by what Zechariah stood for. Through its emotive structures, however, the intentions, wishes, dislikes, and commitments of the text come to the fore, and the ostensibly historical mention of Zechariah is shown to express a particular "'lived' relation to the real which may be neither verified nor

19. Ibid., 94.

falsified."[20] Thus a critical black biblical hermeneutics of liberation is soon aware that the invocation of the priestly connection
through the use of Zechariah represents a particular emotive
enunciation, not a historical statement. It is, however, the contradiction between "the historical" and the use of "the historical" in an ideological discourse that provides a lever for a hermeneutical appropriation of that text in spite of itself.

Third, the black theology of liberation appropriates
Luke 1:5-25 in a *projective* way. It interprets the text in ways that
intend effects conducive to the victory of the liberation struggle
—notwithstanding the class character and ideological commitments of the text. For as Willis and Corrigan have argued concerning the encounter between discourses,

> Having once opened up their territories of meaning to struggle,
> the *same* meaning can never be recouped. The dominant class
> might "choose" the terrain, but not always the outcome.[21]

With the agenda of the text laid bare, we can make hermeneutical connections with similar agendas in the contemporary setting. The usefulness or otherwise of the agenda of the text cannot be decided *a priori*. It has to be tested on the basis of the
demands and experience of the struggle of black working-class
people.

The points made above reconfirm one of the hypothe-
ses of this study: that the texts of the Bible are sites of struggle.
The extent to which such texts may be used against goals other
than middle- and ruling-class ones indicates the nonneutral
character of the texts themselves. Luke 1:5-25 constitutes a study
in ruling-class discourses—their form, intentions, and possible
effects. But again, as Willis and Corrigan so poignantly assert
with regard to appropriations of discourses for socialist construction,

> Starting points . . . are not finishing points. Precisely, in fact, be-
> cause they are not finished, final, completed, *fixed,* they represent
> possible starting points for the socialist project. In the course of

20. Terry Eagleton, "Ideology, Fiction, Narrative," *Social Text* (Summer
1979): 65.
21. Willis and Corrigan, "Orders of Experience," 98.

the latter's long construction they will be transformed. But just as the seemingly impermeable "discourses" of capitalist hegemony are the raw materials through which working class culture comes to know its difference, so too are the cultural forms of resistance won and sustained by the working class, the raw materials for the knowledge and practices of socialist construction. Taking culture seriously means taking it not as we would like it to be—neat, parceled, correct, *ready* (fast food socialism)—but as we find it, and that finding requires more than a single glance. It requires a profanity and a willingness to be surprised by the orders of experience. "Theory is good," said Freud's teacher Charcot, "but it doesn't prevent things from existing." "Discourses" are bad, we are saying, but they do not stop *cultural forms* of resistance from existing. [italics Willis's and Corrigan's][22]

Ruling-class biblical discourses, therefore, should not, by their preponderance among the basic Christian religious texts, stop the existence of religio-cultural forms of resistance. The black working-class culture and history should press the silences between itself and the dominant biblical discourses to speak in favor of victory in the struggle for the liberation of the oppressed and exploited.

LUKE 1:26–2:51

We have already exposed the discursive structures of the infancy narrative on the basis of a polemical criticism or oppositional code derived from a black theology rooted in the black struggle; and we have pointed out the ruling-class interests and morality of the text as it now stands. The question now is: How does a biblical hermeneutics of liberation appropriate the discourses of Luke against the grain and in such a way as to intend the effects that are conducive to the liberation struggle. The only way to do this is to penetrate beneath the texts and go beyond the texts to their silences.

Luke 1:26–2:51 provides a terrain of struggle for black working-class people. As a ruling-class discourse, it cannot be

22. Ibid., 103.

used as a weapon in the struggle for liberation, except negatively. Black working-class people encounter in this text the alienation and conflict with which they have to do battle in contemporary cultural struggles. Thus a politically conscious
community of struggle, rather than appropriating the text unproblematically, chooses to struggle with the dominant forces
within the text to get beyond them to the suppressed oppositional forces. In this way they continue the struggle against the
contemporary ruling class's cultural, political, and economic
discourses on the battleground provided by the signifying practices of the text.

In the black working-class religious situation in South
Africa, the real import of the liberating hermeneutics of the birth
narrative comes into its own during Good Friday. The "Seven
Words on the Cross" tradition, which is the highlight of the
Good Friday services in the black churches in South Africa, in-
cludes Jesus' words to Mary, his mother:

> But standing by the cross of Jesus were his mother, and his
> mother's sister, Mary the wife of Clopas, and Mary Magdalene.
> When Jesus saw his mother, and the disciple whom he loved,
> standing near, he said to his mother, "Woman, behold, your son!"
> Then he said to the disciple, "Behold, your mother!" And from that
> hour the disciple took her to his own home. (Jn. 19:25-27, RSV)

When black preachers expound on this text, they invariably
raise issues that bring tears to the eyes of the so-called illegiti-
mate sons and daughters and their unmarried mothers. A great
deal of weeping and sorrow cover the congregations at this
point. It is important, however, to realize that the sadness expressed at this time is not over the so-called "moral" problem of
illegitimacy. Rather, the sorrow is over the economic disinvest-
ment imposed on a single-parent family by the death of a son or
a daughter. Consequently, the emphasis of the preaching invariably falls on the disciple's response: "And from that hour the
disciple took her to his own home" (v. 27). Black working-class
religious people experience the message of this text (Jn. 19:25-
27) as people who have not read the infancy narrative of Luke.
Their own historical and cultural discourses, circumscribed by
the fact that the majority of black young women under apart-

heid capitalism are single mothers, pushes them beyond Luke's Mary, the wife of Joseph of the Davidic house, to Mary the single parent and possibly a member of the underclasses of Galilee. Thus the black working-class historical and cultural discourses operate on the supposition that, if Jesus had been of the royal blood, there would have been no need to find a disciple to look after Mary in the absence of her real son.

Thus, through struggle with the dominant forces inscribed in the text itself, the oppressed and exploited people today can seek to discover kin struggles in biblical communities. These biblical struggles, then, serve as a source of inspiration for contemporary struggles, and as a warning against their co-optation. The category of the "black struggle" as a hermeneutical factor draws its poetry from a future that in this struggle's collision with the text of Luke 1 and 2 is experienced as an "absence." The visions and ideals of the black struggle are eloquent in the Lukan text by the text's silences about the struggles and aspirations of the oppressed and exploited people of first-century Palestine.

Be that as it may, the dominant class character of the signifying practices of the biblical text does not guarantee the outcome of the struggles. Eagleton says:

> Nothing secures the securing: those privileged signifiers thus become the space of a *struggle*, so that we are cursorily to define ideology as "the class struggle at the level of signifying practices." The transformation of those signifiers may well take the form of a refusal of closure itself, an unleashing of plurality, transgression, and contradiction which dissolves "narrative" into "text"; but its other moment, necessary if we are to avoid a formalistic, essentialist valorizing of "plurality" and "heterogeneity" *in themselves,* and a consequent reversion to some debased *Lebensphilosophie,* is the fight for the installment of alternative, socialist significations, and thus for an alternative, if always provisional, kind of closure. [italics Eagleton's][23]

It is this question of the production of alternative significations that should be at the heart of a biblical hermeneutics of liberation. Within the Christian tradition it strikes at the crucial

23. Eagleton, "Ideology, Fiction, Narrative," 79.

area of the canon of Scripture. It raises the question of the class character and ideological basis of the canon of Scripture. Also, it points to an already ongoing process of the reopening of the canon of Scripture as represented by the interpretations and uses of the Bible in the light of popular experiences of the oppressed. Above all, it calls for a "projective" appropriation of biblical texts in such a way that the absences and silences in these texts may serve as spaces from which the thrust of alternative significations and discourses may be launched.

Epilogue

TWO MAJOR CONCLUSIONS EMERGE FROM THIS STUDY. ONE IS THAT IN a black history and culture characterized by class, race, gender, and age contradictions, and in relation to which some contemporary blacks are contradictorily located, there is not likely to emerge only one black theology of liberation. This conclusion is based on the analyses made in the first three chapters of this book. Chapter One shows how the class and cultural-ideological identifications of some black theologians have kept them enslaved to the biblical hermeneutical assumptions of the very white theology they criticize and seek to replace. Chapter Two further argues that even the new sociological approaches would not represent a step forward, since most of them are still rooted in bourgeois white ideological assumptions. More importantly, Chapter Three demonstrates that black history and culture from the precolonial period to the present have never been monolithic.

Black theologians, as products and inheritors of black history and culture, are differentially inserted into this history and culture. Thus we cannot overstate the need for ideological and theoretical vigilance. For in black theology, as in other discourses of liberation, not all that glitters is gold. This study has underscored the importance of recognizing that a plurality of black theologies of liberation is a reality of the contemporary South African situation as influenced and shaped by black history and culture in addition to bourgeois society. Some black theologies of liberation will be bourgeois in orientation, seeking to fight for the restoration of former black ruling-class positions. The religious roots of such black theologies of liberation are likely to be traceable to such historical movements as the Ethiopian church. Nationalist in character and royalist in ideological perspective, this Ethiopian religious discourse is likely to continue to inspire certain brands of theological opposition among black South Africans. The biblical hermeneutical appropriations of such brands of black theology are likely to coincide with the ideological and political interests of their royalist counterparts in the Bible—such as are found, for example, in many passages in the Psalms.

Other black theologies of liberation will represent more middle-class cultural, ideological, and political perspectives. This strand of black theological opposition has roots historically in the phenomenon of diviners and prophets in black society. More recently, this tradition has been represented by the black intellectual element, many of the representatives being products of Christian mission education. It is a religious discourse and an opposition movement that found explicit political culmination in the philosophy of black consciousness in the late 1960s and early 1970s. The discourse that officially came to be known as the black theology of liberation in South Africa in the 1970s and 1980s is represented by this particular trajectory of the black struggle.

Yet another brand of the black theology of liberation consciously adopts a black working-class perspective. The historical foundations of this strand lie in the struggles of the lowest and often poorest members of the black community, from precolonial times to the present. In contemporary times, and especially under conditions of monopoly capitalism in South Africa, the nondiscursive sociological expression of this religious practice has come in the Zion-Apostolic African churches. The biblical hermeneutics of this religious practice, in the absence of a theoretically well-grounded theological discourse, is a subversive, nonsystematic working-class distortion of the Bible in favor of the struggles of its members.

I would hold that this last brand of black theology is potentially the most genuinely liberating. I would argue, however, that it must first relocate itself more *systematically* and *critically* in the broad black working-class struggle and in an ideological and theoretical framework that is capable of bringing about the material liberation of black working-class people. I would hope that this study will contribute to such a project. Basing itself on an understanding of the concept of "struggle" as a hermeneutical tool, this brand of black theology—in its systematic and critical form—proceeds to apply it to the reading of the Bible. In this way it participates in the struggles of the texts and thus empowers people to participate in the struggles of contemporary communities of faith.

The second major conclusion of this study, which is related to and in some sense follows from the first, is that in a society divided by class, race, and gender, there must certainly be a plurality of biblical hermeneutics. These expressions of hermeneutics function to reproduce or to rationalize or to transform the socioeconomic and political status quo. South Africa is probably the best, though not the only, modern example of a country in which the ruling political group has consciously developed a biblical hermeneutics that reproduces and sustains its ideological and political interests. The theoretical tragedy in South Africa has been that black theologians, in opposing the theology of the dominant white groups, have appealed to the same hermeneutical framework in order to demonstrate a contrary truth. The contrary truth black theologians wish to assert is that God is on the side of the oppressed and not of the oppressors. This study has tried to show, however, that black liberation theology needs an ideologically, epistemologically, and theoretically different biblical hermeneutics.

In searching for this new hermeneutics, I have opted for an approach to the Bible that reads its texts backwards: that is, a biblical hermeneutical method that seeks to discover the questions of which the texts are answers, the problems of which they are solutions. Such a biblical hermeneutics of liberation eschews the intellectual laziness or the deliberate ideological choice that simply colludes with the text without much ado. Rather, it allows a mutual interrogation between text and situation to take place, in the light of the struggles that both represent.

These two conclusions more than confirm the hypotheses that this study set out to test: that the Bible is the product, the record, the site, and the weapon of class, cultural, gender, and racial struggles. And a biblical hermeneutics of liberation that does not take this fact seriously can only falter in its project to emancipate the poor and the exploited of the world. Once more, the simple truth rings out that the poor and exploited must liberate the Bible so that the Bible may liberate them.

Bibliography

Aciman, A. "Deliberating Barthes." *Social Text* (Winter 1984/85):110-117.

Aharoni, Yohanan. "Forerunners of the Limes: Iron Age Fortresses in the Negev." *Israel Exploration Journal* 17 (No. 1, 1967):1-17.

Aharoni, Yohanan, and Ruth Amiran. "A New Scheme for the Sub-Division of the Iron Age in Palestine." *Israel Exploration Journal* 8 (1958):171-184.

Amin, Samir. *Class and Nation, Historically and in the Current Crisis.* London: Heinemann, 1980.

Anderson, P. *Passages from Antiquity to Feudalism.* London: Verso, 1978.

Armstrong, D. *A Trumpet to Arms: Alternative Media in America.* Boston: South End Press, 1981.

Aronowitz, Stanley. "Film: The Art Form of Late Capitalism." *Social Text* (Winter 1979): 110-129.

———. *The Crisis in Historical Materialism.* New York: Praeger, 1982.

Arroyo, G. "Christians, the Church and Revolution." In *Christians and Socialism,* edited by John Eagleson. Maryknoll, NY: Orbis Books, 1975.

Asad, T. "Anthropological texts and ideological problems: an analysis of Cohen on Arab villages in Israel." *Economy and Society* 4 (No. 3, 1975):251-282.

Assmann, Hugo. *Theology for a Nomad Church.* Maryknoll, NY: Orbis, 1976.

Avila, Charles. *Ownership: Early Christian Teaching.* Maryknoll, NY: Orbis, 1983.

Barr, James. "Migras in the Old Testament," *Journal of Semitic Studies* 29 (No. 1, 1984):15-31.

Barrett, Charles Kingsley. *The Epistle to the Romans.* London: Adam & Charles Black, 1971.

Barton, J. *Reading the Old Testament: Method in Biblical Study.* London: Darton, Longmann & Todd, 1984.

Belo, Fernando. *A Materialist Reading of the Gospel of Mark.* Maryknoll, NY: Orbis Books, 1981.

Betori, G. "Modelli interpretativi e pluralita di metodi in esegesi." *Biblica* 63 (1982): 305-328.

Bettelheim, Charles. *Cultural Revolution and Industrial Organization in China: Changes in Management and the Division of Labour.* Translated by Alfred Ehrenfeld. New York: Monthly Review Press, 1974.

Beweging Christenen voor het socialisme, "Wie Oren Heeft om te Horen." *Opstand* 1 (1979).

Blackburn, R., ed. *Ideology in Social Science: Readings in Critical Social Theory.* Fontana, 1978.

Bloch, Marc L. B. *The Historian's Craft.* Manchester: Manchester University Press, 1979.

Boer, Harry R. *The Bible and Higher Criticism.* Grand Rapids: William B. Eerdmans, 1981.

Boesak, Allan. *Farewell to Innocence: A Social-Ethical Study of Black Theology and Black Power.* Johannesburg: Ravan, 1976.

————. *The Finger of God: Sermons on Faith and Responsibility.* Maryknoll, NY: Orbis, 1982.

————. *Black and Reformed. Apartheid, Liberation and the Calvinist Tradition.* Johannesburg: Skotaville, 1984.

Bourne, J. "Towards an anti-racist feminism." *Race and Class* 25 (No. 1, 1983):1-21.

Boyer, J. "Is Hollywood being put out of Business?" *Social Text* (Winter 1984/85):118-127.

Brandon, Samuel G. F. *The Fall of Jerusalem and the Christian Church.* London, 1951.

Braun, R. L. "Solomonic Apologetic in Chronicles." *Journal of Biblical Literature* 92 (1978):503-516.

Braverman, Harry. *Labour and Monopoly Capital: The Degradation of Work in the Twentieth Century.* New York and London: Monthly Review Press, 1974.

Brenkman, J. "Mass Media: From Collective Experience to the Culture of Privatization." *Social Text* (Winter 1979):94-109.

Bright, John. *A History of Israel.* Philadelphia: Westminster Press, 1981.

Brown, J. P. "Techniques of Imperial Control: The Background of the Gospel Event." *Radical Religion* 2 (Nos. 2 & 3, 1975):73-83.

Brown, Raymond E. *The Birth of the Messiah: A Commentary on the Infancy Narratives in Matthew and Luke.* New York: Image Books, 1977.

————. "Luke's Method in the Annunciation Narrative of Chapter One." In *Perspectives on Luke-Acts,* edited by C. H. Talbert. Edinburgh: T. & T. Clark Ltd., 1978.

Brueggemann, Walter. "David and His Theologian." *Catholic Biblical Quarterly* 30 (1968):156-181.

————. *The Prophetic Imagination.* Philadelphia: Fortress Press, 1978.

Bultmann, Rudolf K. *Theology of the New Testament.* 2 vols. London: SCM Press, 1979.

Bundy, C. *The Rise and Fall of the South African Peasantry.* London: Heinemann, 1979.

Bush, R., ed. *The New Black Vote. Politics and Power in Four American Cities.* San Francisco: Synthesis Publications, 1984.

Buthelezi, Manas. "Towards Indigenous Theology in South Africa." In *The Emergent Gospel,* edited by S. Torres and V. Fabella. Maryknoll, NY: Orbis, 1978.

Buttrick, George A., ed. *The Interpreter's Dictionary of the Bible.* 4 vols. New York: Abingdon Press, 1962.

Byres, T. J. "Of Neo-Populist Pipe-Dreams: Daedalus in the Third World and the Myth of Urban Bias." *The Journal of Peasant Studies* 6 (1978-79):210-244.

Bailey, Kenneth E. *Poet and Peasant* and *Through Peasant Eyes: A*

Literary-Cultural Approach to the Parables in Luke. Combined edition. Grand Rapids: William B. Eerdmans, 1983.

Cabral, Amilcar. "The Role of Culture in the Liberation Struggle." *Latin American Research Unit Studies* 1 (No. 3, 1977).

―――. *Revolution in New Guinea: An African People's Struggle.* London: Stage 1, 1979.

―――. "National Liberation and Culture." In *Unity and Struggle.* London: Heinemann, 1980.

Callaway, Mary C. "The Mistress and the Maid: Paul's Allegory of the Midrashic Traditions Behind Galatians 4:21-31." *Radical Religion* 2 (Nos. 2 & 3, 1975):94-101.

Carney, T. F. *The Shape of the Past: Models and Antiquity.* Lawrence, KS: Coronado Press, 1975.

Cassidy, Richard J. *Jesus, Politics, and Society: A Study of Luke's Gospel.* Maryknoll, NY: Orbis, 1983.

Cassidy, Richard J., and P. J. Scharper. *Political Issues in Luke-Acts.* Maryknoll, NY: Orbis Books, 1983.

Casterline, J. B. "Max Weber and Deutero-Isaiah." Master's thesis, Graduate Theological Union, Berkeley, 1972.

Centre for African Studies. *Perspectives on the Southern African Past.* Occasional Papers, No. 2, University of Cape Town, 1979.

Centre for Contemporary Cultural Studies. *The Empire Strikes Back: Race and Racism in 70's Britain.* London: Hutchinson, 1983.

Chaney, Marvin L. "Systemic Study of the Sociology of the Israelite Monarchy." Paper presented at SBL Seminar, "Sociology of the Monarchy," December 1981.

―――. "Latifundialization and Prophetic Diction in Eighth-Century Israel and Judah." Paper presented at SBL/ASOR Seminar, "Sociology of the Monarchy," Anaheim, CA, November 1985.

―――. "The Tenth Commandment as a Prescription of Latifundialization." Paper presented at United Theological College, Bangalore, India, February 1985.

Chase, L. A. *Tired Feet and Dreams: A Tribute to Dr. Martin Luther King, Jr.* Paris: A Bright Idea, 1983.

Claburn, W. E. "The Fiscal Basis of Josiah's Reforms." *Journal of Biblical Literature* 92 (1973):11-22.

Clarke, J., C. Critcher, and R. Johnson, eds. *Working Class Culture: Studies in History and Theory.* London: Hutchinson, 1980.

Clevenot, Michel. *Een Materialistische Benadering van de Bijbel.* Baarn: Ten Have, 1979.

———. *Materialist Approaches to the Bible.* Maryknoll, NY: Orbis Books, 1985.

Cliffe, L., and R. Moorsom. "Rural Class Formation and Ecological Collapse in Botswana." *Review of African Political Economy* 15/16 (May-Dec. 1979):35-52.

Cock, J. *Maids and Madams. A Study in the Politics of Exploitation.* Johannesburg: Ravan, 1980.

Cole, J. G. "Crossroads: From Popular Resistance to Mini-Bantustan." Conference paper, "Western Cape: Roots and Realities," Centre for African Studies, University of Cape Town, 16-18 July 1986.

Comaroff, Jean L. "The Transformation of Land Tenure in Barolong: On the politics of paraproductive relations." SSRC Confernece on Land Tenure in Botswana, Satterthwaite, 1978.

Concordance of the Septuagint. London: Samuel Bagster & Sons, Ltd., 1971.

Cone, James H. *Liberation: A Black Theology of Liberation.* Philadelphia & New York: J. B. Lippincott Company, 1970.

———. *The Spirituals and the Blues: An Interpretation.* New York: Seabury Press, 1972.

———. *God of the Oppressed.* New York: Seabury Press, 1975.

———. "The Black Church and Marxism: What do They have to Say to Each Other?" Institute for Democratic Socialism Occasional Paper, April 1980.

———. "The Gospel and the Liberation of the Poor." *The Christian Century,* Feb. 18, 1981, 162-166.

———. *For My People: Black Theology and the Black Church.* Johannesburg: Skotaville, 1985.

Conrad, E. W. "The Annunciation of Birth and the Birth of the Messiah." *Catholic Biblical Quarterly* 47 (1985):656-663.

Conybeare, Frederic C., and St. G. Stock. *A Grammar of Septuagint Greek.* Grand Rapids: Zondervan, 1980.

Conzelmann, Hans. *The Theology of St. Luke.* London: Faber and Faber, 1960.

Cook, J. "Text and Tradition: A Methodological Problem." *Journal of Northwest Semitic Languages* 9 (1981):3-11.

Cooper, David. "An Interpretation of the Emergent Urban Class Structure in Botswana: A Case Study of Selebi-Phikwe Miners." Ph.D. diss., University of Birmingham, 1982.

Coote, Robert B. *Amos Among the Prophets: Composition and Theology.* Philadelphia: Fortress, 1981.

Cornforth, Maurice C. *Materialism and the Dialectical Method.* New York: International Publishers, 1978.

Cowley, A. E. *Gesenius' Hebrew Grammar.* Oxford: Clarendon Press, 1985.

Cox, Harvey. *The Secular City: A Celebration of its Liberties and an Invitation to its Discipline.* New York: Macmillan, 1965.

Cranfield, C. E. B. *The Gospel according to St. Mark: An Introduction and Commentary.* Cambridge: Cambridge University Press, 1972.

Cross, Frank Moore. *Canaanite Myth and Hebrew Epic. Essays in the History of the Religion of Israel.* Cambridge, MA: Harvard University Press, 1973.

Cross, F. M., and J. T. Milik. "Explorations in the Judean Buge'ah." *Bulletin of the American Schools of Oriental Research* 142 (1956):5-17.

Cross, F. M., et al. *Scrolls from Qumran Cave 1. The Great Isaiah Scroll, The Order of the Community, The Pesher to Habakkuk.* Jerusalem: The Albright Institute of Archaeological Research, and Shrine of the Book, 1974.

Dachs, Anthony J. "Missionary Imperialism in Bechuanaland, 1813–1896." Ph.D. diss., Cambridge University, 1972.

————. "Missionary Imperialism: The Case of Bechuanaland." *Journal of African History* 13 (No. 4, 1972):647-658.

Davis, C. "The Theological Career of Historical Criticism of the Bible." *Cross Currents* (Fall 1982):267-284.

Dearman, J. A. "Prophecy, Property and Politics." Chico: Seminar Papers, *Society of Biblical Literature,* Scholars Press, 1984.

Debray, Regis. *Undesirable Alien.* New York: Viking Press, 1978.

De Geus, C. H. "The Importance of Archeological Research into the Palestinian Agricultural Terraces, with an Excursus on the Hebrew Word *gbi*." *Palestine Exploration Quarterly* 107 (1975).

Deist, Ferdinand E. *Heuristics, Hermeneutics and Authority in the Study of Scripture.* University of Port Elizabeth Research Paper C. 14, 1978.

———. "Idealistic *Theologiegeschichte*, Ideology Critique and the Dating of Oracles of Salvation." *OTWSA* 22, 23 (1980): 53-90.

———. "Bybelinterpretasie en Ideologiekritiek. 'n Hermeneutiese Oefening." Unpublished paper, University of South Africa, no date.

Denby, C. *Indignant Heart: A Black Worker's Journal.* Boston: South End Press, 1978.

De Ste. Croix, G. E. M. *The Class Struggle in the Ancient Greek World.* Ithaca, NY: Cornell University Press, 1981.

De Vaux, Roland. "Les Hurrites de L'Histoire et les Horites de la Bible." *Revue Biblique* 74 (1967):481-503.

———. *Ancient Israel: Its Life and Institutions.* London: Darton, Longman & Todd, 1978.

Dever, William G. "The Impact of the 'New Archeology' on Syro-Palestinian Archeology." *Bulletin of American School of Oriental Research* 242 (1982):15-29.

Dietrich, W. *Jesaia und de Politik.* München: Chr. Kaiser, 1976.

Dixon, Marlene. *Things Which are Done in Secret.* n.p.: Black Rose Books, 1976.

———. *The Future of Women.* San Francisco: Synthesis, 1983.

DuBois, W. E. B. *Black Reconstruction in America, 1860-1880.* New York: Atheneum, 1983.

Dubow, Saul. *Land, Labour and Merchant Capital.* Centre for African Studies Communications, No. 6, University of Cape Town, 1982.

Duke, F. "Historiography as Kulturkampf: The Fischer Thesis, German Democracy and the Authoritarian State." *Literature and History* 6 (No. 1, 1980):94-110.

Durkheim, Emile. *The Elementary Forms of the Religious Life.* New York: Collier Books, 1961.

Dwane, Sigquibo. "Christology and Liberation." *Journal of Theology for Southern Africa* 35 (1981):29-37.

Eagleton, Terry. *Criticism and Ideology.* London:Verso, 1976.

———. "Ideology, Fiction, Narrative." *Social Text* (Summer 1979):62-80.

————. *Walter Benjamin, or Towards a Revolutionary Criticism.* London: Verso, 1981.

————. *The Rape of Clarissa.* Minneapolis: University of Minnesota Press, 1982.

————. *Literary Theory.* Minneapolis: University of Minnesota Press, 1983.

————. *The Function of Criticism.* London: Verso, 1984.

Eagleton, Terry, A. Assites, and G. McLennan. "E.P. Thompson's Poverty of Theory: A Symposium." *Literature and History* 5 (No. 2, 1979):139-164.

Elliot, John Hall. *A Home for the Homeless: A Sociological Exegesis of I Peter: Its Situation and Strategy.* London: SCM Press, 1982.

Ellison, Ralph. "Juneteenth." *Quarterly Review of Literature* (Fall 1984):262-276.

Engels, Friedrich. *The German Revolutions.* Chicago & London: University of Chicago Press, 1967.

————. *The Condition of the Working Class in England.* London: Granada, 1981.

Engnell, Ivan. "The 'Ebed Yahweh Songs and the Suffering Messiah in 'Deutero-Isaiah.'" *John Rylands University Library of Manchester Bulletin* 31 (1948):54-93.

Ermath, M. "The Transformation of Hermeneutics: 19th Century Ancients and 20th Century Moderns." *The Monist* 64 (No. 2, 1981):175-193.

Evans, C. F. *Explorations in Theology* 2. London: SCM Press, 1977.

Even-Ari, Michael, et al. "The Ancient Desert Agriculture of the Negev. III, Early Beginnings." *Israel Exploration Journal* 8 (1958):231-253.

Fehervary, H. "Enlightenment or Entanglement: History and Aesthetics in Bertolt Brecht and Heines Muller." *New German Critique* 8 (Spring 1976):80-109.

Ferré, Frederick, and Rita H. Matnagnon. *God and Global Justice.* New York: Paragon House, 1985.

Fierro Bardaji, Alfredo. *The Militant Gospel: An Analysis of Contemporary Political Theologies.* London: SCM Press, 1977.

Fiorenza, Elisabeth Schüssler. *Bread Not Stone: The Challenge of Feminist Biblical Interpretation.* Boston: Beacon Press, 1984.

Fitzmyer, Joseph A. *The Gospel According to Luke I-IX: The Anchor Bible.* New York: Doubleday and Co., 1979.

Fohrer, Georg. *History of Israelite Religion.* London: S.P.C.K., 1973.

————. *Introduction to the Old Testament.* London: SPCK, 1983.

Foner, Philip S. *American Socialism and Black Americans: From the Age of Jackson to World War II.* Westport & London: Greenwood Press, 1977.

Fong, N. "Chinatown: Theology Emerging out of Community." *Radical Religion* 5 (No. 2, 1980):30-37.

Ford, Josephine Massyngberde. *My Enemy is My Guest: Jesus and Violence in Luke.* Maryknoll, NY: Orbis Books, 1984.

Foster-Carter, A. "The Modes of Production Controversy." *New Left Review* 107 (1978):47-77.

Frank, Andrew G. *Capitalism and Underdevelopment in Latin America: Historical Studies of Chile and Brazil.* New York and London: Monthly Review Press, 1969.

Freedman, David Noel, and D. F. Graf. *Palestine in Transition: The Emergence of Ancient Israel.* Sheffield: Almond Press, 1983.

Frisk, F. S. "The Rechabites Reconsidered." *Journal of Biblical Literature* 90 (1971):279-287.

Gager, John G. *Kingdom and Community: The Social World of Early Christianity.* Englewood Cliffs, NJ: Prentice-Hall, 1975.

Gandy, D. Ross. *Marx and History: From Primitive Society to the Communist Future.* Austin & London: University of Texas Press, 1979.

Gay, Peter. *The Enlightenment: An Interpretation.* New York: Alfred A. Knopf, 1966.

Gehman, Henry S. "Arlos in the Septuagint, and its Relation to the Hebrew Original." *Vetus Testamentum* 4 (1954):337-348.

Genovese, Eugene D. *The Political Economy of Slavery: Studies in the Economy and Society of the Slave South.* New York: Vintage Books, 1967.

————. *Roll, Jordan, Roll: The World the Slaves Made.* New York:Vintage Books, 1976.

Gill, R. *Theology and Social Structure.* London and Oxford: Mowbray, 1977.

Gilroy, Paul. "Steppin' out of Babylon--Race, Class, and Autonomy." In *The Empire Strikes Back,* Centre for Contemporary Social Studies. London: Hutchinson, 1982.

Gitlin, Todd. *The Whole World is Watching: Mass Media in the making and unmaking of the New Left.* Berkeley and Los Angeles: University of California Press, 1980.

Gnuse, R. *You Shall Not Steal: Community and Property in the Biblical Tradition.* Maryknoll, NY: Orbis Books, 1985.

Gort, J. D., C. M. Veenhuizen, and A. Wessels. *Wie Zeggen de Mensen, dot Ik Ben? Westerse, Joodse, Aziatische, Afrikaanse, Latunsamerikaanse Beelden van Jezus Christus.* Sektie Missiologie en Evangelistiek Theologische Faculteit der Vrije Universiteit, 1981/82.

Gottwald, Norman K. "Domain Assumptions and Societal Models in the Study of Premonarchic Israel." *Vetus Testamentum Supplement* 28 (1974).

———. *The Tribes of Yahweh: A Sociology of the Religion of Liberated Israel, 1250-1050 B.C.* Maryknoll, NY: Orbis Books, 1979.

———. "Sociological Method in the Study of Ancient Israel." In *Encounter with Text,* edited by M. J. Buss. Philadelphia: Fortress Press, 1979.

———. "'Church and State' in Ancient Israel: Example or Caution in our Age?" Department of Religion Lecture Series, University of Florida, Gainesville, 12 January 1981.

———. "John Bright's New Revision of 'A History of Israel.'" *Biblical Archeology Review* (July/August 1982):56-61.

———. "Sociological Method in Biblical Research and Contemporary Peace Studies." *American Baptist Quarterly* 2 (No. 2, June 1983):168-184.

———. "Social History of the United Monarchy: An application of H. A. Landsberger's Framework for the analysis of peasant movements to the participation of free agrarians in the introduction of the monarchy to ancient Israel." Paper presented at SBL Seminar on "Sociology of the Monarchy," 20 December 1983.

———. "Two Models for the Origins of Ancient Israel: Social Revolution or Frontier Development." In *The Quest for the Kingdom of God: Studies in Honour of George E. Mendenhall,* edited by H. B. Huffmon, et al. Winona Lake, IN: Eisenbrauns, 1983.

———. "Social Matrix and Canonical Shape." *Theology Today* 42 (No. 3, 1985):307-321.

———. *The Hebrew Bible: A Socio-Literary Introduction.* Philadelphia: Fortress Press, 1985.

————. "Review Article of Irving M. Zeitlin, 'Ancient Judaism: Biblical Criticism from Max Weber to the Present.'" Unpublished paper, New York Theological Seminary, New York, 8 July 1985.

————. "Socio-Historical Precision in the Biblical Grounding of Liberation Theologies." Address presented at Catholic Biblical Association of America, San Francisco, August 1985.

————. "Contemporary Studies of Social Class and Social Stratification and a Hypothesis about Social Class in Monarchic Israel." ASOR-SBL Seminar on "Sociology of the Monarchy," 25 November 1985.

Gottwald, N. K., ed. *The Bible and Liberation: Political and Social Hermeneutics.* Maryknoll, NY: Orbis, 1983.

Gqubule, Simon. "What is Black Theology?" *Journal of Theology for Southern Africa* 8 (1974):16-23.

Gramsci, Antonio. *Selections from the Prison Notebooks.* New York: International Publishers, 1983.

Grant, Frederick C. *The Economic Background of the Gospels.* New York: Russell and Russell, 1926.

Greenspahn, Frederick E. "Recent Scholarship on the History of Premonarchic Israel." *Journal of Reform Judaism* (Spring 1983):81-93.

Greenwood, W. *Love on the Dole.* Harmondsworth: Penguin Books, 1983.

Gutiérrez, Gustavo. *A Theology of Liberation: History, Politics and Salvation.* London: SCM Press, 1975.

Gutkind, P., and P. Waterman. *African Social Studies: A Radical Reader.* New York and London: Monthly Review Press, 1977.

Hall, Stuart. "Encoding and Decoding in the Television Discourse." Paper presented to the Council of Europe Colloquy on "Training in the Critical Reading of Televisual Language," University of Leicester, September 1973.

————. "Pluralism, Race and Class in Caribbean Society." In *Race and Class in Post-Colonial Society: A Study of Ethnic Group Relations in the English-speaking Caribbean, Bolivia, Chile and Mexico.* Paris: UNESCO, 1977.

————. "The 'Political' and the 'Economic' in Marx's Theory of Classes." In *Class and Class Structure,* edited by A. Hunt. London: Lawrence and Wishart, 1977.

————. *Policing the Crisis*. London: Macmillan, 1978.

————. "Cold Comfort Farm." *New Socialist* 32 (Nov. 1985):10-13.

Hall, Stuart, and T. Jefferson, eds. *Resistance Through Rituals: Youth Subcultures in Post-war Britain*. London: Hutchinson, 1982.

Harari, Josué V., ed. *Textual Strategies. Perspectives in Post-Structuralist Criticism*. Ithaca, NY: Cornell University Press, 1981.

Har-El, M. "The Valley of the Craftsmen (*Ge' Haharasim*)." *Palestine Exploration Quarterly* 109 (1977):75-86.

Harrington, Daniel J. "Some New Voices in New Testament Interpretation." *Anglican Theological Review* 64 (No. 3, 1982):362-370.

Harris, Zellig S. *Development of the Canaanite Dialects. An Investigation in Linguistic History*. Millwood, NY: Kraus Reprint Co., 1978.

Hayes, John Haralson. "The Tradition of Zion's Inviolability." *Journal of Biblical Literature* 82 (1963):419-426.

Hengel, Martin. *Judaism and Hellenism*. London: SCM Press, 1974.

Herrmann, S. *A History of Israel in Old Testament Times*. London: SCM Press, 1975.

Herzog, Frederick. "Liberation Hermeneutics as Ideology Critique." *Interpretation* 28 (1974):387-403.

Hill, M. *A Sociology of Religion*. London: Heinemann, 1976.

Hilton, R., ed. *The Transition from Feudalism to Capitalism*. London: Verso, 1978.

Hilton-Barber, Barbara. "Images of War." *Vula!* (June 1986):32-35.

Hindess, Barry, and Paul Q. Hirst. *Pre-Capitalist Modes of Production*. London: Routledge & Kegan Paul, 1979.

Hohendal, Peter U. "The Use Value of Contemporary and Future Literary Criticism." *New German Critique* 7 (Winter 1976).

Hollenbach, P. "Recent Historical Jesus Studies and the Social Sciences." In *Society of Biblical Literature 1983 Seminar Papers*, edited by K. H. Richards. No. 22, Scholars Press, Chico, 1983.

Hopkins, David C. "The Dynamics of Agriculture in Monarchical Israel." *SBL 1983 Seminar Papers*, edited by K. H. Richards. No. 22, Scholars Press, Chico, 1983.

————. *The Highlands of Canaan. Agricultural Life in the Early Iron Age*. Sheffield: Almond, 1985.

Horsley, G. H. Richard. "Divergent Views on the Nature of the Greek of the Bible." *Biblica* 65 (1984):393-403.

Institute for Contextual Theology. "Final Statement of the Black Theology Seminar." *ICT News* 1 (No. 2, 1983).

James, W. "Life Trajectories of a Working Class: South Africa, 1969-1981." Centre for African Studies, University of Cape Town, 5 Sept. 1984.

Jameson, Fredric. "Reification and Utopia in Mass Culture." *Social Text* (Winter 1979):130-148.

―――. *The Political Unconscious: Narrative as a Socially Symbolic Act.* Ithaca, NY: Cornell University Press, 1981.

Jay, E. G. *New Testament Greek: An Introductory Grammar.* London: S.P.C.K., 1965.

Jeppesen, Knud. "The Verb *ya' ad* in Nahum 1, 10 and Micah 6, 9." *Biblica* 65 (1984):571-574.

―――. "New Aspects of Micah Research." *Journal for the Study of the Old Testament* 8 (1978):3-32.

Jeremias, Joachim. *Jerusalem in the Time of Jesus: An Investigation into Economic and Social Conditions during the New Testament Period.* Philadelphia: Fortress Press, 1969.

Jerushalmi, I. *The Aramaic Sections of Ezra and Daniel.* Cincinnati, OH: Hebrew Union College–Jewish Institute of Religion, 1982.

Joll, James. *Gramsci.* Glasgow: Fontana Paperbacks, 1977.

Judge, Edwin A. "The Social Identity of the First Christians: A Question of Method in Religious History." *Journal of Religious History* 20 (1980):201-217.

Kaiser, Otto. *Der Prophet Jesaja: Kapitel 1-12.* Göttingen: Bandenhoef & Ruprecht, 1970.

―――. *Introduction to the Old Testament: A Presentation of its Results and Problems* (translated by J. Sturdy). Oxford: Basil Blackwell, 1975.

Karis, Thomas, and G. M. Carter. *From Protest to Challenge: Documents of African Politics in South Africa, 1882-1964.* Stanford: Hoover Institution Press, 1973.

Karris, Robert O. "Poor and Rich: The Lukan Sitz im Leben." In Talbert, C. H. (ed.), *Perspectives on Luke-Acts.* Edinburgh: T. & T. Clark Ltd., 1978.

Kautsky, Karl. *Foundations of Christianity.* New York & London: Monthly Review Press, 1972.

Keegan, Tim. "The Restructuring of Agrarian Class Relations in a Colonial Economy: The Orange River Colony, 1902–1910." *Journal of Southern African Studies* 5 (1978-79): 234-254.

Klausner, Joseph. *Jesus of Nazareth.* New York: Macmillan Company, 1925.

Knodler-Bunte, E. "The Proletarian Public Sphere and Political Organization: An Analysis of Oskar Negt and Alexander Kluge's 'The Public Sphere and Experience.'" *New German Critique* 1-2 (1975): 51-75.

Krikler, Jeremy. "A Class Destroyed, A Class Restored: The Relationship of Agrarian Class Struggle to the Destruction of the Boer Landowning Class during the South African War and its Reconstruction Thereafter." Paper presented at Centre for African Studies, University of Cape Town, 13 Aug. 1986.

Kümmel, Werner G. *Introduction to the New Testament.* London: SCM Press, 1979.

Laclau, E. *Politics and Ideology in Marxist Theory: Capitalism-Fascism-Populism.* London: Verso, 1982.

Landes, G. M. *A Student's Vocabulary of Biblical Hebrew.* New York: Charles Scribner's Sons, 1961.

Lang, Bernhard. "The Social Organization of Peasant Poverty in Biblical Israel." *Journal for the Study of Old Testament* 24 (1982): 47-63.

Langlamet, F. "Les Recits de L'Institution de la Royaute (I Sam. VII-XII)." *Revue Biblique* 77 (1970): 161-200.

Lebulu, J. L. "Religion as the Dominant Element of the Superstructure among the Pare of Tanzania." *Social Compass* 26 (No. 4, 1979): 417-459.

Lee, R. B. *The !Kung San: Men, Women and Work in a Foraging Society.* Cambridge: Cambridge University Press, 1980.

Lemche, N. P. "David's Rise." *Journal for the Study of Old Testament* 10 (1978): 2-25.

Linder, M. *Anti-Samuelson.* New York: Urizen Books, 1977.

Lohfink, Norbert. "Zur deuteronomistischen Zentralisationsformel." *Biblica* 65 (1984): 297-329.

Lohse, Eduard. *The New Testament Environment*. London: SCM Press, 1976.

Lukacs, György. *History and Class Consciousness: Studies in Marxist Dialectics*. Translated by R. Livingstone. Cambridge, MA: MIT Press, 1983.

Machery, P. *A Theory of Literary Production*. London: Routledge & Kegan Paul, 1978.

MacPherson, Crawford Brough. *The Political Theory of Possessive Individualism: Hobbes to Locke*. Oxford: Oxford University Press, 1977.

Mafeje, Archie. "The Problem of Anthropology in Historical Perspective: An Inquiry into the Growth of the Social Sciences." *Canadian Journal of African Studies* 10 (No. 2, 1976): 307-333.

Magesa, L. "The Bible and a Liberation Theology for Africa." *African Ecclesiastical Review* 19 (1977): 217-222.

Magubane, Bernard M. *The Political Economy of Race and Class in South Africa*. New York & London: Monthly Review Press, 1979.

Majeke, N. *The Role of the Missionaries in Conquest*. Johannesburg: Society of Young Africa, 1952.

Malina, Bruce J. "The Social Sciences and Biblical Interpretation." In *The Bible and Liberation,* edited by N. K. Gottwald. Maryknoll, NY: Orbis Books, 1983.

———. "The Gospel of John in Sociolinguistic Perspective." Centre for Hermeneutical Studies in Hellenistic and Modern Culture, Colloquy 48, Graduate Theological Union & University of California, Berkeley, CA, 1984.

Manikkam, T. "Towards an Indian Hermeneutics of the Bible." *Jeevadhara* 12 (1982): 94-104.

Mansueto, Anthony. "From Historical Criticism to Historical Materialism." Paper presented at Graduate Theological Union, Berkeley, CA, 1983.

Marfoe, Leon. "The Integrative Transformation: Patterns of Socio-political Organization in Southern Syria." *BASOR* 234 (1979).

Marks, Shula. *The Ambiguities of Dependence in South Africa: Class, Nationalism and the State in Twentieth-Century Natal*. Johannesburg: Ravan, 1986.

————. "Patriotism, Patriarchy and Purity. Natal and the Politics of Cultural Nationalism." Paper presented at Centre for African Studies, University of Cape Town, 23 July 1986.

Marks, Shula, and A. Atmore, eds. *Economy and Society in Pre-Industrial South Africa*. London: Longman, 1980.

Marks, Shula, and Richard Rathbone, eds. *Industrialisation and Social Change in South Africa: African Class Formation, Culture and Consciousness, 1870-1930*. London: Longman, 1982.

Marks, Shula, and Stanley Trapido. "Lord Milner and the South African State." In *Working Papers in Southern African Studies*, Vol. 2, edited by P. Bonner. Johannesburg: Ravan Press, 1981.

Marquardt, F.-W. *Theologie und Sozialismus: Das Beispiel Karl Barths*. München: Kaiser, 1972.

Marshall, Alfred. *The R.S.V. Interlinear Greek-English New Testament*. (The Nestle Greek Text with a Literal English Translation.) London: Samuel Bagster & Sons, Ltd., 1972.

Marx, Karl. *Capital, Vol. 1: The Process of Capitalist Production*. New York: International Publishers, 1967.

————. *Der Grundrisse*. Edited and translated by D. McLennan. New York: Harper Torchbooks, 1971.

————. *Wage-Labour and Capital and Value: Price and Profit*. New York: International Publishers, 1976.

————. *Economic and Philosophic Manuscripts of 1844*. Moscow: Progress, and London: Lawrence & Wishart, 1981.

————. *A Contribution to the Critique of Political Economy*. Moscow: Progress, and London: Lawrence & Wishart, 1981.

Marx, Karl, and Friedrich Engels. *The German Ideology*. New York: International Publishers, 1947.

————. *On Religion*. New York: Schocken Books, 1964.

————. *Selected Works in One Volume*. Moscow: Progress, and London: Lawrence & Wishart, 1968.

Marzoni, C. "The Vatican as a Left Ally?" *Monthly Review* 34 (July/August 1982): 1-42.

Maughan-Brown, D. *Land, Freedom & Fiction. History and Ideology in Kenya*. London: Zed Books, 1985.

Mayer, Anton. *Der zensierte Jesus: Soziologie des Neuen Testaments*. Olten und Freiburg im Breisgau: Walter Verlag, 1983.

————. *Betroffen vom zensierten Jesus. Signale eines neuen religiosen Aufbruchs.* Olten und Freiburg im Breisgau: Walter Verlag, 1985.

Maylam, P. *A History of the African People of South Africa: From the Early Iron Age to the 1970's.* London: Croom Helm, and Cape Town & Johannesburg: David Philip, 1986.

Mays, James Luther. *Micah: A Commentary.* Philadelphia: Westminster Press, 1976.

McAfee Brown, Robert. *Theology in a New Key: Responding to Liberation Themes.* Philadelphia: Westminster Press, 1978.

McCarter, Peter Kyle. "The Apology of David." *Journal of Biblical Literature* 99 (1980): 489-504.

McFadden, P. "Women Workers in Southern Africa." *Journal of African Marxists,* 4 Sept. 1982:54-62.

McKale, M. "Culture and Human Liberation," *Radical Religion* 5 (No. 2, 1980): 5-15.

McLellan, David. *Marxism after Marx.* 2nd ed. London and Basingstoke: Macmillan, 1980.

McLennan, G. *Marxism and the Methodologies of History.* London: Verso, 1981.

Meeks, Wayne A., ed. *Zur Soziologie des Urchristentums.* Munchen: Chr. Kaiser Verlag, 1979.

————. *The First Urban Christians.* New Haven: Yale University Press, 1983.

Meillassoux, C. "The Social Organisation of the Peasantry: The Economic Basis of Kinship." *The Journal of Peasant Studies* 1 (No. 1, 1973): 81-90.

Metzger, Bruce M. *The New Testament: Its Background, Growth and Content.* Nashville: Abingdon, 1965.

————. *Lexical Aids for Students of New Testament Greek.* Princeton, NJ: Theological Book Agency, 1983.

Meyers, Carol L. "Procreation, Production and Protection: Male-Female Balance in Early Israel." *Journal of the American Academy of Religion* 41 (No. 4, 1983): 569-593.

Mgojo, Elliot K. M., "Prolegomenon to the Study of Black Theology." *Journal of Theology for Southern Africa* 21 (1977): 25-32.

Míguez Bonino, José. *Room to be People: An Interpretation of the Message of the Bible for Today's World.* Philadelphia: Fortress, 1979.

210

Miller, David. "Ideology and the Problem of False Consciousness." *Political Studies* 20 (No. 4, 1972): 432-447.

Moeti, M. T. "Ethiopianism: Separatist Roots of African Nationalism." Ph.D. diss., Syracuse University, 1981.

Mofokeng, Takatso A. *The Crucified among the Crossbearers: Towards a Black Christology.* Kampen: Uitgeversmaatschappij J. H. Kok, 1983.

Mogoba, Stanley. "The Faith of Urban Blacks." Master's thesis, University of Bristol, 1978.

Mosala, Itumeleng J. "Social Justice in the Early Israelite Monarchy as Illustrated by the Reign of David." Master's thesis, University of Manchester, 1980.

Mosala, I. J., and Buti Tlhagale. *The Unquestionable Right to be Free: Essays in Black Theology.* Johannesburg: Skotaville, 1986.

Mosothoane, Ephraim K. "The Use of Scripture in Black Theology." In *Scripture and the Use of Scripture.* Pretoria: Unisa, 1979.

Motlhabi, Mokgethi. *The Theory and Practice of Black Resistance to Apartheid: A Social-Ethical Analysis.* Johannesburg: Skotaville, 1984.

Mottu, Henri. "Jeremiah vs. Hananiah: Ideology and Truth in Old Testament Prophecy." *Radical Religion* 2 (Nos. 2 & 3, 1975):58-67.

Muraoka, T. "Notes and Studies on Septuagint Lexicography and Patristics." *Journal of Theological Studies* 35 (1984):441-449.

Murray, N. U. "The Nature of Hegemonic Ideology: the Church Missionary Society in Colonial Kenya." Paper presented at Southern African Universities Social Science Conference, Gaborone, 1980.

Negt, O., and A. Kluge. *Offentlichkeit und Erfahrung: Zur Organisationsanalyse von burgerlicher und proletarischer Offentlichkeit.* Frankfurt am Main: Suhrkamp Verlag, 1972.

Nelson, Richard D. "Josiah in the Book of Joshua." *Journal of Biblical Literature* 100 (No. 4, 1981):531-540.

Ngugi Wa Thiong, O. *Petals of Blood.* London: Heinemann, 1977.
———. *Homecoming.* London: Heinemann, 1978.
———. "Mau Mau is Coming Back: The Revolutionary Significance of 20th October 1952 in Kenya Today." *Journal of African Marxists,* 4 Sept. 1983:18-44.

————. *Barrel of Pen: Resistance to Repression in Neo-Colonial Kenya.* Trenton, NJ: Africa World Press, 1983.

Nicholson, C. E. "A World of Artifacts: The Rape of the Lock as Social History." *Literature and History* 5 (No. 2, 1979):183-193.

Nicholson, Ernest Wilson. "The Meaning of the Expression *'am hā'āreṣ* in the Old Testament." *Journal of Semitic Studies* 10 (1965):59-66.

Nineham, Dennis E. *The Use and Abuse of the Bible: A Study of the Bible in an age of rapid cultural change.* London: SPCK, 1978.

Noko, Ishmael. "The Concept of God in Black Theology." Ph.D. diss., McGill University, 1977.

Nolan, Albert. *Jesus Before Christianity: The Gospel of Liberation.* London: Darton, Longman & Todd, 1980.

Nolutshungu, Sam C. *Changing South Africa.* Cape Town and Johannesburg: David Philip, 1983.

Ntshebe, Lulamile Ephraim. "In Search of Humanity: A View of Protest." Master's thesis, Rhodes University, Grahamstown, 1980.

Nunn, H. P. V. *A Short Syntax of New Testament Greek.* 5th ed. Cambridge: Cambridge University Press, 1983.

Nzimiro, I. "Against the Mystification of Class." *Journal of African Marxists,* 4 Sept. 1983:94-102.

Oden, R. A., Jr. "Hermeneutics and Historiography: Germany and America." In *Seminar Papers: Society of Biblical Literature.* Chico: Scholars Press, 1980.

Odendaal, A. *Vukani Bantu! The Beginnings of Black Protest Politics in South Africa to 1912.* Cape Town and Johannesburg: David Philip, 1984.

O'Meara, D. *Volkskapitalisme: Class, Capital and Ideology in the Development of Afrikaner Nationalism 1934-1948.* Johannesburg: Ravan, 1983.

Ousmane, S. *God's Bits of Wood.* London: Heinemann, 1976.

Pereppadan, J. "The Contribution of Paul Ricoeur to Biblical Hermeneutics." *Jeevadhara* 12 (1982):156-163.

Perrin, Norman. *The New Testament: An Introduction.* New York: Harcourt Brace Jovanovich, 1974.

Phillips, H. Y. "The Bagaseleka Barolong's Search for a Homeland." B.A. thesis, University of Botswana, Lesotho and Swaziland, 1976.

Pixley, George V. *God's Kingdom: A Guide for Biblical Study.* Maryknoll, NY: Orbis Books, 1977.

Plaatje, S. T. *Native Life in South Africa.* Johannesburg: Ravan, 1982.

Plamenatz, John P. *Ideology.* London and Basingdale: Macmillan, 1979.

Premnath, Devadasan N. "The Process of Latifundialization mirrored in the Oracles pertaining to 8th Century B.C.E. in the Books of Amos, Hosea, Isaiah and Micah." Th.D. diss., Graduate Theological Union, Berkeley, CA, 1984.

Ranger, Terence O. "Religious Studies and Political Economy: The Mwari Cult and the Peasant Experience." Paper presented at Conference on the Interactions of History and Anthropology in Southern Africa, Manchester, Sept. 1980.

Rast, Walter E. *Joshua, Judges, Samuel, Kings.* Philadelphia: Fortress Press, 1978.

Redalie, Yann. "Conversion or Liberation? Notes on Acts 16:11-40." *Radical Religion* 2 (Nos. 2 & 3, 1975):102-108.

Roberts, J. J. M. "The Davidic Origin of the Zion Tradition." *Journal of Biblical Literature* 92 (1973):329-343.

Robinson, C. J. *Black Marxism. The Making of the Black Radical Tradition.* London: Zed Press, 1983.

Robinson, T. H. *Paradigms and Exercises in Syriac Grammar.* 4th ed., rev. by L. H. Brockington. Oxford: Clarendon Press, 1975.

Rodney, W. *How Europe Underdeveloped Africa.* Washington: Howard University Press, 1974.

Rohrbaugh, Richard L. "Methodological Considerations in the Debate over the Social Class Status of Early Christians." *Journal of American Academy of Religion* 52 (No. 3, 1984):519-546.

Rorty, Richard. "Nineteenth Century Idealism and Twentieth Century Textualism." *The Monist* 64 (No. 2, 1981):155-174.

Rosenthal, F. *A Grammar of Biblical Aramaic.* Wiesbaden: Otto Harrassowitz, 1974.

Rostagno, Sergio. "The Bible: Is an Interclass Reading Legitimate?" *Racial Religion* 2 (Nos. 2 & 3, 1975):19-25.

Rothenburg, B. "Metals and Metallurgy." In *Investigations at Lachish,* edited by Yohanan Aharoni. Tel Aviv: Gateway Publishers, 1975.

Roumain, J. *Masters of the Dew.* London: Heinemann, 1978.

Sanders, James A. *Torah and Canon.* Philadelphia: Fortress, 1972.
——. "Text and Canon: Concepts and Method." *Journal of Biblical Literature* 98 (No. 1, 1979):5-29.
——. *Canon and Community. A Guide to Canonical Criticism.* Philadelphia: Fortress Press, 1984.
Saul, J. S. *The State and Revolution in Eastern Africa.* London: Heinemann, 1979.
Sayres, Sohnya, et al., eds. *The 60's Without Apology.* Minneapolis: University of Minnesota Press, 1984.
Schalkwyk, D. "The Flight from Politics: An Analysis of the South African Reception of 'Poppie Nongema.'" *Journal of Southern African Studies* 12 (No. 2, 1986):183-195.
Scharper, P. and S., eds. *The Gospel in Art by the Peasants of Solentiname.* Maryknoll, NY: Orbis, 1984.
Schoeffeleers, J. Matthew. "African Christology." Paper presented at Free University, Amsterdam, 1981.
Schottroff, W., and W. Stegemann, eds. *God of the Lowly: Socio-Historical Interpretations of the Bible.* Translated by M. J. O'Connell. Maryknoll, NY: Orbis Books, 1984.
Scroggs, Robin. "Sociological Interpretation of the New Testament: The Present State of Research." *New Testament Studies* 26 (1979/80):164-179.
Segundo, Juan Luis. *The Liberation of Theology.* Maryknoll, NY: Orbis, 1976.
Setiloane, Gabriel M. *The Image of God Among the Sotho-Tswana.* Rotterdam: A. A. Balkema, 1976.
Shanin, T., ed. *Peasants and Peasant Societies.* London: Penguin, 1979.
Shillington, K. *The Colonisation of the Southern Tswana 1870-1900.* Johannesburg: Ravan, 1983.
Shoup, L. H. *The Carter Presidency and Beyond: Power and Politics in the 1980's.* Palo Alto, CA: Ramparts Press, 1980.
Silver, M. *Prophets and Markets: The Political Economy of Ancient Israel.* Boston, The Hague, London: Kluwer-Nijhoff, 1983.
Stade, B. "Bemerkungen über des Buch Micha." *Zeitschrift für die alttestamentliche Wissenschaft* (1881):161-176.
Stager, L. T. "Farming in the Judean Desert during the Iron Age."

Bulletin of the American Schools of Oriental Research 221 (1976):145-158.

Stámbaugh, John E. "Social Relations in the City of the Early Principate: State of Research." *Seminar Paper: Society of Biblical Literature.* Chico: Scholars Press, 1980.

Stech-Wheeler, T., et al. "Iron at Taanach and Early Iron Metallurgy in the Eastern Mediterranean." *American Journal of Archaeology* 85 (1981):245-268.

Stiebing, W. H. "The End of the Mycenean Age." *Biblical Archeologist* (Winter 1980):7-21.

Stoch, A. "The Limits of Historical-Critical Exegesis." *Biblical Theology Bulletin* 13 (1983):28-31.

Szymanski, A. J., and T. G. Geortzel. *Sociology.* New York: Van Nostrand Co., 1979.

Talbert, Charles H. *Literary Patterns, Theological Themes and the Genre of Luke-Acts.* Chicago: SBL and Scholars Press, 1974.

————, ed. *Perspectives on Luke-Acts.* Edinburgh: T. & T. Clark Ltd., 1978.

————, ed. *Luke-Acts: New Perspectives from the Society of Biblical Literature Seminar.* New York: Crossroad, 1984.

Tamez, Elsa. *Bible of the Oppressed.* Maryknoll, NY: Orbis, 1982.

Terray, Emmanuel. *Marxism and Primitive Societies.* New York & London: Monthly Review Press, 1972.

Theissen, Gerhard. *Sociology of Early Palestinian Christianity.* Philadelphia: Fortress Press, 1978.

————. "The Sociological Interpretation of Religious Traditions: Its Methodological Problems as Exemplified in Early Christianity." In *The Social Setting of Pauline Christianity.* Philadelphia: Fortress Press, 1982.

————. "Lokal- und Sozialkolorit in der Geschichte von der syrophonikischen Frau (Mk 7:24-30)." *Zeitschrift für die neutestamentliche Wissenschaft* 75 (No. 314, 1984):202-225.

Thompson, Thomas L. "The Background to the Patriarchs: A Reply to William Dever and Malcolm Clark." *Journal for the Study of the Old Testament* 9 (1978):2-43.

Thorion-Vardi, T. "The Use of the Tenses in the Zadokite Documents." *Revue de Qumran* 12 (No. 45, June 1985):85-88.

Tlhagale, Buti. "Towards a Black Theology of Labour." In *Black*

Theology Revisited. Institute for Contextual Theology Report, 1984.

Torres, Sergio, and Virginia Fabella. *The Emergent Gospel: Theology from the Underside of History.* Maryknoll, NY: Orbis, 1978.

Torres, Sergio, and John Eagleson, eds. *The Challenge of Basic Christian Communities.* Maryknoll, NY: Orbis, 1981.

Tracy, David. *The Analogical Imagination.* London: SCM Press, 1981.

Turkowski, L. "Peasant Agriculture in the Judean Hills." *Palestine Exploration Quarterly* 101 (1969):21-33, 101-112.

Tutu, Desmond M. *Hope and Suffering: Sermons and Speeches.* Grand Rapids: Eerdmans, 1984.

Tyson, J. B. "Source Criticism of the Gospel of Luke." In *Perspectives on Luke-Acts,* edited by Charles H. Talbert. Edinburgh: T. & T. Clark Ltd., 1978.

Van der Lingen, A. "David en Saul in I Samuel 16–II Samuel 5: Verhalen in politiek en religie." Rijksuniversiteit te Groningen, 1983.

Van der Woude, A. S. "Micah in Dispute with the Pseudo-Prophets." *Vetus Testamentum* 19 (1969):244-260.

Von Onselen, C. *Studies in the Social and Economic History of the Witwatersrand 1886-1914: Vol. I, New Babylon; Vol. II, New Nineveh.* Johannesburg: Ravan, 1982.

Von Rad, Gerhard. *Old Testament Theology.* 2 vols. London: SCM Press, 1975.

Waetjen, Herman C. *The Origin and Destiny of Humanness: An Interpretation of the Gospel According to Matthew.* San Rafael, CA: Crystal Press, 1978.

Waldbaum, Jane C. "The First Archeological Appearance of Iron." In *The Coming of the Age of Iron,* edited by T. A. Wertime and J. D. Muhly. New Haven: Yale University Press, 1980.

Watson, Wilfred G. E. *Classical Hebrew Poetry: A Guide to its Techniques.* Sheffield: JSOT Supplement Series 26, 1984.

———. "Allusion, Irony and Wordplay in Micah 1:7." *Biblica* 65 (1984):103-105.

Weber, Max. *Basic Conceptions in Sociology.* Secaucus, NJ: The Citadel Press, 1962.

———. *Economy and Society.* New York: Bedminster Press, 1968.

———. *The Protestant Ethic and the Spirit of Capitalism.* London: George Allen & Unwin, 1976.

————. *The Sociology of Religion.* Translated by E. Fischoff. Boston: Beacon Press, 1964.

Weil, G. E. *Massorah Gedolah,* luxta Codicem Leningradensem, B19a, Volumen 1, Pontificum Institutum Biblicum, Rome, 1971.

Weingreen, J. *A Practical Grammar for Classical Hebrew.* 2nd ed. Oxford: Clarendon Press, 1975.

Weiser, Artur. *Introduction to the Old Testament: The Canon, the Apocrypha and Pseudepigrapha.* London: Darton, Longman and Todd, 1961.

Weiss, D. "Marx vs Smith on the Division of Labour." *Monthly Review* 28 (No. 3, 1976):104-118.

Wenham, John W. *The Elements of New Testament Greek.* Cambridge: Cambridge University Press, 1970.

West, Cornel. "Ethics, Historicism and the Marxist Tradition." Ph.D. diss., Princeton University, 1980.

————. *Prophesy Deliverance: An Afro-American Revolutionary Christianity.* Philadelphia: The Westminster Press, 1982.

————. "Fredric Jameson's Marxist Hermeneutics." *Boundary 2: A Journal of Post-Modern Literature* (Winter 1983):177-200.

————. "Reconstructing the American Left: The Challenge of Jesse Jackson." *Social Text* (Winter 1984/85):3-19.

White, L. J. "Biblical Theologians and Theologies of Liberation: Pt. I: Canon-Supporting Framework." *Biblical Theology Bulletin* 2 (1981):35-40.

————. "Biblical Theologians and Theologies of Liberation: Pt. II: Midrash Applies Text to Context." *Biblical Theology Bulletin* 2 (1981):98-103.

————. "Historical and Literary Criticism: A Theological Response." *Biblical Theology Bulletin* 13 (1983):32-34.

Whitelam, Keith W. *The Just King: Monarchical Judicial Authority in Ancient Israel.* Sheffield: JSOT Press, Supplement Series 12, 1979.

Wifall, W. R. "The Tribes of Yahweh: A Synchronic Study with a Diachronic Title." *Zeitschrift für die alttestamentliche Wissenschaft* 95 (No. 2, 1983):197-209.

Wilde, J. "The Social World of Mark's Gospel: A Word about Method." In *Society of Biblical Literature Seminar Papers.* Chico: Scholars Press, 1978.

Willis, Paul, and Philip Corrigan. "Orders of Experience: The

Differences of Working Class Cultural Forms." *Social Text* (Spring & Summer 1983):85-103.

Wilmore, Gayraud S., and James Cone. *Black Theology: A Documentary History, 1966-1979.* Maryknoll, NY: Orbis, 1979.

Wilson, Robert R. *Prophecy and Society in Ancient Israel.* Philadelphia: Fortress Press, 1980.

————. *Sociological Approaches to the Old Testament.* Philadelphia: Fortress Press, 1984.

Wimbush, Vincent L. "Historical Study as Liberation: A Methodological Proposal for an Afro-Christian Biblical Hermeneutic." Paper presented at Claremont School of Theology, Jan. 1985.

Winter, D. *Hope in Captivity: The Prophetic Church in Latin America.* London: Epworth Press, 1977.

Witbooi, B. "The Decline of the Khoikhoi in South Africa from Freedom to Bondage." Master's thesis, Graduate Theological Union, Berkeley, CA, 1983.

————. "Liminality, Christianity and the Khoikhoi Tribes." In *Hammering Swords into Ploughshares: Essays in Honour of Archbishop Desmond Tutu,* edited by I. J. Mosala and B. Tlhagale. Grand Rapids: Eerdmans, 1987.

Wolff, Hans Walter. *Anthropology of the Old Testament.* London: SCM Press, 1974.

————. *Joel and Amos.* Philadelphia: Fortress Press, 1977.

————. *Mit Micha Reden: Prophetie einst und heute.* München: Chr. Kaiser Verlag, 1975.

Wolff, Robert Paul. *Understanding Rawls: A Reconstruction and Critique of 'A Theory of Justice.'* Princeton, NJ: Princeton University Press, 1977.

Wright, J. H. "The Bible and the Hermeneutical Horizon: The Use of Scripture in Theology." *Theological Studies* 43 (1982):651-672.

Würthwein, Ernst. *The Text of the Old Testament: An Introduction to Kittel-Kahle's Biblia Hebraica.* Translated by P. R. Ackroyd. Oxford: Basil Blackwell, 1957.

Young, I. "Socialist Feminism and the Limits of Dual Systems Theory." *Radical Religion* 5 (No. 2, 1980):38-49.